The John Colet Archive · 4

The John Colet Archive
of American Literature
1620-1920

Number 4, Spring-Summer 1975

Barrett Wendell

Literature, Society, and Politics: Selected Essays

Edited by Robert T. Self

THE JOHN COLET PRESS

For Moose

The John Colet Archive of American Literature,
a quarterly series, presents the tangible yields of
current scholarly inquiry into the distant reaches
of American literary history. By the selective
recovery of near-forgotten works in compact,
inexpensive modern editions, the Archive is
intended to enrich, modestly but measurably, the
working literary heritage of the American people.
Correspondence may be addressed to The Director,
The John Colet Press, Box 80101, Como Station,
St. Paul, Minnesota 55108.

Preface

It is the fashion today, or rather the business, to reprint
the books of those secondary writers in English and American
literature upon whom literary arbiters no longer look with
much interest. In many cases, the uncritical reproduction of
those works provides little more information or understanding for the student than earlier critical neglect. As a prominent and influential teacher of creative writing and literature
at Harvard from 1880 to 1917, as a well-known national and
international lecturer, as a pioneer in the study and teaching
of American literary history, Barrett Wendell (1855-1921)
deserves not only the attention of the reprint houses but the
respect of the literary historian and the appreciation of the
student. Since his death Wendell has suffered neglect as well
as attack from the modern literary establishment as the last
stalwart of the Genteel Tradition in late nineteenth-century
American letters. Until recently his famous works English
Composition (1891), Cotton Mather (1891), and A Literary
History of America (1900) have been out of print, and his
contributions to the development of the pedagogy of English
composition, to the serious study of American literary history, and to the renaissance in twentieth-century American
literature have been ignored or missed altogether.
  This book offers a representative sampling of Wendell's
writing, covering the chronological as well as the thematic
and subjective development of his concerns. The introduction
seeks to trace the outlines of Wendell's life, to locate Wendell within the academic and cultural milieux of his time,
and to provide a brief critical and analytical context for the

essays printed here. Ideally the introduction and essays will
quicken the reader's interest in the complexities of Wendell's
life and work during one of the most dynamic and chaotic periods of American life, and will give him a new appreciation
for both Wendell's oft-noted failures and his lesser-known
but influential achievements.

   I owe a large debt to C. Carroll Hollis of the University of
North Carolina for first arousing and guiding my interest in
Barrett Wendell. I wish also to thank the Council of Academic
Deans at Northern Illinois University for the grant which
helped fund the research and clerical work for the book, and
to thank Charles Scribners' Sons and the Barrett Wendell
estate for permission to publish these essays. But words are
insufficient to express the encouragement and assistance
given me in this work by my wife Lois.

                                        Robert T. Self

Northern Illinois University

Contents

Introduction

I

Fred Lewis Pattee described James Russell Lowell as a "Janus figure caught midway between two generations and standing comfortably with neither."[1] The estimate even better describes one of Lowell's students and heirs apparent to the Brahmin throne: Barrett Wendell's lifetime spanned the years between the publication of Whitman's Leaves of Grass and of Eliot's Poems, almost exactly the distance from the first American "renaissance," the "literature of the new nation," to the second, the "literature of the whole nation." But the day of apostolic succession that brought William Dean Howells into the hallowed circle of James T. Fields and Lowell in 1867 was over when Wendell came of age ten years later. His life and career illustrate the uncertainties and complexities generated by an era of rapid and wholesale transition, when, as Thomas Beer observed, the values of Henry and William James gave way to those of the other James brothers, Jesse and Frank. Wendell represents the debilitation of a genteel mind divided between an idealistic appreciation of the classical and Puritan past and a sensitivity for the new material energy, between moral idealism and crass materialism, between intellect and sentiment, between aesthetic taste and mass culture. He reveals the difficulty of an older generation in understanding and appreciating the revolutionary voice of a younger generation, and at the same time makes clear the role played by the past in preparing the way for the future.

Barrett Wendell was born August 5, 1855, in Boston, de-
scended from New York Dutch traders and merchants, a New
England governor, a Harvard president, and the Puritan divine John Rogers. His father worked his way from poverty to
ownership of the successful Jacob Wendell textiles firm,
which provided an environment of affluent respectability for
young Wendell and allowed him to visit "Longfellow's Europe"
three times and fall in love with it before he graduated from
college. From his youth Wendell was never strong: a lifelong
spinal disability he attributed to genetic inheritance, and the
pain of walking which necessitated his famous, often carica-
tured cane dated from a back injury during his teens. His
third trip to Europe in 1872 followed a nervous breakdown
during his freshman year at Harvard, from which after an
undistinguished undergraduate career he graduated in 1877.

Following graduation he spent a year in the Harvard Law
School and from 1878 to 1880 read law in New York and Boston law firms. The year 1880 was an important one for Wendell:
he failed the bar examinations, married Edith Greenough
of a prominent Boston family, and received a desperately
needed job as a theme reader under his former professor
Adams Sherman Hill. Thus, inadvertently, began Wendell's
thirty-seven-year career at Harvard, a career never quite
secure in Wendell's mind, as evidenced by his oft-repeated
defensiveness toward the specialized Ph.D. orientation of the
university and his consternation at not being promoted to full
professor until some twenty years after joining the faculty.
He became an assistant professor in 1888, but almost lost
his job altogether in 1893 because of a personality clash with
Harvard Overseer Phillips Brooks.

Wendell's lifelong interest in politics reveals the same
changing philosophic perspectives that emerge from his academic career. In the early 1880s as a Mugwump he came
under harsh criticism from the Boston newspapers because
his novel Rankell's Remains seemed to contain a malicious
parody of the Republican convention that nominated James G.
Blaine. He supported Cleveland in 1884 and described himself as a "blind democrat." But by 1893, with his fourth child
on the way, his reappointment at Harvard uncertain, the

country in economic crisis, Wendell began to sound the conservative and despairing notes that increasingly characterized his outlook. He feared the loss of classical values in the
new undergraduate curriculum at Harvard, the loss of social
order in the demands of the working çlass, the loss of traditional democracy in the "doctrinaire socialism" of Woodrow
Wilson. Even his old friend Theodore Roosevelt, whom he had
acclaimed earlier as a new American hero, he came finally to
view as dangerously radical.

These conservative, even reactionary views underlie much
of Wendell's literary, political, and social writing in the last
twenty years of his life. He was, however, one of the most
prominent academicians of his day—intimate with men such
as William Dean Howells, Brooks and Henry Adams, William
James, Henry Cabot Lodge, and well known through the national and international dissemination of his ideas in books,
magazines, newspapers, and lectures. His successful lectureships at Cambridge in 1902-1903 and the Sorbonne in
1904-1905 led a publicity-conscious Germany to offer him a
lectureship at the University of Berlin in 1914. Unlike his
former professor James Russell Lowell, however, he was
unable to translate his academic career into a diplomatic
one. Even though his retirement in 1917 was a major event
in official Harvard, cultural and political history had passed
him by and his fame at the time of his death February 8, 1921,
was already gone.

Wendell was a Tory, the "last of the Brahmins," an academic representative of the Genteel Tradition. He appreciated
the Puritan and Transcendentalist values of earlier Boston but
found them largely sterile, and had little stomach for the
emerging America Whitman so enthusiastically celebrated.
Bewildered, uncertain, he knew not whether to look forward
to a democratic future or back to an aristocratic past; the
present was indistinguishably cultural sunset or sunrise. He
felt: "We are passed into an ethnologic era as new as that of
fire, of the wheel, of metal. Not inconceivably, the trouble
men of your time feel, and of mine, is only that we must con-
front the new era with the ideas of the old. But it needs
strong faith to feel buoyant."[2] An outworn tradition may be

of little concern to the forgers of new tradition, as many of
the young writers in the early twentieth century felt, but
Wendell lacked confidence in either. Indeed at thirty-eight he
lamented: "I feel a certain regret that I had not the fortune
to be born fifty years earlier. Then I could eagerly have
joined in the expression of faith in the future which made New
England literature promise something."[3] In many respects,
then, Wendell's life and career are as meaningful as his published work. Thomas Beer called him "rather an emblem than
a man." He is the nineteenth-century man of letters caught
between a dead world and one yet unborn, a man like T. S.
Eliot's Prufrock for whom "talking of Michelangelo" meant
but a shadow of the old culture and a man awakened by the
"human voices" of the new century.

The events of Wendell's life are not so important, however,
as the "temperamental facts" of his career, and central to
those facts is a sense of failure which caused him to retreat
into a mode of aristocratic sophistication and eccentric exaggeration. His father had made a solid fortune in the post-
Civil War business world of Boston, a world for which Wendell had no aptitude. Toward the end of his career he still felt
his father's disappointment: "At 63 I have never displayed
the economic powers for which he ever so buoyantly hoped."[4]
After failing his bar examination he attained his appointment
at Harvard only through an accidental meeting with a former
professor who chanced to need an assistant. His first published works as a Harvard instructor were two disastrously
bad gothic novels, and when driven finally to scholarship to
secure promotion, he discovered his Bachelor of Arts degree
afforded inferior status by the new standards of textual criticism and Germanic scholarship. He denounced the Ph.D. as
the "Hun in the university," and forever presented himself
arrogantly—and defensively—as a "mere man of letters,"
a man whom George Santayana described as a "stray soul in
official Harvard." At the end of that career which brought him
many honors and international recognition (including an honorary doctorate from Harvard) he described himself as
always "profoundly in the wrong" and felt his thirty-seven
years at Harvard a failure.

Stuart Sherman called Wendell's importance paradoxical:
"I find the most important tokens of Wendell's humanity not
in his fortunate and effective and happy external career but in
the series of his failures and in the record of impulses which
bore little fruit."[5] As with many late nineteenth-century
writers below the rank of James and Howells, as with Henry
Adams and his pose of reticence and failure, much of Wendell's importance lies in his tragic qualities, and his "success" in the twentieth century has derived largely from his
representation of the late nineteenth-century failure in criticism. H.L. Mencken accurately analyzed his conflict: "Sen-
timentally and emotionally, he was moved powerfully by the
New England tradition, and felt a strong impulse to defend it
against the world. Intellectually, he saw clearly that it was
in collapse around him—worse, that it had been full of defects and weaknesses even when, by his own doctrines, it had
been strong. The result was his endless shuffling between
worship and ribaldry."[6] His teaching and appearance illustrated this ambivalence of Wendell's mind; students remembered him as conservative, iconoclastic, eccentric, ribald
and witty. He cut a fashionable figure, but part of that fash-
ionableness was the eccentric, the affected: his red hair
parted down the middle; his long, violent strides across the
front of his classroom; his furiously twirling watch-fob; his
English-looking clothes and spats; his "most exaggerated"
accent and what Mencken called his "whinnying voice." He
would suddenly shatter the calm of class with an obscenity
and always painted his lectures with off-color analogies. His
manners puzzled and delighted students. Santayana wondered
about his colleague, benefactor, and former teacher, "how far
was Wendell a fool and how far was he a martyr?" His eccen-
tricities, his "Rabelaisian comments," his "judicious indis-
cretions," his affectations in dress and manner cloaked his
uncertainty and insecurity. They served him as a defense
against the demands of his heritage and against his personal
sense of weakness and inadequacy. To realize the meaning of
these mannerisms is to recognize beneath his "arabesque of
temperamental opinion" a more complex man than literary
history has suspected.

II

Yet the major irony is that while Wendell felt himself out of joint with the new spirit in American culture, he was inextricably bound up in that transition between old and new. He was a product of that transition, a prime example of the debilitation caused by major transitional periods, and at the same time he was one of the figures who sped to arms the coming revolution in literature. If Adams and Wendell saw in the new century a world they could not like or accept, the rebellion that reached full volume by the 1920s was engineered and directed by men like Van Wyck Brooks, T. S. Eliot, and e. e. cummings, who at Harvard were fed a diet of rebellion by teachers too weak to rebel themselves. Wendell's efforts as a teacher and administrator at Harvard from 1880 to 1917 show him to be not only a man of doubt and weakness, but a man of vast influence. Hardly just a "provincial schoolmaster," Wendell was one of the major forces in the development of a strong English department at Harvard. With Bliss Perry, Fred Robinson, Francis Childs, George Lyman Kittredge, and George Pierce Baker, Wendell was part of Charles William Eliot's golden age. George Baker wrote of his former teacher: "Born and bred a conservative in social matters, he was yet a reorganizer intellectually. Steadily, his life long, an inculcator of that which is deadliest to conservatism, —independent, fresh, constructive thinking, —he was one of the most stimulating teachers Harvard has ever known."[7]

Wendell fought President Eliot's famous elective system as too specialized for undergraduates and destructively chaotic in its expansion and splintering of the curriculum. Santayana finally left Harvard in 1912 after being told to teach the "facts" of philosophy. Wendell, too, disliked the "eccentric historical perspective" that merely lists dates and events; for him the "ideal fruit" of studying history "should be reasoning about history." Consequently, in 1904, with faculty from government, history, and comparative literature,

Wendell helped pioneer not only the general-education approach to university training but the field of American studies as well. Harvard's honors degree in literature and history, with Wendell as its chairman till his retirement, was an interdisciplinary program animated by Wendell's concern to "think things together."

Wendell's versatility as a teacher is also clear from the diversity of his published work, most of which derived from his courses. It may have been the flux in higher education or the rapid growth in new courses that caused Wendell in thirty-seven years to teach some twenty different courses, everything from Beowulf to the present—survey courses, courses in Shakespeare, the seventeenth and eighteenth centuries, the Romantics, comparative literature courses from Homer to Kipling, composition courses, and the first American literature course at Harvard.

His book English Composition came out of his famous courses English 12 (Elective Composition) and English 5 (Advanced Composition). Wendell's teaching of creative writing made Harvard a mecca for students who wanted to write. Frank Norris moved with his mother to Cambridge specifically to enroll in Harvard's well-known writing courses. Robert Frost sought special permission to enroll in Wendell's course, and the novelist Robert Herrick wrote: "My personal debt to Mr. Wendell is of the largest. . . . He taught me my profession, teaching, and he also gave me my first and greatest inspiration in my art."[8] The text itself, in print until 1942, proved equally popular and influential. It has served as a model approach for rhetoric and composition in college writing courses since its publication in 1891. Even Wendell felt "this not very important book has proved a landmark. . . . It has stood the test of time."[9] As late as 1945 Santayana speculated: "A change of tone [in American writing] there has certainly been in the last thirty years, and who knows how much of it may not be due to Barrett Wendell?[10]

Similarly in American literature Wendell played a pioneering role. His name has missed the attention it deserves among the ranks of that small handful generally associated with the rising interest in American literature (Joseph W.

Beach at Minnesota, William P. Trent at Columbia, William
Cairns at Wisconsin, Fred Lewis Pattee at Pennsylvania
State, Moses Coit Tyler at Michigan, and Arthur H. Quinn at
Pennsylvania). The indifferent success of late nineteenth-
century American literature courses was not shared at Harvard, where in 1897, when he was Chairman of English,
Wendell began his reading course English 20c (Research in
the Literary History of America) and in 1898 his English 33
(Literary History of America), offered continuously to undergraduates, and from 1911 to graduates, until his retirement
in 1917. As usual the results of a course became a book, this
time the famous—and infamous—Literary History of America,
which along with its school-text version also remained in
print into the forties. The book is significantly flawed, as
will be seen, but Wendell nevertheless was one of the first
serious instructors of American literature, and the work itself aroused fruitful counterattacks and greatly advanced the
prestige of its subject in American colleges.

The nature and extent of his direct influence upon individual
students, however, would assure Wendell a significant if
secondary place in American literary history had he written
no books at all. H. L. Mencken maintained that Wendell
"opened paths that he was unable to traverse himself. Stur-
dier men, following him, were soon marching far ahead of
him."[11] Students there were certainly whom Wendell repelled,
but such students, according to the more positive reminis-
cence of their classmates, were the conventional and intolerant, for there was something playful about Wendell's mind;
he was always posturing to shatter illusions and undisputed
authority, to reveal hypocrisy, to stimulate individual thinking. He embodied the irony of a man whom critics and indeed
his own self-portrait depict as hating change and who at the
same time committed himself to the most liberal of goals,
the encouragement of students to think for themselves. In his
composition courses he cared less whether students learned
how to write than that they acquire "this real knowledge of
individual awareness and response." For all his aristocratic
tendencies and his love for the "gentle past," he was a rebel:
"He was witheringly intolerant of the conventional for its own
sake, moral timidity, the commonplace, or worship of the

letter instead of the spirit."[12] It is easy to see in retrospect
that while Van Wyck Brooks and Bernard DeVoto condemned
the Barrett Wendells for not giving them a program for revolution, the older Harvard nonetheless gave them the weapons
with which to rebel. Wendell was sentimental about the past,
but knew it "the most delusive of iridescent fantasies" to hope
for its return. He hated the ugliness of reform-conscious
America, but seeing the job of education as an effort to
achieve "the nearest possible adjustment of man to his environment," he urged his students to question the past and attend to the present.

One of Wendell's basic premises as a teacher of writing—
that "a teacher or pupil keep himself alive to the truth that
what he is striving to accomplish is no less than an act of
creative imagination"[13]—was not without efficacy in a younger
generation. Though he felt in 1908 a "growing impotence of
diffusion," there was already at Harvard an undergraduate
named Eliot who would soon emerge as a leader in a new literary renaissance, and Wendell, not the isolated genteel
academician here, could himself say that "the enthusiastic
diffusion of the moment has broken the old bonds; . . . for
they would never have been broken if they had not been almost
worn out."[14] The list of men who followed Wendell is both impressive and ironic since the success of their work meant the
eclipsing of their former teacher: George Santayana, Joel
Spingarn, Van Wyck Brooks, John Macy, T. S. Eliot, John
Dos Passos, V. L. Parrington, e. e. cummings are men
whose work marks the emergence of a new criticism and
creativity in the twentieth century, and are major represen-
tatives of generations of men who

> . . . studied under the guidance of a fastidious instructor
> who was always watchful for individuality, for fine phras-
> ing, for craftsmanship . . . , a source of profound stim-
> ulation. It was not scholarly inspiration. It was not as an
> educational process that they felt the work. It was an artis-
> tic, or creative inspiration.[15]

Wendell's influence on a wide range of students is easily
documented. John Lomax left the encouragement of Wendell's
American literature class to begin a long and major career

in the study of western ballads. John M. Manly expressed
indebtedness to Wendell for giving him "three of the most valuable things a teacher can give a student: ideas, inspiration
to independent thinking, and an example of the possibility,
and value of seeing a work of literature under both its historical and permanent aspects."[16] And he acknowledged in the
preface to his Specimens of the Shakespearian Drama (1897)
that Wendell "first awakened my interest in the subject of
these volumes." The well-known Yale professor William Lyon
Phelps expressed his debt to Wendell and his fondness for his
former teacher in his Autobiography (1939). Kenneth Murdock self-consciously followed Wendell to carry on the Harvard tradition of Puritan studies. Sir Arthur Quiller-Couch,
a student of Wendell through his books, dedicated Shakespeare's Workmanship (1917) to Wendell "in gratitude for
many pleasures of insight directed by his illuminating com-
monsense."

Horace M. Kallen—immigrant Jewish philosopher and a
founder of the New School for Social Research, a colleague
of Thorstein Veblen, Charles Beard, and James Harvey Robinson—offered one of the most striking testimonies to Wendell's concerns and efforts as a teacher. His lifelong friendship, said Kallen, "stood the test of radical divergences in
outlook and aspiration to the very end," and those differences
were major between the conservative Bostonian and the Jew
with positive concerns for labor, the problems of minorities,
American pluralism, and the American Civil Liberties Union.
The liberal Kallen, perhaps more than any other of his students, illustrated the ideal results of Wendell's principles.
Kallen has written:

> He freed my surprised mind for ways of perceiving the
> American Idea and for the art of saying anything I saw
> which gave a new turn to my appraisal of myself as a free
> man among other men. I learned soon that the figure of
> this man of letters, with his cane and his pince-nez, his
> difficult articulation . . . and the Tory-like stance of his
> protesting spirit, shaped up, in the sight of many, as ex-
> aggerated snobbery. I found this a superficial if not an
> illusory image.[17]

Wendell's belief that American drama was "rather sleeping
than dead" led him to urge the power and possibility of drama
on his students. Much of the undergraduate interest in Ibsen,
Strindberg, and the new European drama arose from Wendell's interest. Evidence that his dramatic concerns fell on
fertile ground is amply presented in the chapter entitled
"Wendell Points the Way" in Wisner Kinne's biography of
George Pierce Baker.[18] A student and then a colleague of
Wendell's, the young Baker in the late 1890s had published
two books on speech and argumentation without much success.
Wendell's strong advice then pointed him in the direction of
drama. He too recognized his appreciation for Wendell's
stimulation in his dedication of The Development of Shakespeare as a Dramatist (1907), and in a letter to Wendell
stated: "More and more I have come to see that my teaching
at all and any success which has been mine as a teacher I owe
to you . . . for correction, stimulation, even inspiration in
the past, and for thirty odd years, I thank you."[19] Just as
Wendell inspired Baker, so Baker inspired several generations of budding playwrights: his famous Harvard 47 work-
shop produced playwrights like Eugene O'Neill and became
a seminal force in the new drama emerging so clearly by the
end of the twenties.

Wendell also exerted influence outside the classroom. He
served as Charles Scribner's main contact in Cambridge,
introducing to the New York publisher colleagues and proté-
gés like George Herbert Palmer, William Vaughn Moody,
and Robert Morss Lovett. His contact with Scribner's secured the young Santayana a contract for his first book, The
Sense of Beauty. And Wendell's strong appreciation for a
first volume of poems entitled The Torrent and the Night
Before led him actively to campaign for Scribner's acceptance of Edwin Arlington Robinson's Captain Craig, though
finally not even Theodore Roosevelt could persuade editor
W. C. Brownell to publish it.

The lengthy correspondence between Wendell and Amy Lowell from 1915 to 1919 uncovers an even more direct link between the defender of old New England and one of the prime
movers in the poetry of the new century. While Wendell, to

Van Wyck Brooks, stood for the seekers of "lost trails" in American literature, Amy Lowell was the "prime minister of the republic of poets."[20] No two individuals could have been further apart than the Wendell who stood for all that was sterile in Boston culture and the Lowell who represented all its health. But in 1915 Lowell sent Wendell a copy of Six French Poets with a note: "You have taught me so much in your books and conversation, ever since I was a child, that I insist upon being considered in some sort your pupil."[21]

Their correspondence is illuminating, for Lowell there professed a serious indebtedness to her lifelong friend. She wrote in response to his criticism of her "excess of vivacity," "that criticism of yours was one of the best I ever had," and in 1917 she sent Wendell her Tendencies in Modern American Poetry and wondered, "if it is not too much trouble, I will be very glad to have you tell me what you think of it, as I value your opinion very much." Wendell's response is typical of the long, detailed criticism that passed between them; writing in the shaky hand of illness, her "friendly conservative" found that "the question is whether you have done a Literati, more thoughtful than Poe's . . . , or have cast the first light on ways to be. . . . That you have done work one would be glad to have done oneself is sure." Wendell's long letter and Lowell's seven-page response dealt frankly with her sense of a "new movement," characterized by a "marked Americanism," about which Wendell was quietly doubtful and Lowell clearly enthusiastic.

Van Wyck Brooks found two Bostons in the pre-World War days: one, the dying gasp of Brahmin Boston, the other a milieu of taste, culture, dissent that was soon to flower in the work of T. S. Eliot. Wendell may be the epitome of the first group, the narrow aristocrats looking to a dead past. Yet Wendell's relationship with the other, more vital Boston is clear in his correspondence with Amy Lowell. As will be seen, too, his writings demonstrate that his appreciation for the New England past was not uncritical, his belief in a Puritan dogmatism not all personal. Wendell in fact is not unlike Brooks's Epigoni "in their revolt from democracy and realism, their desire to expunge all remnants of the Puritan

past."[22] But Wendell with his admiration for the British
crown, his enthusiasm for the classics, his appreciation of
the hierarchic church, parallels a famous royalist, classicist,
Anglo-Catholic of the thirties. When, then, Warner Berthoff
says that "the grounding of [Eliot's] thought in polite opinion
of the '80s and '90s is always worth noting," it is important to
recognize Wendell's place in the Lowell-Eliot continuum.[23]
Indeed, the recollection that Brooks too came out of that
same Harvard tradition raises the question whether Brooks,
like Pound with Whitman, owed a debt to a teacher he could
not easily admire.

At the turn of the century the new poetry still smacked of
the Bohemian, and Wendell's status seemed assured: the
media widely reviewed and the public read his books; students filled his classes to overflowing year after year. He
lectured three times under the august auspices of the Lowell
Institute; he gave the Clark lectures at Trinity College, Cambridge, in 1902-1903; in 1904-1905 he inaugurated with great
success the Hyde Foundation lectures at the Sorbonne; and he
received honorary doctorates from Columbia, Harvard, and
Strasbourg.

But by the 1920's William Dean Howells had become the
"grand old lady" of American literature, and Wendell suffered even greater damage at the hands of the new "makers
and finders": the last of the Boston Brahmins, defender of
a "cramped and sickly" tradition, Wendell was afflicted with
"grandfather of the brain," and his Literary History was "the
last testament of the old school." Forgotten now was the
courage with which Howells championed the new realism
from the Editor's Study of Harper's, the courage of Ernest
Clarence Stedman's emphatic praise of Whitman in 1880,
the vigor of Barrett Wendell's continuing defense of the Puritan spirit in a tradition whose form he knew had become
sterile. Weakness, timidity, lack of curiosity became cli-
chés for anti-Victorians. Brooks called Boston too "cha-
grined" to notice the rising new generation. Pattee claimed
the genteel writers missed completely the insights of new
literature after the war, and for V. L. Parrington the Boston
mentality attended to nothing of significance and vitality in

American life. Such views culminated in 1930 with Sinclair
Lewis's Nobel discussion of "The American Fear of Literature."

Certainly the efforts of the young manifesto-givers in the
early twentieth century to find a usable past demonstrate the
necessity of the young artist to interpret his past in the light
of present personal needs and social demands. That there
was justice in their accusations against the "grandfathers" in
the academies even the grandfathers themselves recognized.
But Wendell's career and influence indicate that the Genteel
Era was not so simple and harmful to American letters as the
Brooks-DeVoto generation charged. As Morton Zabel noted:
"From the vantage point of 1960 it is possible to look back on
a large portion of this activity [in the 1920s and 1930s] with
detachment or objectivity and discount a good deal of what
was then urgent, vital, and challenging."[24]

Wendell believed the world had bypassed Yankee New England, and such a realization presented him with a challenge,
as many anti-Victorian critics have argued, to renewed vigor
in defense of the fading culture, but a challenge also for the
future. He wrote:

> The great moments seem to me those when energy, which
> has been confined by tradition, breaks the outworn bonds
> of it. This was the case in New England, when New England
> was memorable. Nothing but conscious knowledge of ortho-
> doxy could have made Emerson what he was.[25]

And such, Wendell felt, was the case with Dante, with Shakespeare, with Wordsworth, as their reaction against the past,
their use of the past, found expression in vital new forms.
Such was the case with the writers of the twentieth-century
renaissance as they used and reacted against the cultural
orthodoxy which Wendell both defended and distrusted. By
his expression of faith in the future Wendell helped pave the
way, as teacher, critic, and literary historian, for the generation that followed him.

III

The essays included in this collection are grouped first by common concerns—the Puritans; composition; the "touch-stone" authors represented here by Shakespeare; American literary history; politics, society, and literature—and within those groupings they are arranged chronologically. The essays present Wendell in all his diversity and ambivalence: in subject matter from Shakespeare to popular journalism; in critical viewpoint between the provincial prejudices of a consummate Tory and the literary illumination of a cultural historian; in personal temperament from "heart-felt sympathy" for Cotton Mather to Brahmin distaste for the "anarchistic" Whitman. The strengths and weaknesses fostered by his heritage, his era, his personality are all here. Wendell originally delivered the essays as lectures in his classrooms, or under the auspices of the Lowell Institute, or during his Cambridge and Paris lectureships or on one of the many speaking engagements that carried him from New York to California and South Carolina. Because he seldom bothered to revise for the press, his writings give the impression often that type was set directly from his speaking notes, so that the eccentricity, exaggeration, wit and insights so famous to generations of his students still emerge. These selections come from the first editions of their publication in book form, that form representing as well as any Wendell's care that his writing coincide with his thought.

Wendell's first book, Cotton Mather, the Puritan Priest (1891) set liberal Harvard on its ear, inasmuch as Mather was one of Harvard's least admired ancestors. Wendell undertook sympathetically "to tell what manner of man he was, what manner of world he lived in, why—with all his oddities and failings that are so grotesque to us—he seems worth remembering." After the rise of Unitarianism and Transcendentalism, Mather had come to represent all that was superstitious and tyrannical in the Calvinist tradition, yet by a thorough

and balanced presentation of Mather's own writings (many
given scholarly consideration for the first time in his study),
Wendell attempted to show that Mather "never ceased striving, amid endless stumbling and errors, to do his duty."
These essays reflect Wendell's long fascination with Mather
and the Puritans, an interest which gained him the ire of
twentieth-century critics like Van Wyck Brooks, H.L. Mencken, and V.L. Parrington, who saw the American "fear of
experience," the timidity of American literature, rooted in
the unhappy influence of Puritanism. Nevertheless, Wendell's remains one of the best studies of Cotton Mather and
is a major document in the Harvard tradition of serious attention to the Puritans, carried on by Wendell's successors
Kenneth Murdock and Perry Miller.

Wendell is clearly aware of Mather's faults—"self-seeking, vain, arrogant, inconsistent"—but his initial concern is
how so "profoundly fatalistic a creed could possibly prove a
motive strong enough to result not only in individual lives but
in a corporate life, that was destined to grow into a national
life, of passionate enthusiasm, and of abnormal moral as
well as material activity." His answer has psychological
validity; the "unrecognized impulse of selfish human curiosity" created the need if not the reality to demonstrate individual election. In Wendell's own day religion was losing the
battle with science, and only recently has humanistic psychology returned to an understanding of the kind of passionate,
imaginative ideality Wendell finds in Puritanism and its
healthy "disregard for that fine adjustment of phrase to fact
which our modern scientific spirit of veracity assumes for
the moment to be eternally the chief of cardinal virtues."
Wendell's insight into the profundity of Puritan spirituality,
the intense emotional reality of its intercourse with demons
and angels, its awareness of the spiritual lessons in the
natural world led him to an early appreciation of William
James's Varieties of Religious Experience. It also provided
him clues to the Puritan failure. The conflicts among "devout
free thought," spiritual imagination, and the incessant demands of the "petty material facts" of everyday life, focused
by an anthropomorphic desire to express concretely the un-

knowable, eventually and inevitably resulted in the exhaustion of that imagination.

Puritanism gave way to Common Law; the doctrine of election came to be upheld not by grace but by material success. Still, for Wendell, the ideality underlying the spiritual and imaginative enthusiasm of the Puritans survived in what he called "national inexperience," an innocence of the debilitating social forces of an old Europe, reinforced by a faith in what ought to be. This thesis, more fully developed in later years, evoked the hostility of the young "literary radicals" later, for whom the weakness in American literature derived from its failure to grapple frankly with the realities of everyday life. It locates Wendell's concepts of the development of American democracy and the dilemmas inherent in it, and helps clarify his statement to William James: "I love the memory of Cotton Mather; and should be happier in a world that hadn't been graced by Channing or Emerson."[26] His study was a self-conscious counter to the Germanic scholarship he detested, an attempt to seek not the sterile facts but the "subjective matters" of Mather and his faith. Moreover, Wendell crystallized his own uncertainties; like Mather he saw around him the breakup of the old faith resulting in personal conflict:

> Pure in motive, noble in purpose, his whole life was one unending effort to strengthen in himself that phase of human nature whose inner token is a riot of mystical emotion, whose outward signs are unwitting manifestations of unfettered credulity and unmeant fraud.

As the heir to Brahmin New England Wendell too struggled with the conflict of traditional authority and the formlessness of change and experiment. Mather had real faith to sustain him but Wendell in his own life fell back on "histrionic insincerity," wanting to play the role of cultural priest "who can at will seem to be what in truth he is not." The Puritan conflicts he dramatized in these essays call attention once again to the tension between American dream and American reality, between yesterday's green breast of a new world and tomorrow's ashheaps.

While Wendell's studies in Puritanism reveal the sensitive historian, his English Composition (1891) conveys the humanistic and influential teacher. The two essays here, "The Elements and the Qualities of Style" and "Elegance," are the first and last chapters of his long-printed book, an answer to the wrong-headed, rules-oriented approach of the older rhetorics. Wendell's thesis states that the way to good writing "is not to load your memory with bewilderingly innumerable rules, but to firmly grasp a very few simple, elastic general principles." His lack of concern with rules was a major departure from the earlier texts, best represented by his old professor Adams Sherman Hill's Principles of Rhetoric and Their Applications (1876). Hill worked inductively. His text is jammed full of correct and incorrect examples of writing which led to briefly stated but emphatic rules of composition. Wendell, on the other hand, worked deductively, beginning with the desired effect and employing whatever rhetorical techniques are necessary to achieve it. While the book has been called the last line of conservative defense against a disintegrating classical education under Harvard's Elective System, many contemporary reactions decried Wendell's failure to be more doctrinaire. His descriptive approach to language and its symbolic aspects predated Jespersen, and he may have been the earliest rhetorician to appeal to the "average man" for his evidence that "It is me" is idiomatically acceptable—though one critic hoped he did not reflect the "best Cambridge usage."

"Good use" for Wendell means relativity, general principles not rules, not right versus wrong but better versus worse: how accurately something expresses what the writer has to say. Language is not static but a matter of fashion; dictionaries do not detail legislation but common law. Like Hill, Wendell is concerned with words, sentences, and paragraphs, but a major innovation in English Composition is an extra step—the whole composition (which Wendell in his writing classes tended to call "themes"). He specifies "clearness," "force," and "elegance" as the general principles governing whole compositions: the effective essay is intellectually understandable, emotionally engaging, and aesthetically pleasing. The final effectiveness of any writing is "the result of a constant though generally unconscious struggle between good use and the principles of composition. In words, of course good use is absolute; in sentences, though it relaxes its authority, it remains very powerful; in paragraphs its authority becomes very feeble; in whole compositions, it may roughly be said to coincide with the principles."

Perhaps this kind of relativity derived from Wendell's almost metaphysical starting point. Style "means simply the expression of thought or emotion in written words." Writing captures in material form those immaterial realities and is ultimately individual and creative. Thus Wendell's approach, too, for teaching composition as well as his influence on young creative writers:

> This matter of composition is as far from a dull and lifeless business as earthly matters can be; . . . he who scribbles a dozen words, just as truly as he who writes an epic, performs . . . that most wonderful of things—gives a material body to some reality which till that moment was unmaterial, executes all unconscious of the power for which divine is none too grand a word, a lasting act of creative imagination.

In "Elegance" Wendell articulates not only a theory of composition but a poetics as well; he understands the symbolic impulse of Romanticism when he points out the inadequacy of words to express truth: "the expression of thought and feelings in words can never be complete," and "we are apt to forget that the noblest expression of the noblest art is as petty a thing beside the great infinite expanse of truth that the masters strive to express." He also echoes the vague genteel attitude toward beauty as "charm," "grace," "ease." And genteel squeamishness is there when he notes that euphemism, despite its inelegance, prevents one's mentioning "hateful things needlessly."

But Wendell's theory here allies him more with Henry James, T. S. Eliot, and formalist criticism than with the genteel writers. Henry James uses the word "execution," where Wendell says "adaptation":

> The more exquisitely style is adapted to the thought it
> symbolizes the better we can make our words and compo-
> sitions denote and connote in other human minds the mean-
> ing they denote and connote in ours, the greater charm
> style will have, merely as a work of art. In a single
> phrase, the secret of elegance lies in adaptation.

Wendell's word indicates a formalistic theory of expression.
The genteel figure may speak in the single passage where he
condemns Maupassant for describing "according to our standards . . . very abominable subjects," subjects about which
"the better plan is to ask ourselves whether we may not best
of all leave [them] . . . unmentioned." Many critics stop
here and cite Wendell for prudishness, but do so at the ex-
pense of the Wendell caught somewhere between this Victorian attitude and the stance which decried euphemisms as
aesthetically degrading in literature, the Wendell within
whom warred a didactic humanism and an aesthetic creativity. The critic, Wendell says, must ascertain a writer's
purpose before attacking his methods, and "the purpose of
not a few admirable artists is so detestable that on grounds
of morality and decency we may utterly condemn their work;
but this fact does not, in my opinion, at all affect the value
of their work as a work of art. . . . And some of the stories
that are in themselves the most hateful can give, and rightly,
to the technical critic the keenest delight."
Here was Howells's conflict between larger aesthetic
standards and more provincial didactic standards, but this
was essentially aesthetic criticism; it recalled Coleridge's
organic approach; it anticipated T. S. Eliot's "objective cor-
relative," where the reader sees through those written words
to the thought and feeling which they incarnate; and it marked
perhaps Wendell's most successful integration of the ideal
and the real, that tension which disturbed him throughout his
entire career.

In his review of Edward Eggleston's The Transit of Civilization, Wendell wrote:

> The historian of a past civilization must somehow bring
> himself into imaginative sympathy with the human spirit of
> the times with which he deals, until he understands not only
> bare facts but also how those facts made the living men feel
> who knew them in the flesh.[27]

This statement very accurately describes Wendell's method
in the classroom and in his literary histories. He repeatedly
urged the need "to think things together," to see the data of
literature and history "in their mutual relations," for history "is the ultimate base of all literature, just as all literature might be described as the voice of history." His mixed
mind wavered between the "dilettantish" impressionist and
the "pedantic" scholar, but his study of Cotton Mather reveals how well at his best he could balance broad research in
forgotten manuscripts with a personal appreciation for the
real man.

All of his literary histories were developed around specific
cultural theses, most of which may be traced to the intellectual current of the late nineteenth century. Wendell, who
found Hippolyte Taine "admirable," "always precise, always
intelligent, and above all incessantly suggestive," continually
employed Taine's triad of race, place, and moment to structure his histories. Literature for Wendell, as for Taine, was
part of the organized unity of historical process. The evolutionary ideas, too, of Ferdinand Brunetière, Charles Darwin,
Herbert Spencer, and John Fiske were widespread in the
1880s and 1890s and figured largely in the "scientific" concerns of William Dean Howells, Thomas Sargent Perry,
Hamlin Garland, and Wendell. Literature, conceived as a
product of society, was seen to be like society, continually
in flux, evolving in two ways: progressively (and for some
Darwinian critics competitively) through its socially determined origins, and cyclically (with growth, proliferation,
maturity, decay) through its particular genre. While individual genres moved inevitably through the birth-death pattern
giving way subsequently to another genre or a new variant of
the same kind, social progress continued from the communal
to the individual, the homogeneous to the heterogeneous, the

simple to the complex, the undifferentiated to the differenti-
ated, and both aspects of evolution progressed from general
and abstract through particular and concrete to imitation and
artifice. And Wendell in this context speaks of

> how imagination breaks the limits of old conventions, and
> of how, after a brief period when imagination and sense of
> fact have been immortally fused, a crushing sense of fact
> slowly and inexorably checks the further aspirations of
> imagination, imposing new conventions on an art which is
> no longer free.[28]

Wendell's Shakspere aims at a "coherent" view of the
poet's life and works, at seeing Shakespeare "as he saw himself," which entails analysis of Elizabethan "commonplaces
of human experience," the Elizabethan drama, its audience
and its stage. As opposed to Taine's view of Shakespeare as
a "superhuman" of "inordinate" and "extravagant" genius,
Wendell's wants to keep in mind that admiration of genius
may lead people fatally to "forget the truth that Shakspere's
work really emanated from a living man." But the whole work
develops rigid system. Following the lead of J.A.Symonds's
rigorous description of the biological development of Elizabethan drama, Wendell calls that drama "one of the most
completely typical phenomena in the whole history of fine
arts. It took little more than half a century to emerge from
archaic tradition, to develop into great imaginative vitality,
and to decline into a formal tradition"—"a remarkably typical
example of artistic evolution." At a time when England as a
nation was emerging from the medieval into the modern
world, from a provincial to an imperial power, he finds conditions satisfying both aspects of evolution, social and generic.

Shakespeare's career, too, Wendell finds to correspond
exactly, in its rise and fall, to the national drama; he
"worked with intrinsic fidelity to the greater laws which govern actual life." Unlike Edward Dowden, in his famous book
Shakspere: His Mind and Art (1875) which divides the poet's
career into four successively better periods, Wendell marks
off four periods of a different sort in the poet's career: a

period of early experimentation, one of increasing imaginative force, a high period of fused imaginative, spiritual, and
psychological force, and lastly a period of decline. Just as
the chronology from Marlowe through Shakespeare to Webster
is important, the chronology of Shakespeare's plays becomes
crucial to illustrate the "growth," "maturity," "decline" of
his drama. Two Gentlemen of Verona reveals originality and
versatility of character in Shakespeare's "apprenticeship."
A Midsummer Night's Dream demonstrates an increasing
concentration of his power with concrete words. Hamlet,
King Lear, Othello illustrate "tremendous power both of will
and artistic expression," and with The Tempest and A Win-
ter's Tale the "old spontaneous power was fatally gone."
Wendell's system suffers from a rigidity that often distorts,
yet he is clearly aware of the temporality of his approach:

> Just now the study of literary evolution happens to be the
> fashion, or at least to appeal to the temper of the day. The
> temper in question is new and probably transient. Shak-
> spere was a supreme figure long before it existed; he will
> remain such long after it has taken its place among the
> curiosities of the past.

The thing that makes Shakespeare a poet for all ages, however, is his genius, that craft which makes his work seen
through whatever system seem constantly new, and makes
the critic tend to "forget that it was made for any other condition than those amid which, generation after generation, we
find it."

Among late nineteenth-century critics Robert Falk recognizes three groups: the "literary democrats," the neo-
humanists, and the "objective-impressionists."[29] Wendell's
use of science, his evolutionary criticism, his Taine-like
attention to sociological factors place him in the first camp,
without its faith in progress or any confidence in democratic
mediocrity. His attention to broader human characteristics
than race, place, and time and his awareness of European
tradition locate him with W. C. Brownell, George Woodberry,
and Brander Matthews in the second group, though he himself
posits few universal standards of value. And his criticism

both impressionistic and analytic recalls the work of Henry
James in the last group, though by far without the insight or
technical sense of James. While Wendell never explicitly
enunciated his theoretical position, his work on Shakespeare
demonstrates his eclectic participation in many aspects of
the critical scene in his day. The movement in American literary criticism from James Russell Lowell and Whitman to
T. S. Eliot was far more complex than the familiar battle for
realism, the genteel adulation of beauty, the liberal reaction
against Victorian prudery, or aesthetic humanism in the
twenties—though certainly these facets marked the general
outline of seventy years of criticism. From the historical,
aesthetic criticism of Lowell, the critical path ran through
the optimism of Spencerian evolution where men like James,
Howells, Lanier sought the "romantic vision of the real";
through the highwater mark of realism in the eighties cham-
pioning the democratic average in American life; through the
collectivist and utopian concerns of Howells, Garland, and
Norris; to the neo-romantic revival and poetic revolution
prior to the First World War. The basic critical thrust in
these decades came between the romantic and realistic, between Stedman's devotees of beauty, culture, and business
and Howells's school of reality, democracy, and progress.
And Barrett Wendell, characteristically ambivalent, shared
something with them all.

In a letter to William James in 1900, Wendell described
his Literary History of America as "characteristic—a bewildering confusion of superficiality and insight, which somehow
neutralize each other until nobody is pleased. . . . In sentiment it is Tory, pro-slavery, and imperialistic; all of which
I fear I am myself."[30] Young literary historians of the
twenties and thirties denounced the book for just those reasons: its New England biases; its aristocratic, narrowly
anglophile perspectives; its genteel racism; its negative and
misplaced assessment of American literature. "Real" American literary history is said to begin in 1915 with John Macy's
more national, more judicial Spirit of American Literature;
for writers like Parrington, Fred Pattee, and Robert Spiller,

Wendell stood on the other side of their efforts fully, accurately, and "objectively" to scrutinize the American past
using the tools of modern scholarship. The Introduction and
Conclusion to Wendell's History illustrate the book's weaknesses and faults, but also its strengths.

Drawing on the general popularity of Taine's historical
criticism, Wendell is primarily concerned with the felt experience of American life, the environment, the people, the
centuries of American letters. His dichotomy between the
ideal and the real surfaces again as he describes American
absorption with "right and rights," the ideals of morality and
government which like its language America shares with England: "For better or worse the ideals which underlie our
blundering conscious life must always be the ideals which
underlie the conscious life of the mother country." While literature means "the lasting expression in words of the meaning of life," Wendell intends American life, but because of
the shared English language his concern becomes, What has
America added to English literature? His method then is historical and comparative: "An important phase of our study
must accordingly be that which attempts to trace and to understand the changes in the native character of the Americans
and of the English." At base what was criticized as his Anglo-
Saxon prejudice may be seen as his attempt by contrast to
describe the American character. In a real sense he too, like
the literary historians of the early twentieth century, asks,
"In what sense is our literature distinctively American?"

The characteristics which he discovers are spontaneous
creation, versatile power, and idealistic enthusiasm, all de-
riving from the initial English settlers of America during the
Renaissance. America retained those traits (while the English moved from Renaissance to Revolution, Restoration, and
finally, in the nineteenth century, Reform) because of what
he terms "national inexperience"; this is the unifying thesis
of his study. And though the Literary History suffers, as do
the histories of Charles Richardson and William Trent, from
too much focus on New England rather than the whole nation,
though it is disproportionately weighted toward Boston values
and tends to discuss an author's biography more than his art,

Wendell's theme of national inexperience is indeed an attempt
to define, describe, and trace the development of American
culture.

   His Sorbonne lectures provide a definition for that phrase
which courses throughout Wendell's commentaries on American literature:

> Variations in environment which alter national organisms
> I have grown accustomed to describe to myself by the term
> national experience. By national inexperience, accordingly,
> I mean at once the absence of such altering and distorting
> environment, and a certain relaxation of external pres-
> sure, which prevents fixity of habit; this is evident even in
> individual American life.[31]

Such inexperience existed "only under conditions where the
pressure of external fact, social, political, and economic,
is relaxed, —under conditions, in short, where the individual
type is for a while stronger than environment." The characteristic, along with the American power to absorb immigrants, maintained as vital much of the Elizabethan and Puritan vigor while the Civil War and Protectorate in England
"destroyed a youthful world" of the Renaissance. National
inexperience one way meant "social stagnation," but it "does
not mean, of course, that human life has not existed here in
all its real complexities. It means that hitherto our commu-
nities have generally been so far from over-crowded, and
our people so free to make their way whither they could and
would, that in America the material problems of life have
presented themselves less regularly than in Europe."

   Wendell shared the opinion of many later critics as to the
effects of this national inexperience. On one hand its value
was clear: when, for two hundred years, intellectual tyranny
had kept the native mind cramped within the limits of tradition, Emerson fearlessly stood forth as the chief representative of that movement which asserted the right of every
individual "to think, to feel, to speak, to ask for himself,
confident that so far as each acts in sincerity good will ensue." But that same vigor of innocence was also its weakness. Like Henry James's view earlier in the well-known

Hawthorne essay, Wendell's view was also the one expressed later by T. S. Eliot: "Their world was thin; it was not corrupt enough."[32]

The conflicting values of Wendell's mind and of his critical postures emerge in his essays in the Literary History on Hawthorne and Whitman and in the late essay on Poe. That his criticism is also more than merely the accident of Anglo-Saxon and Brahmin prejudice is clearer here, for these artists evoke all of Wendell's hostility and force his critical integrity to work all the harder to assert their worth. The general content of his views toward these three writers is not necessarily unique. It is hard to praise his increasingly positive attitude toward Poe, for instance, since despite a tentative appreciation of the Virginia poet and author whom Howells could not accept, that shifting perspective paralleled the general critical shift in judgments from George Woodberry's important study in 1885 to his revised version of that work in the Poe centenary year, 1909. Hawthorne had long been a New England favorite, and Wendell's view of his provincialism postdates James's famous study. Even in the case of Whitman, such genteel writers as Stedman had managed as early as 1880 to work up an enthusiasm for the Good Grey Poet. The value of Wendell's book—despite its infamous negativity—lies in its positive criticism of the more important authors discussed, and in the view that these criticisms yield of the Boston historian attempting to balance honesty and prejudice, of the Brahmin aware that a safe old New England was dead and not certain what kind of new century was coming to light. Beneath the aristocratic stance, there is the honest critic whose approach to "pure" American letters rests on the realization that for American writers "to give their expression resemblance of reality they had no medieval relics to guide them, no enduring local traditions, thick and strong about them. They were compelled to rely on sheer force of creative imagination."[33]

In his first book on American literature, Stelligeri (1893), Wendell used the negative terms "fantastic and meretricious," "falsity," "sham," "wild," "freakish," to illustrate his feelings toward Edgar Allan Poe. By 1900, however, he

could speak in the <u>Literary History</u> of Poe's haunted imagination as "handled with something like mastery." The flaws in
Poe's work are staginess, unnecessarily ornamental verse,
morbidity, "lack of spiritual insight." Wendell is put off by
Poe's inferior social position and his southern origins, yet
he explicitly cites his Americanness as a function of the <u>His-
tory</u>'s theme; Poe's "freedom from lubricity," his unaffect-
ed tone depend on that freedom from complex social pressure
Wendell calls national inexperience. Poe's power is of "unusual technical mastery," and as he concludes the chapter
Wendell's generally final note of equivocation yields to positive assessment:

> Though Poe's power was great, however, his chief merits
> prove merits of refinement. Even through a time so recent
> as his, refinement of temper, conscientiousness of form,
> and instructive neglect of actual fact remained the most
> characteristic traits . . . of American letters.

But Wendell took up Poe again in his Sorbonne lectures
four years later when he compared him favorably with Shelley, and the equivocation of his 1900 essay gives way in Wendell's 1908 centennial address to the assertion of Poe's unchallenged position in permanent literature. The change may
have been sparked by positive French reaction encountered
during the Hyde lectureship, but change there is. Time and
again in the <u>Literary History</u> his evaluation of a writer's
worth coincides with observations on the artist's social
class. That Poe was never of "the better sort" may have obscured Wendell's earlier vision, but in 1908 he asserts, "we
are apt nowadays, when concerned with literature, to pass
our time even less fruitfully than if we were still grammarians, in researches little removed from the impertinence of
gossip." But not this time, for the "Poe whom we are met to
celebrate is not the man but his work." He rather simply
describes Poe as a Romantic who alone can capture "the fascinating, fantastic, elusive, incessant mystery of that which
must forever envision human consciousness, unseen, unknowable, impalpable, implacable, undeniable." This ability
"asserts his nationality" because it is so "serenely free of

material condition and tradition."

This last essay on Poe is a strange collection of positions, however. Wendell's real lack of ease with Poe is apparent when he calls Poe's mood "bafflingly elusive." He typically provides a long essay on English literary history to set up the Romantic tradition—from which he then isolates Poe. He goes so far as to admit that the literature of New England, "American though we may all gladly assert it in its nobler phases, is, first of all, not American or national, but local." This sentiment either contradicts the views in his Literary History and indicates a marked growth in Wendell's outlook, or else it tends to take the sting out of his final assertion to a Virginia audience that "Poe's individuality is too intense for universal appeal." There is in the whole essay a wordiness, a vagueness that seems on one hand conciliatory toward his southern listeners, and on the other hand defensive since any lack of sympathy for Poe he notes must derive from a deficiency of individual response to the poet. The result, when Wendell at last states his "reverence" for Poe as a wondrous "harbinger of American spiritual reunion," is the same ambivalence that struggles to appreciate real artistry despite his temperamental uneasiness with that artistry.

Wendell's attitude toward Hawthorne shows less of that usual equivocating. Solitary, imaginative, Hawthorne not only expresses his "meanings in words of which the beauty seems sure to grow with the years," he articulates the "inalienable emotional heritage of Puritanism." Summarizing the roles of writers in the New England Renaissance Wendell designates Emerson its prophet, Whittier its reformer, Longfellow its academic poet, Lowell its humanist, and Holmes its rationalist. Hawthorne stands above these as eminently its artist, "an artist who lived for nearly fifty years only in his native country, daily stirred to attempt expression of what our Yankee life meant. Of all our men of letters he was the most indigenous; of all, the least imitative."

He was gifted with a "pervasive sense of form" and the romantic temperament so typically native in America and traceable to "the darkly passionate idealism of the Puritans,"

whose sense of depravity and eternal retribution always
haunted Hawthorne. In his solitary nature, his sense of the
mysteries of life and sin, his self-searching instinct, Wendell finds Hawthorne a reflection of the essential Puritan
spirit, though he makes no specific analysis of Hawthorne's
fiction to illustrate that spirit or his artistry.

He asserts Hawthorne to be essentially American in his
self-conscious awareness of form; "starved of antiquity,"
living in "isolated, aesthetically starved New England,"
Hawthorne combines classical precision of form, artistic
craftsmanship, with limited vision to express with beauty the
facts and sense of mystery that lie beyond physical human
life. Wendell probably is far more positive about Hawthorne's
craft than Poe's because it subsumes a Puritan sensitivity.
He even becomes philosophical to explicate this combination
of Puritan consciousness and aesthetic form: "though artistic conscience be very different from moral, the two have in
common an aspiration toward beauty." The Thomistic concept
of ethics and aesthetics underlies Wendell's appreciation for
Hawthorne's artistic concern with "beauty of conduct" and
"beauty of expression." There is incompleteness in the formal
substance of this romantic sentiment, however; "one grows
aware . . . of its unmistakable rusticity; in turns of thought
as well as of phrase one feels monotony, provincialism, a
certain thinness"—attributable to the isolated quality of his
own and of American life. Hawthorne's art proves to be
characteristic of provincial, inexperienced New England
whose ideals, heritage, habit of conscious form, and awareness of mystery and sin "impelled him constantly to realise
in his work those forms of beauty which should most beautifully embody the ideals of his incessantly creative imagination," to express "the deepest temper of that New England
race which brought him forth."

Wendell's long chapter on Whitman reveals greater ambivalence, greater personal struggle than the essays on Hawthorne and Poe, for here the pressures of his New England
predilections, his view of the literary strengths inherent in
national inexperience, his aristocratic bias against the new
"privileged" classes, and his conservative interpretation of

American democracy militate against his ability to say anything very positive about the Brooklyn poet. Indeed his comments on Whitman evoked heated response from Horace
Traubel and sparked a long attack on Wendell at the international meeting of the Walt Whitman Fellowship in New York
in 1902. The main speaker at that gathering saw one more
handicap to Wendell's ability to appreciate Whitman: "We
might once in a while have literature considered from the
standpoint of the man of the world, the man free from academic traditions and undominated by the accepted canons of
the literary reviewer."[34] While the whole Literary History
shows Wendell struggling to overcome those very standards,
the biases here are clear: Whitman, the son of a carpenter,
grew up "close to the most considerable and corrupt centre
of population on his native continent." His reading public
"was at once limited, fastidiously overcultivated, and apt
to be of foreign birth" and his "dogma of equality" represents
clearly a "complete confusion of values."

Although in 1893 in Stelligeri Wendell devotes almost the
entirety of his observation on Whitman to a positive assessment, his chapter in 1900 almost totally smothers any praise
under a blanket of negative criticism. He reiterates his often
stated belief in the American continuation of a conservative
English, not radical French, political theory. Consequently
he can hardly be enthusiastic about Whitman's idea that "as
God made everything, one thing is just as good as another."
Wendell reacts scornfully to the belief of "salvation in the
new, life-saving ideal of equality," and notes ironically that
"among prophets of equality Whitman has the paradoxical
merit of eminence."

Equally repellent and irritating to Wendell is Whitman's
"eccentricity." For instance, the famous fifth section of Song
of Myself mixes "undoubtedly tender feeling"—"beautiful
uncut hair of graves"—with "such rubbish" as the "handkerchief of the Lord," the total impression being "an inextricable hodge-podge . . . [of] beautiful phrases and silly gabble,
tender imagination and insolent commonplace." Here for
Wendell is confusion of both poetic and political values, only
compounded by Whitman's eccentricity of form.

Especially in the matter of that form, however, can be
seen the ambiguity of Wendell's stance and the possibility in
Whitman not of poetic failure but of innovation. Some lines
Wendell describes as "confused, inarticulate, and surging in
a mad kind of rhythm which sounds as if hexameters were
trying to bubble through sewage." But the divergent forces of
his mind almost surface completely in one passage where he
shifts from Whitman's "amorphously meaningless" jargon to
his diction approaching "inevitable union of thought and
phrase," to the isolation of such passages, finally to observe
that Whitman "leaves you with a sense of new realities concerning which you must do your thinking for yourself"—and
all this in one paragraph! And although the Whitman Fellowship speaker himself had to admit that he knew not whether
Whitman's verse-form marked "anticipation of what the future will prefer and adopt,"[35] to Wendell, Whitman "seems
not only native but even promising." Interestingly Wendell
does not conclude the chapter directly in his own words, but
chooses to quote, without citation, his own favorable comment from the earlier Stelligeri describing Whitman finally
as "the only one who points out the stuff of which perhaps the
new American literature of the future may in time be made."

In the early years of the twentieth century Barrett Wendell
was the widely known author of English Composition and the
Literary History of America, but the essay "Democracy" ex-
poses the Wendell who increasingly in the second decade
came to stand for a narrow-minded, reactionary establishment at a time when national optimism came to be designated
the Age of Innocence. With the publication of Liberty, Union,
and Democracy (1906), The Privileged Classes (1908), and
The Mystery of Education (1909) his reputation acquired the
tenor of notoriety. Reviewers called him "low in his mind"
and "clouded in doubt" over the nation's future. Scribner's
regretfully decided not to publish any more of his "disastrously unpromising" articles in the last years of his career.
Boston by 1900 was overwhelmingly populated by Irish and
other European immigrants. Like many other New Englanders
of his day Wendell viewed this influx of aliens with alarm.

Furthermore the working masses of the country he called a
tyrannous privileged class who threatened to supplant the old
"taxation without representation" by "representation without
taxation." To Wendell the demands of unions were an attack
on the basic strengths of democracy, freedom of contract and
private property. His fear of the lower classes appears often
in his last writings. The fickleness of the people, their in-
ability to respect authority "is all in Coriolanus," and the
distinction between people of the "better sort" and the worse,
between upper and lower class, is between "intelligence,
industry, ability, character," and "stupidity, sloth, ineffi-
ciency, and weakness."[36] But in the Literary History Wendell
notes both the Federalist fears of anarchy on the election of
Jefferson and the fact that his election "really started our
permanent progress," and while he puts down the masses as
a new privileged class, he equally condemns aristocratic and
proletarian privilege: "that both aspects of privilege are
ominously threatening can hardly be questioned."

The contradictions that are Wendell's, early and late, between the aristocratic, Tory fear of the masses and his distrust of people in high places, between the snobbery of a
gentleman and the equalitarianism of a teacher, between cultured, provincial old Boston and the vulgar West, cannot in
any case be understood merely as distinctions between good
and bad traits in American ideality. The critical battle-lines
of the twentieth century—humanists versus Marxists, the
Parringtons and Menckens versus the Babbitts and Mores—
have rather enforced such distinctions, even though American
"reality" no less than American "dream," old Boston no less
than new frontier, Hamiltonian no less than Jeffersonian
democracy still constitute the American mind. Wendell's
Liberty, Union, and Democracy aims to show that "the native
character of America is marked and unbroken from the foundation of colonies in Virginia and New England," just as Parrington's Main Currents in American Thought finds a contin-
uous development of the American mind; but Wendell's is a
Hamiltonian and Parrington's a Jeffersonian tradition. Wendell diverges from the more liberal concepts of the New
World man, the yeoman as the source of national strength,

and looks back at the sources of early American idealism to document his faith not only in equality but in excellence. We cannot deny the fact of ideas like Wendell's in our national culture. The drive for democratic equality has always been tempered by more or less aristocratic concepts of leadership and creativity; indeed, as the economic interpreters of the Constitution point out, the formal basis of our government is at least a function of the conservative, aristocratic interests, and at best the function of a compromise between Hamiltonian and Jeffersonian tradition.

Wendell's democratic ideal means social order but not social obstruction, and he is fully aware of a democratic problem inherent in the difference between freedom and equality: "However fervently Americans may have believed that all men are created equal, they have never gone so far as to insist that all men must permanently remain so." The true embodiment of this ideal is Abraham Lincoln; his words about government of, by, and for the people reiterate Wendell's belief that the American ideal means "none unworthily secure" or "undeservedly oppressed," and that Lincoln himself illustrates the American "chiaroscuro appreciation of decent obscurity." While unfortunately Wendell was unable— because of class prejudice or ignorance of actual conditions— to recognize the economic oppression growing in a rapidly industrializing nation, Wendell still defines American government as one "not of authority but of consent," a government that respects "not the tyranny of any one class over any other, but the consent of all classes—none secured by inflexible privilege—to exist together under a system trusted by all to act as guardian and agent of their common welfare."[37]

The conservative temper of Wendell's mind within the context of his own day may seem reactionary. The widespread strikes of the fifteen years prior to the publication of his book had made clear the existence if not the plight of the working class. More important, however, was the fact that the nineties saw the publication of outspoken appeals for the working class by Riis, Garland, Howells, Bellamy, Norris, Crane, and Dreiser, and almost simultaneously with Wendell's book Upton Sinclair published The Jungle. Muckraking

articles filled the national magazines. As a matter of fact,
Wendell's view of the Revolution was included in a <u>Cosmo-
politan</u> attack on "the revolutionary teachings submitted with
academic warrant by our great universities."[38] These were
also Republican days, however, and Wendell's political
theory was not at great variance with those of many of his
contemporaries; indeed, William Graham Sumner articulated
similar views with greater insight, complexity, and effectiveness. But they were days of confidence, and Wendell's fears
emerge in this essay far more strikingly than any confidence
in his own views. This is the Wendell so easily and necessarily attacked in the next twenty years. The essay reveals a
man like Henry Adams, who wrote in a letter to Wendell:

> We roll on the ground and sprinkle dust on our heads in
> consciousness of our miserable state, but we can get no
> help. The disease has reached a point where we are obli-
> gated to compose our music for ourselves alone, and of
> course this sort of composition means that we go on re-
> peating our faults. No echo whatever comes back.[39]

There were many echoes to Wendell's next book, however:
<u>The France of Today</u> proved an important book in Franco-
American relations and was considered by Wendell his best
work. J. J. Jusserand, the French ambassador and author,
claimed that no American "had ever understood the French
people as he understood and explained them."[40] The French
translation of the book, Wendell's honorary degree from
France, his lectureship offer from Berlin, the republica-
tion of the book in the postwar twenties, all testify to its
value.

The essay here, "The Relation of Literature to Life," again
illuminates Wendell's comparative concern to illustrate the
meaning of life as expressed by a particular national temper.
The American system avows liberty and individuality and consequently the American audience prefers not to read about
individuals but about characters who represent an attitude,
a set of values, ideals. The French society is more struc-
tured, thus a French audience prefers characters out of the

ordinary. Wendell states that French literature differs from everyday life:

> Literature, in general, must concern itself with interesting exceptions to the commonplace. Of these the most interesting, on the whole, arise from the vagrant tendencies of affection between men and women. If such incidents were not exceptional, they would not be interesting.

Such a view might confirm the suspicion of Wendell's critics that the only "ordinary" life from which literature might with interest diverge in the France of the Third Republic was that of the bourgeoisie, but it certainly absolves that class of the charge of personal licentiousness. On the other hand, Wendell makes a distinction, rather popular among the "custodians of culture," between the average French and American reader, that what is palatable to one is immoral to the other: "The public to whom French literature is addressed, in short, is always assumed to be mature," and so with the French appreciation of candor. "The difference is that we are disposed to display our reverence for youth by excessive attention to our library shelves, and that the French display theirs by the more summary process of keeping the library doors shut." He ties these observations into general national tendencies: "Our whole conception of education implies our belief that literature should be addressed to everybody who can and will read it"—especially of course the sixteen-year-old schoolgirl—but "their whole conception of education implies their contrary belief that literature should be addressed only to those who have outgrown domestic supervision."

Characteristic of his analytical method, however, Wendell goes beyond any Bostonian prudery to say "they think our novels hypocritical, and theirs seem to us corrupt; and both of us are wrong"; both views derive from national character and do not necessarily reflect the value of the respective literatures. Indeed, our Boston Puritan can describe modern French literature as "that great body of literature—in many respects the most admirable of modern times," revealing classical awareness of form and care for expression and an effort "not to increase the wealth of society, but to enlarge

its intelligence, and above all to intensify its aesthetic pleasure." And in the days of American neo-romantic fiction he
can correctly charge American literature—as a function of
its audience—with "the ephemeral vivacity of popular journalism." This is not the writer seeking the past, nor even the
man whose critical powers were enervated by the clash of
cultures. He condemns contemporary, popular American fiction and praises the very literature neo-romantic critics
were claiming American writers had finally gotten out of
their blood.

IV

To identify Barrett Wendell demands transcending the negative criticism generated about him and his age by writers of
the twentieth century, in order to discover the man of ambivalence, of contradictions, of surprises, of importance in the
history of American letters. He has generally been remembered as the last of the Boston Brahmins, an epithet which in
terms of Wendell's appreciation for the achievements of the
New England past is not untrue. But the positive aspects of
his career have seldom been recognized: his infamous negativity about the quality of American literature was more than
balanced by his belief that national American expression,
American "inexperience," in 1900 was approaching the
achievement of experience; his Literary History helped bring
about a reconsideration of American literary tradition and
sparked new interest in the study of American literature. His
English Composition, far from reiterating traditional principles of rhetoric, initiated modern methods of teaching
composition in the universities. With an intellectual appreciation for Puritan culture, he expressed no sterile Victorian
prudishness, but produced one of the best of all biographies
of Cotton Mather. His despair over the influx of foreign immigrants and the threat to property implied by universal suffrage hardly outweighed his unflagging faith in democratic
excellence. His prejudicial faith in the superior ability of the

"better sort" did not deny excellence in minorities, nor did his supremely Tory sympathies prevent his congenial encouragement of younger liberal intellectuals. Even his appreciation for the good and moral in literature failed to blind him to the transcendent aesthetic qualities of Poe and Whitman.

The large numbers of major literary and social critics and writers of the twenties who came out of Wendell's Harvard and in most cases his classes underline the accuracy of Walter Eaton's assertion that "what Wendell did for Harvard was actually to make a place there . . . in which the artist could find encouragement and counsel."[41] Certainly Wendell struggled with an outworn tradition—this is representative of much that characterizes the genteel decades—but his importance as a figure in American literary history goes beyond that. To say as Van Wyck Brooks did early and Martin Green recently that Wendell and his fellow Bostonians were writing in the wrong tradition and that "theirs was no mood to build a vigorous New England culture,"[42] is seriously to undervalue the tradition—of literary standards, of aesthetic integrity, of artistic aristocracy, even of cultural alienation—which Wendell defended and which men like T. S. Eliot voiced anew in the twenties.

Wendell experienced the reality of Matthew Arnold's lines in "Stanzas from the Grande Chartreuse": "Wandering between two worlds, one dead, /The other powerless to be born." Like his friend Henry Adams, who felt himself to be living in a "weak transitional period," he keenly felt the pressure of change but lacked the confidence to assert its ultimate direction. This stance appears repeatedly in Wendell's writing; the future "shall prove most tremendously whether at this moment of crescent democratic force our world is passing into the dusk of a new barbarism, or into the dawn of a new dispensation." Wendell, like much of late nineteenth-century Boston, feared the future but could not deny its hope.

As Henry F. May observes, "the line from Norton to T. S. Eliot was unbroken,"[43] and Wendell, who certainly shared Norton's views, provides in his life and work an adequate description of Boston and Harvard values between the times

of James Russell Lowell and T. S. Eliot. In the transitional
anxiety of the late nineteenth century, Wendell cherished the
myths of the past but doubted their efficacy for the twentieth
century, and his life and writings vacillated accordingly between despair and optimism, seldom resolved but maintained
in ironic tension. Yet as he himself wrote, an era such as
his own belongs "surely not among the things that are great,
but just as surely among the things that are significant. It is
the moments of inspiration that are great, but not less significant than the great moments are the periods of preparation."[44] Wendell self-consciously wore the masks of eccentric gadfly, artist, and alchemist; yet as he remarked about
his teaching of composition, "it took alchemy to make chemistry."[45] His traits and his professional concerns are central
elements of the particular twentieth-century chemistry called
Modernism. If at the turn of the new century its outward
forms were weak, the tradition of Charles Eliot Norton and
James Russell Lowell still lived, and Barrett Wendell para-
doxically marks both its end and its continuance.

Notes

1. Fred Lewis Pattee, "A Call for a Literary Historian," in The Reinterpretation of American Literature, ed. Norman Foerster (New York, 1928), p. 21.

2. Letter to Sir Robert White-Thomson, 22 November 1908, in Mark A. DeWolfe Howe, Barrett Wendell and His Letters (Boston, 1924), p. 198.

3. Letter to Robert Thomson, 17 December 1893, in Howe, p. 109.

4. "Recollections of My Father," MS in the Houghton Library, Harvard University, p. 126.

5. Stuart P. Sherman, "Barrett Wendell: Farewell, New England Gentleman," Critical Woodcuts (New York, 1926), p. 252.

6. H. L. Mencken, "The Last New Englander," Prejudices, Fifth Series (New York, 1926), p. 250.

7. George P. Baker, "Barrett Wendell (1855-1921)," Harvard Graduates' Magazine, XXIX (June 1921), 536.

8. Robert Herrick, letter to George P. Baker, 28 May 1917, in a collection of tributes presented to Wendell on his retirement 15 June 1917, Houghton Library, Harvard University.

9. The Mystery of Education (New York, 1909), pp. 163-164.

10. George Santayana, Persons and Places, 2 vols. (New York, 1945), II, 172.

11. Mencken, p. 254.

12. Baker, p. 574.

13. English Composition (New York, 1891), p. 306.

14. The Privileged Classes (New York, 1908), p. 268.

15. Walter Pritchard Eaton, "Barrett Wendell," The American Mercury, V (August 1925), 450.

16. Letter to George Baker, 12 June 1917, Wendell Retirement Tributes.

17. Horace M. Kallen, "Journey to Another World," in College in a Yard, ed. Brooks Atkinson (Cambridge, 1957), pp. 118-119.

18. Wisner Payne Kinne, George Pierce Baker and the American Theatre (Cambridge, 1954), pp. 34-35, 45.

19. 15 June 1917, Wendell Retirement Tributes.

20. Van Wyck Brooks, New England: Indian Summer (New York, 1940), pp. 426-427, 533.

21. 21 November 1915, in Robert T. Self, ed., "The Correspondence of Amy Lowell and Barrett Wendell, 1915-1919," New England Quarterly, 47 (March 1974), 67.

22. Brooks, p. 437.

23. Warner Berthoff, The Ferment of Realism (New York, 1965), p. 10.

24. Morton D. Zabel, Introduction, Literary Opinion in America, 2 vols. (New York, 1962), I, xii.

25. Letter to Frederick Schenck, 28 August 1906, in Howe, p. 178.

26. Letter to William James, 25 October 1900, in Mark A. DeWolfe Howe, ed., "A Packet of Wendell-James Letters," Scribner's Magazine, LXXXIV (December 1928), 678.

27. In American Historical Review, VI (July 1901), 803-804.

28. The Temper of the Seventeenth Century in English Literature (New York, 1904), p. 50.

29. Robert P. Falk, "The Literary Criticism of the Genteel Decades, 1870-1900," in The Development of American Literary Criticism, ed. Floyd Stovall (Chapel Hill, 1955), p. 154.

30. 25 October 1900, "Wendell-James Letters," p. 677.

31. 6 December 1904, "Collection of Lectures on American Literature," Harvard University Archives.

32. T. S. Eliot, "American Literature," The Athenaeum, 25 April 1919, p. 237.

33. The Mystery of Education, p. 236.

34. George F. Smith, "A Harvard View of Whitman," The Conservator, 13 (August 1902), 85.

35. George F. Smith, "A Harvard View of Whitman," The Conservator, 13 (September 1902), 103.

36. The Privileged Classes, p. 50.

37. The France of Today (New York, 1907), p. 370.

38. Harold Bolce, "Polyglots in the Temples of Babel," Cosmopolitan, XLVII (June 1909), 52-65.

39. Quoted in Henry Adams and His Friends, ed. Harold Dean Cater (Boston, 1947), p. 644.

40. J. J. Jusserand, "Barrett Wendell's France," New York Times, 23 November 1907, p. 742.

41. Eaton, p. 450.

42. Martin Green, The Problem of Boston (New York, 1966), p. 177.

43. Henry F. May, The End of American Innocence (Chicago, 1959), p. 36.

44. Barrett Wendell, "Lectures in English 7, Eighteenth Century English Literature," lecture of 1 October 1890, Harvard University Archives.

45. The Mystery of Education, p. 178.

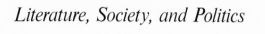

Literature, Society, and Politics

Cotton Mather,
the Puritan Priest

Before Cotton Mather's tomb was fairly closed, then, men who had known him best were whispering among themselves other than good things concerning the dead. Posterity has held them right. A subtle priest, self-seeking, vain, arrogant, inconsistent, mischievous in his eternal business, many have called him: even if honest, dreadfully deluded and grotesquely lacking in judgment, is what those mostly say who say the best. And if we had only public records to guide us, I should be disposed to assent.

The son of Increase Mather, the grandson of John Cotton and of Richard Mather, sprung of a race of chosen vessels of the Lord, himself a chosen vessel before his boyhood was fairly closed, intoxicated with such adulation as Urian Oakes spoke when, the youngest of Harvard graduates, he took his degree, he began his half-century of earthly work. Full of the traditions of the fathers, he pressed on, divinely authorized to lead the people of God in the path of salvation: whoever would not follow was godless. Then he saw his father's great work in England; and meanwhile did great work at home. He saw the tyranny of Andros fall: his prayers were answered. He saw Phipps come with the new Charter: New England was saved. Now he might lead on more confidently still. And he plunged into the horrors of witchcraft. And he saw theocracy fall with poor Sir William Phipps. And he saw Harvard College lost to the cause of the fathers. And he saw the very churches of Boston preaching new doctrines, full of delusion. For five and thirty years he saw the clergy of New England started on the course in which they still travel: from a position where the influence of the church was greater than anywhere else in the world, to one where the influence of the church has become almost imperceptible. And he fought against fate with every weapon he could clutch; and he believed his own advancement was what God needed to restore His kingdom; and some of the blows he struck—and for aught I know many of them—may have been foul ones.

But before we can judge him aright, we must strive to see him as he saw himself. This is what I have tried to do. I have told his story perhaps too much in his own words. By no other means could I show so simply what seems to me the truth: that with a depth of human nature which makes him above most men who have lived a brother man to all of us, he never ceased striving, amid endless stumblings and errors, to do his duty.

It was his lot to possess a mind and a temperament more restlessly active than most men ever know. With this nature, it was his lot to live all his life in a petty provincial town, further removed from the great current of contemporary life than any spot to-day in the civilized world. And this he never realized; nor have any of those realized who have sat to judge him. His grandfathers, and the other founders of New England, came from the midst of the seething England which was soon to dethrone the Stuarts, full of the passion of a contest that had been to every one of them the greatest of earthly realities. His father's life had brought the elder man face to face with kings and bishops: Increase Mather had fought hard to preserve and to perpetuate a Puritanism whose pristine freshness was still within his own memory. But when Cotton Mather's time came, Puritanism—like Anglicanism itself—was already not the great reality it had once been: it had become a tradition. The world travels faster nowadays. The Civil War is already such a tradition to us.

This great tradition of Puritanism he fought so passionately to defend had in it the seeds of a grim, untruthful formalism, which has made it seem to many men of later times a gloomy delusion, fruitful only of limitation and of cant. Those

who see in it only or chiefly this, forget what even to Cotton
Mather himself was its greatest truth. Few human philoso-
phies have been more essentially ideal; few systems formu-
lated by men have so strenuously kept before the minds of
those who accept them the transitory unreality of those
things which human beings can perceive, the eternal and
infinite reality of the Divine universe that lies beyond human
ken. Once learn this, and nothing on this earth is so great
as to deserve a care, when we think of the infinite realities
beyond; nor anything on this earth so mean as not to be a
manifestation of divine truth. At once contemptible and reverend, this earthly life of ours is but the fragment of an instant in the timeless eternities of God. But to the Puritans,
it was an instant in which the infinite mercy of God, with
free grace mitigating His infinite justice, gave every living
man the chance and the hope of finding in himself the signs
of eternal salvation. It is not every man who can rise to such
heights of idealism as this: whoever cannot or will not so
rise, whoever cannot feel beneath the austere pettiness of
Puritanism the passionate enthusiasm that made things unseen—Hell and Heaven, the Devil, and the Angels, and God—
greater realities than anything this side of eternity, can
never even guess what Puritanism meant.

On its earthly side, however, Puritanism had a trait which
has been more generally recognized, though not, perhaps,
more fully understood. In its origin it was Protestant. It
began, and it gained earthly strength, in a passionate revolt
of human thought from those phases of ecclesiastical tradition which human experience had proved false and wicked.
God's word contains God's truth, the first Protestants
cried; we will read it for ourselves, none but God shall be
our guide. So, Bible in hand, they led the way for who would
follow; and when they were gone far enough to muster their
forces, they would have cried halt. But what authority had
they to stop the progress they had urged? God's world contains God's truth, cried those of their followers whose spirit
came nearest to that of the leaders: let us read it there, and
read it each for himself; none but God shall be our guide.
And those who press ever onward, seeking God's truth each

for himself, are the Protestants of to-day. Protestantism
can have no priesthood.

This truth Cotton Mather never guessed. To this day honest Protestant Christians are blind to it. Nor did he guess,
either, some other truths which modern Protestant Christi-
anity equally fails to recognize. The priestly office, let it
derive its authority from Rome or Canterbury, Geneva or
Utah, demands in those who exercise it even most fervently
a trait which in its most obvious form the priests are the
first to condemn, —histrionic insincerity. Placed before men
as an accredited spiritual leader, the priest—whatever his
mood or his character—must conduct himself, at least in his
public functions, as if he were what no human being ever was
or can be, —wholly given up to the service of God. And the
adulation of the worshippers who see in him an ever present
minister of God strengthens him year by year in the power
in which applause strengthens the actor: the power of seeming at will to be what in the depths of his heart he is not. To
gain this power, to strengthen it, is part of the priest's
duty. And there is no way of strengthening it so certain as
the way Cotton Mather took, like the saints of Rome before
him. Day after day, week after week, month after month,
year after year, he cast himself in the dust before the Lord;
he strained his eyes for a fleeting glimpse of the robes and
crowns of God's angels, his ears for the faintest echo of
their celestial music. Pure in motive, noble in purpose, his
whole life was one unending effort to strengthen in himself
that phase of human nature whose inner token is a riot of
mystical emotion, whose outward signs are unwitting mani-
festations of unfettered credulity and unmeant fraud.

Yet it is not as a sly and superstitious priest that I remember him to-day: any more than I think that slyness and
superstition to-day make up the character of a Christian
minister. In the first place, the passionate idealism to which
he held with all his heart—like honest priests since the world
began—coloured, and glorified, and made divine, even the
meanest things in the petty earthly life he knew. A squatting
dog brought him a message straight from the throne of God.
In the second place, the life he lived—with all its grotesque

pettiness—was the life which had in it the seeds of that great continental life in which lies the chief hope of the modern world. To understand the America of to-day, we must know the New England of the fathers; to know the first New England of the fathers, there is no better way than to study this man,—its last, its most typical incarnation. And as we study him, and then look back at the figure that emerges from the dusty books and manuscripts of two centuries ago, the final trait of him, that hides the rest, is this: strenuously, devoutly, he did what he deemed his duty.

All about him he saw ever crescent disappointment and sorrow and earthly failure; but he never lost heart, not ever for a moment ceased effort, with word and deed alike, to do good to mankind. Fructuosus—be fruitful, do God's work here on earth—was his last command to his son. And the incessant training of his career in the art that in its meaner form he would have been the first to execrate,—the art of the actor, who can at will seem to be what in truth he is not,—made him what it makes good ministers to-day. More than other men they can sympathize with mankind: in agony, in sorrow, in sin, men turn to them for aid, for counsel, for charity in all its divinest forms. And this the saintly actors give as no other men can, thus doing good unspeakably reverend. The very weakness of their calling, so palpable to those who have not known their beneficence,—so fruitful of obloquy and execration in those who neither share their faith nor will let themselves sympathize,—makes them more blessed to mankind than a thousand of their more candid fellows. Out of evil God brings good: it is the histrionic insincerity of priesthood that brings to unhappy men the Divine sympathy of priests. And in his ministry Cotton Mather never faltered: with ever growing earnestness, he went through that grim and sorrowful old New England, in every deliberate thought and act ministering to the bodies and the souls of the people of God. Fructuosus—fruitful—is the final word for him.

And what fruit has his priesthood borne that is with us to-day? New England is far enough from the stern creed in which alone he saw hope of salvation. But not long ago an

old friend, talking of the New England that both of us love,
spoke a phrase I like to remember: "We have here," he
said, "what the world has never seen before: we have devout
free thought." It is the Protestantism of the fathers that has
won us our freedom. But freedom alone were a curse. It is
the faithful earnestness of the Puritan priesthood that has
kept our freedom from straying into that pert irreverence
which elsewhere than here has made so many who cast aside
the false cast with it the true. And among the Puritan priests
there was never one, I believe, more faithfully earnest than
this Cotton Mather.

One hundred and sixty-three years have passed since he
was laid in his father's tomb on Copp's Hill. And few of us
to-day can believe that he is gone to such a little company of
God's elect as would make the heaven he preached of. If he
be, then, when by chance he looks back at the earth where
he laboured, he must see a sight that for the instant should
dim the joys of Paradise. But there are not a few to-day who
dream of a heaven in whose blessedness all the fetters of
humanity are broken; where what is best in men waxes better than men can even dream, amid the ever-growing glories
of eternal freedom from sin, and weakness, and sorrow.
And if by chance his eyes have opened again in a heaven like
this, and if from thence he looks back to an earth where his
sins and errors have borne little fruit, but where the de-
voutness of the free thought of New England speaks still for
what was best in his human life, he sees, I like to think,
little that should disturb the great serenity of his peace.

Some Neglected
Characteristics of
the New England Puritans

On February 15, 1728, the Reverend Benjamin Colman, first minister of the Brattle Street church, preached the Boston lecture in memory of Cotton Mather, who had died two days before. Cotton Mather had lived all his life in Boston; there is no record, they say, of his ever having travelled farther from home than Ipswich or Andover or Plymouth. Of sensitive temperament, and both by constitution and by conviction devoted to the traditions in which he was trained, he certainly presented, to a degree nowhere common, a conveniently exaggerated type of the characteristics that marked the society of which he formed a part. But Benjamin Colman, at least in earlier life, was of different mettle. After graduation at Harvard College he had passed some years in England, at a time when clever Dissenters could see good company. In Boston, whither he had returned late in 1699 to take charge of the new church subsequently known as the Brattle Street, he had been so liberal—at least in matters of discipline—as to impress the Mathers, who were the leaders of the strictly orthodox party, as a dangerous Radical. It is not too much, perhaps, to say that his ministerial career marks the beginning of that movement in the Boston churches which, a century later, became Unitarianism and

9

put Calvinism, at best, hopelessly out of fashion. In view of
this, his lecture on Cotton Mather becomes curious.

His text is the translation of Enoch: "And Enoch walked
with God, and he was not, for God took him." From these
words he draws inferences that enable him to expound the
career and character of the patriarch, with edifying precision, to the length of four closely printed pages. But what he
chiefly insists on is that Enoch's blessed fate

> "must be resolved into the good pleasure of God, His wise
> and sovereign will; and to be sure it was not for any merit
> or desert in Enoch's holy walking with God. Enoch de-
> served to have died for his sins as well as any before or
> after him. . . . Elias was a man of like passions with
> others. . . . It was not due to the righteousness of either
> that they were taken without seeing death. Before that God
> formed them in the belly he designed them their transla-
> tion."

In other words, the Boston divine, who at times seems the
most Radical of his generation, feels bound, as a matter of
course, to begin his eulogy on the most distinguished of his
fellow-ministers by an assertion in the most concrete terms
of the doctrine of election.

II

Beyond question this doctrine was never, for many hours,
absent from the mind of Cotton Mather, nor often from that
of Samuel Sewall, the two worthies of the period then drawing to a close whose diaries are best preserved. Beyond
question, too, these men were, in this respect, not peculiar, but typical of their time. There is hardly a figure in the
first century of Boston history whose conduct and opinions
can present themselves, to modern temperaments, as com-
prehensibly human, unless we keep this doctrine constantly
in mind; and keep it in mind, too, not as a verbal dogma,
but as a living reality. It is worth our while, then, to recall
exactly what it was.

In the beginning, the Puritans believed, God created man, responsible to Him, with perfect freedom of will. Adam, in the fall, exerted his will in opposition to the will of God. Thereby Adam and all his posterity merited eternal punishment. As a mark of that punishment they lost the power of exerting the will in harmony with the will of God, without losing their hereditary responsibility to Him. But God, in His infinite mercy, was pleased to mitigate His justice. Through the mediation of Christ certain human beings, chosen at God's pleasure, might be relieved of the just penalty of sin, ancestral and personal, and received into everlasting salvation. These were the elect; none others could be saved, nor could any acts of the elect impair their salvation.

All this is familiar enough. What puzzles posterity about it is how so profoundly fatalistic a creed could possibly prove a motive power strong enough to result not only in individual lives but in a corporate life, that was destined to grow into a national life, of passionate enthusiasm, and of abnormal moral as well as material activity.

To understand this nowadays we must emphasize a fact generally neglected by the writers of New England history: namely, the test by which the elect could be recognized. The test of election, the Puritans believed, was ability to exert the will in true harmony with the will of God—a proof of emancipation from the hereditary curse of the children of Adam; whoever could at any time do right, and want to, had ground for hope that he might be saved. But even the elect were infected with the hereditary sin of humanity; and besides, no wile of the Devil was more constant than that which deceived men into believing themselves regenerate when in truth they were not. The task of assuring one's self of election, then, could end only with life.

III

Colman, in his funeral lecture, states this doctrine very specifically:

"To walk with God means, in all the parts and instances

of a sober, righteous, and godly life, and constancy therein
all our days. We walk with God in a sincere, universal,
and persevering obedience to the written Word and revealed
law of God; and blessed are the undefiled in the way that
walk in the law of the Lord. To walk is not to take a step or
two, nor is it for a day or a year, but for the whole life,
all our days. We must walk and work while the day lasts;
the light is given for this. How much does it concern us,
then, to ask ourselves whether we have indeed begun this
walk with God and to Him? Whither are we going? What are
we doing? How do we live and act; and what will become of
us a few days hence? Will God take us; take us on the
wings of angels and in their arms to His own presence and
glory; or will death drag us out of the body and devils take
us away to their abodes of darkness and of fire unquenchable?"

The Puritans themselves would probably have told us, as
their lineal religious followers sometimes tell us to-day, in
both cases with perfect honesty of intention, that this specifically asserts the duty of man to give himself up to God, with
no other purpose than to advance God's glory. Such a statement does not explain in modern terms why any living man
ever really did so. Few facts, indeed, seem much truer to
modern minds than that human beings do what they do not
want to do only when some humanly overpowering motive
makes self-denial, in the end, the line of least resistance.
And looking at Colman's teaching in a modern spirit we may
see in it, without much trouble, an appeal to an everyday
human motive which goes farther than most things else to
explain the apparent inconsistency of Puritan doctrine and
Puritan character. In short, what he does, and what all the
Puritan preachers do, is to assume the doctrine of election;
to declare the test of election to be ability to walk with God,
to exert the will in true harmony with His; and then, by
every means known to their rhetoric, to stimulate in every
one of their hearers the elementary and absorbing passion of
curiosity, concerning self-preservation.

IV

In the diary of Cotton Mather, a most characteristic Puritan document, this trait appears in a form almost incredibly exaggerated. We have in these manuscripts a pretty full account of him from eighteen to sixty-one. The number of private fasts he kept was enormous. It is not too much to say that they were at least weekly throughout those forty-three years. For twenty-two of those years he habitually held vigils, too,—all-night watches in his library of ecstatic prayer and effort to penetrate the veil that is between God and man. And this was but a little part of his passionate effort to walk with God. And the only modernly comprehensible motive to account for all this passion is the one he records in a self-examination at the age of forty-two:

"I am afraid," he writes, "of allowing my soul a wish of evil to the worst of all [my enemies]. . . . Q. Whether the man that can find these marks upon himself may not conclude himself marked out for the city of God?"

The same trait appears in Increase Mather; the same in that vastly less emotional personage, Samuel Sewall; the same reveals itself distinctly in almost every godly portrait in that quaint gallery of worthies that fills so much of Cotton Mather's "Magnalia."

V

This book, with all its obvious faults and errors, remains, on the whole, the chief literary monument of New England Puritanism. It has been rather the fashion, of late years, to criticise it as a modern historical document; as a record of actual fact. As such it is certainly untrustworthy from beginning to end. So modern critics are generally disposed to put it aside as worthless, and incidentally, to apply the same adjective to its author. Psychologically, however, the "Magnalia" is a document of such historic value that an earnest student of Puritan New England cannot safely neglect it. Any work of serious literature, we are beginning to see, must inevitably express, at least in its implications, the conditions of the society wherein it was produced. And these it often expresses in a conveniently generalized form where they may be better studied than in individual phases from which posterity, as best it may, would draw what it is apt to think more accurate, because more conscious, inductions. This is the aspect in which the "Magnalia" is most significant. As a piece of literature it possesses two traits which should follow directly from the fundamental self-curiosity of the Puritan character. Within arbitrary and rigidly defined limits it is intensely imaginative; and it displays throughout a serene disregard for that fine adjustment of phrase to fact which our modern scientific spirit of veracity assumes for the moment to be eternally the chief of the cardinal virtues.

VI

To understand the peculiar nature of its intensely imaginative quality we may best, perhaps, refer not to itself but to the passage from Colman's funeral discourse to which we last directed our attention. The quality is so constant among the Puritans that you may find it almost anywhere.

"Will God," he writes, "take us . . . on the wings of angels and in their arms to His own presence and glory? or will death drag us out of the body, and devils take us away to their abodes of darkness and of fire unquenchable?"

This sounds commonplace enough, nowadays. But a gentleman who once visited Goethe at Weimar, has told me that Goethe's first question was whether it were a fact that in America there were still people who believed in actual winged and crowned angels; and that when he answered, as

was then true, that he believed in them himself, Goethe
looked at him with an expression he can never forget and ex-
claimed, "Das ist wunderbar!" Which exclamation, my
friend says, began his emancipation from Puritan anthropo-
morphism. To come nearer our own time, it is not a dozen
years since in a Boston newspaper somebody wrote in a very
serious obituary notice concerning a secretary of the American Board of Foreign Missions, that "few men on entering
heaven will find a wider circle of personal acquaintance or
a larger number of those under indirect obligations."

These things all go together: Colman's angels and devils,
the material angels of the American boy of 1830, the white
chokered old missionary receiving in staid social formality
the emancipated spirits of the Polynesian elect, and the godly ministers and magistrates of our Puritan Plutarch. In
earlier and later forms they are concrete examples of the
way in which the faculty we call imagination, exerting itself
for generations within the limits of what after all was an intensely anthropomorphic creed, will first create for itself
concrete images, only less material than the bronze and
marble ones iconoclasm casts down; and then, while denying that bronze or marble can be symbolic, will passionately
and honestly assert its own images to be real. Nowadays we
are apt to look on all these images—material and immaterial
alike—as only symbols. But Cotton Mather at least once was
rewarded, in ecstasy, by an actual vision of an angel—wings,
robes, crown, and all; and there is no reason to question
that Colman, who was well on with his preparation for college at this moment of Cotton Mather's highest ecstasy,
actually believed his devils to be waiting, with hoofs and
horns and tridents, for such of humanity as the unspeakable
free grace of his just God had not undeservedly released,
with Enoch, from the ancestral penalty of human sin.

When Cotton Mather drew his godly portraits, they stood
for figures so vivid in his imagination that he had no more
suspicion of their actual truth than of the elements of fiction
and invention which a modern eye detects in his God, his
angels, his devils. When Colman spoke of "abodes of darkness and of fire unquenchable," he spoke of something that

to the Puritans represented a fact as concrete as the Tower
of London, or as the George II of whom in the same lecture
he writes thus:

> "What an honor should we account it if our earthly
> prince would allow us to walk after him in his garden?
> Only a few select and favorite nobles have the honor done
> them."

And it is not a little significant of the exhaustion of human
power that must follow constant, overwrought intensity of
exercise that Colman failed to remark the strict incompati-
bility of darkness and unquenchable flames.

To consider this exercise of imagination in another and
more modern spirit, what it amounted to was this: Only by
incessant assurance and reassurance that the will was exerting itself in harmony with the will of God could the insa-
tiable curiosity to know whether God's free grace were ours
be for a moment stayed. God's way of contemplating things
heavenly, earthly, infernal, belongs to that class of perceptions to which so many modern thinkers give the convenient
name unknowable; it is a thing which, true or false, can
never be verified by either observation or experiment. But
the God of the Puritans, for all he was a spirit, was a
white-bearded spirit, with limbs and passions,—still "le
père éternel de l'école italienne," who had made man in His
visible image. To them His will in regard to all things,
great and small, was a thing not only that might be known,
but—if life were to possess any meaning—that must be
known; and that being known must be proclaimed. In the intense, incessant effort that followed to formulate the unknowable in concrete, anthropomorphic terms, imagination
exhausted itself. What we call the prosaic colorlessness of
Puritan life is merely external. The subjective life of the
Puritans was intensely, passionately ideal; blazing with an
emotional enthusiasm constantly stimulated by the unrecognized impulse of selfish human curiosity. If you want proof
of it, ask yourselves how otherwise people who after all are
not far from us in years and in blood could have survived
the discipline and the public devotions which were to them
what meat and drink are to the starving.

VII

The difficulty that followed these godly emotional debauches
is obvious. To the Puritans the concrete images thus created
in moments of abnormal ecstasy were more real and unspeakably more important than any facts of actual life.
Yet these images, in each case inevitably the creation of a
single brain, could neither be confirmed by any general
process of human observation, nor tested by any general
process of experiment. Each seer could tell what he himself
saw; that was all. For the rest, these visions were such as
human language has only metaphoric terms to describe. The
consent that governs the meaning of words demands, for
precision, wide identity of experience. We all know the in-
sidious temptation to impressive inaccuracy of statement
which besets whoever has had a solitary adventure with a
fish or a snake. Spiritual experiences are inevitably solitary. Inevitably, too, they cannot be precisely described.
Given these truths, given the fundamental errors of human
nature, given too the passionate Puritan conviction that an
exact account of spiritual experience is the only valid evidence you can give of your eternal salvation, and you get two
pretty obvious results.

The first was never better phrased than by Increase Mather, perhaps the most canny of the Puritan divines whose
career is recorded. In early life he habitually recorded the
heavenly afflations that rewarded his ecstatic prayers.

"As I was praying," he wrote once, "my heart was ex-
ceedingly melted, and methoughts saw God before my eyes
in an inexpressible manner, so that I was afraid I should
have fallen into a trance in my study."—"In his latter
years," adds Cotton Mather, writing of him, "he did not
record so many of these heavenly afflations, because they
grew so frequent with him. And he also found . . . that
the flights of a soul rapt up into a more intimate conversation with heaven are such as cannot be exactly remembered with the happy partakers of them."

The second appears very clearly in what Colman wrote of
Cotton Mather, with whom in his day he had waged fierce
fights:

"But here love to Christ and His servant commands me
to draw a veil over every failing; for who is without them?
Not ascending Elijah himself, who was a man of like passions with his brethren, the prophets; and we have his
mantle left us wherewith to cover the defects and infirm-
ities of others after their translation in spirit. These God
remembers no more, and why should we? and he blots out
none of their good deeds, and no more should we."

Nil de mortuis nisi bonum, in other words, is God's will
—and not merely a Latin apothegm. In other words still, it
is God's will that the whole truth should never be spoken.

VIII

The traits thus hastily specified are incessant activity, within rigid limits, of anthropomorphic imagination, strained
to the utmost by life-long efforts concretely to formulate the
unknowable; and a sense of veracity weakened at once by
incessant dogmatic assertion of unprovable fact and by constant conviction that only such truth should be spoken as was
agreeable to the disposition of God. These traits appear
throughout the "Magnalia." And whoever does not recognize
in the "Magnalia" an image not to be neglected of the Puritan
character can never seriously understand the Puritans.
These traits, as we have seen, both follow directly from
unquestioning acceptance, in its most concrete form, of the
doctrine of election at a time when its freshness had not
faded into theological tradition. Doubts assailed the Puritans
often enough, but, like Increase Mather, the Puritans met
doubts not by reasoning—"it puts too much respect upon a
devil, to argue and parley with him, on a point which the
devil himself believes and trembles at"—but by "flat contra-
diction." And the energy that, during the first century of

Boston history, fortified them to contradictions as incessant as temptations, sprang, we may believe, from no mystic cause, but from nothing more marvellous at bottom than the almost incredible stimulus which acceptance of this fundamental doctrine gave to self-searching, self-seeking curiosity.

IX

In discussing these old New Englanders one is apt to speak as if, historically, they were a unique class. It is perhaps worth while, then, for one who cannot profess to be a trained student of history, distinctly to disclaim any such elementary error. Human affairs, people think nowadays, are as much questions of cause and effect as any other phenomena observable by science. Similar conditions will produce similar characters anywhere. And this old hierarchy of ours will very probably prove more like than unlike the other hierarchies that by and by serious students will have studied comparatively. In none of them, any more than in this, will such fundamental traits as we have tried to detect prove to be the sole ones. In no serious study of corporate character can the serious student for a moment forget, for one thing, the crushing, distorting influence of those petty material facts to which we give the convenient name of every-day life. And certainly these concrete facts are generally more profitable subjects of study than such subjective matters as we have dealt with here. What is more, of course, such extreme traits as we have touched on characterized chiefly the leaders—the clergy, the priestly class. During the first century of New England history, however, the influence of this class can hardly be overstated. And just because the concrete facts commonly engross professional students and makers of history, it sometimes seems that such aspects of history as we have glanced at—aspects that in this case reveal themselves with startling distinctness to an unprofessional explorer of Puritan records—have been perhaps unduly neglected.

Note

[General note appended to the original text:] The passages
from Colman are cited from "The Holy Walk and Glorious
Translation of Blessed Enoch." (Boston: J. Phillips & T.
Hancock, 1728.) The other citations are referred to authorities in my "Life of Cotton Mather." (New York: Dodd,
Mead & Co., 1891.) From this is taken directly the account
of the Puritan creed.

The Elements and
the Qualities of Style

During the past ten years I have been chiefly occupied in
teaching, to undergraduates of Harvard College, the principles of English Composition. In the course of that time I
have been asked a great many questions concerning the art,
mostly by friends who found themselves writing for publication. Widely different as these inquiries have naturally been,
they have possessed in common one trait sufficiently marked
to place them, in my memory, in a single group: almost
without exception, they have concerned themselves with
matters of detail. Is this word or that admissible? Why, in
a piece of writing I once published, did I permit myself to
use the apparently commercial phrase "at any rate"? Are
not words of Saxon origin invariably preferable to all others?
Should sentences be long or short? These random memories
are sufficient examples of many hundreds of inquiries.

They have in common, as I have just said, the trait of
concerning themselves almost wholly with matters of detail.
They have too another trait: generally, if not invariably,
they involve a tacit assumption that any given case must be
either right or wrong.

These two traits—the one indicative of rather surprising
ignorance of the nature of the matter in hand, the other of
a profound error—are what has prompted me to prepare this
book. Year by year I have seen more and more clearly that
although the work of a teacher or a technical critic of style
concerns itself largely with the correction of erratic detail,

21

the really important thing for one who would grasp the subject to master is not a matter of detail at all, but a very
simple body of general principles under which details readily group themselves. I have seen too that although a small
part of the corrections and criticisms I have had to make
are concerned with matters of positive error, by far the
greater, and incalculably the more important part are concerned with what I may call matters of discretion. The question is not whether a given word or sentence is eternally
right or wrong; but rather how accurately it expresses what
the writer has to say,—whether the language we use may not
afford a different and perhaps a better means of phrasing his
idea.

The truth is that in rhetoric, as distinguished from gram-
mar, by far the greater part of the questions that arise concern not right or wrong, but better or worse; and that the
way to know what is better or worse in any given case is not
to load your memory with bewilderingly innumerable rules,
but firmly to grasp a very few simple, elastic general principles. Consciously or not, these principles, I believe, are
observed by thoroughly effective writers. Of course, nothing
but long and patient practice can make anybody certain of
writing, or of practising any art, well. Of course too if the
principles I state be, as I believe them, fundamental, whoever practises much cannot help in some degree observing
them; but the experience of ten years' teaching leads me
more and more to the belief that a knowledge of the principles is a very great help in practice.

I may best begin, I think, by stating these principles as
briefly and as generally as I can. Then I shall try to show
how they apply to the more important specific cases that
present themselves to writers. Each case, I think, presents
them in a somewhat new light. Certainly, without considering them in various aspects we can hardly appreciate their
full scope. First of all, it will be convenient to fix a term
which shall express the whole subject under consideration.
I know of none more precise than Style. A good deal of usage, to be sure, and rather good usage too, gives color to
the general impression that style means good style, just as

criticism is often taken to mean unfavorable criticism, or
manners to mean civil behavior. Very excellent authorities
sometimes declare that a given writer has style, and another none; only a little while ago, I heard a decidedly careful
talker congratulate himself on having at last discovered, in
this closing decade of the nineteenth century, a correspond-
ent who, in spite of our thickening environment of newspapers and telegrams, wrote letters that possessed style.
I dwell on this common meaning of the word style for two
reasons: in the first place, clearly to define the sense in
which I mean not to use the word; in the second place, to
emphasize the fact, which we shall find to be highly important, that in the present state of the English language hardly
any word not unintelligibly technical can be trusted to express a precise meaning without the aid of definition. Style,
as I shall use the term, means simply the expression of
thought or emotion in written words; it applies equally to an
epic, a sermon, a love-letter, an invitation to an evening
party.

   This definition brings us face to face with an obvious trait
which the art we are considering shares with all the other
arts of expression,—painting, sculpture, architecture, music, and indeed those humbler arts, not commonly recognized as fine, where the workman conceives something not
yet in existence (a machine, a flower-pot, a sauce) and
proceeds, by collaboration of brain and hand, to give it material existence. Thought and emotion, the substance of what
style expresses, are things so common, so incessant in
earthly experience, that we trouble ourselves to consider
them as little as we bother our heads about the marvels of
sunrise, of the growth of flowers or men, of the mystery of
sin or death, when they do not happen to touch our pockets
or our affections. But for all that they are with us from
morning till night, and not seldom from night till morning,—
for all that together they make up the total sum of what to
most of us is a very commonplace affair, our earthly existence,—thought and emotion, when we stop to consider them,
are the most fascinatingly marvellous facts that human
beings can contemplate. They are real beyond all other

realities. What things are, no man can ever know; analyzed
by astronomy, the material universe vanishes in infinite
systems of spheres revolving about one another throughout
infinitely extended regions of space, in obedience to law that
may be recognized, but not comprehended; analyzed by phys-
ics, this same material universe vanishes again in infinitely
small systems of molecules bound together by the same
mysterious forces that govern the stellar universe. The
more we study the more we learn that neither the heavens
nor the very paper on which I write these words are what
they seem, and that what they really are is far beyond the
perception of any faculty which the history of the human race
can lead us rationally to hope for even in our most remote
posterity. But what we think of all these marvels, the forms
in which they present themselves to us, we know as we know
nothing else. Our whole lives, from the day when our eyes
first open to the sunlight, are constant series of thoughts,
sometimes seemingly springing from within ourselves, often
seeming to come from without ourselves, through the medium of those senses that in careless moods we are apt to
think so comprehensive. To each and all of us, the final reality of life is the thought, which, with the endless surge of
emotion, —now tempestuous, again almost imperceptible, —
makes up conscious existence.

Final realities though they be, however, thought and emotion are essentially things that in our habitual thoughtless-
ness we are apt to call unreal. As we know them, they are
immaterial. No systems can measure their extent or their
bulk; and though they are in some degree conditioned by
time, it is so slightly that we may almost say—as in a single
instant our thought ranges from primeval nebulae to cosmic
death and celestial eternity—they are free from time-limit,
as well as from the limits of space. Real at once, then, and
unreal, or better, real and intangible, real yet immaterial,
each of us who will stop to think must find the thought and
the emotion that together make that fresh marvel, —himself.
Each of us, I say purposely; for there is one more thing
that we must remember here. Like one another as we seem,
like one another as the courses of our lives may look, there

are no two human beings who tread quite the same road from
the cradle to the grave. No one of us in any group has come
from quite the same origin as any other; no two, be they
twin brothers or husband and wife, can go thence by quite
the same path. The laws of space and of time forbid; unspeakably more the still more mysterious laws of thought
forbid that any two of us should know and feel just the same
experience in this world. If two or three of us, habitually
together, suddenly utter the same word, we are surprised.
The thought and emotion of every living being, then, is an
immaterial reality, eternally different from every other in
the universe; and this is the reality that style must express.

And style, we remember, must express this reality in
written words; and written words are things as tangible, as
material, as the thought and emotion behind them is immaterial, evanescent, elusive. The task of the writer, then, is
a far more subtle and wonderful thing than we are apt to
think it: nothing less than to create a material body, that all
men may see, for an eternally immaterial reality that only
through this imperfect symbol can ever reveal itself to any
but the one human being who knows it he knows not how.

When a piece of style—a poem, a book, an essay, a letter—is once in existence, it may perhaps best be considered
for the moment from the point of view of readers, of those
to whom it is addressed. Any piece of style, we all know,
impresses us in a fairly distinct way, which we rarely take
the trouble to define. Most readers never know more about
it than that it interests or pleases them, or bores or annoys.
A little consideration, however, will show, I think, that the
undefined impression which any piece of style makes may
always be resolved into three parts. Present in widely different degrees in different pieces of style, no one of these
factors can ever, I believe, be asserted quite absent. In the
first place, you either understand the piece of style before
you, or do not understand it, or feel more or less in doubt
whether you understand it or not. In the second place, you
are either interested, or bored, or left indifferent. Finally,
you are either pleased, or displeased, or doubtful whether
you are pleased or not. And the more you analyze your

impressions of style the more you will find, unless your experience differs surprisingly from most, that the third state
of things I suggest—indifference or doubt—is the rarest. In
short, every piece of style may be said to impress readers
in three ways,—intellectually, emotionally, aesthetically;
to appeal to their understanding, their feelings, their taste.
Every quality of style that I know of may be reduced to one
of these three classes; and these three—and these three
only—are different enough to deserve distinct and careful
consideration. Briefly, then, I may say that the qualities of
style are three,—intellectual, emotional, and aesthetic. It
is convenient to name these qualities; the terms I choose are
on the whole the best I have found,—those which Professor
Hill, of Harvard College, uses in the most sensible treatment of the art of composition I have yet found in print. To
the intellectual quality of style he gives the name "Clearness;" to the emotional, "Force;" to the aesthetic, "Elegance."

   To define this generalization, a concrete example is perhaps worth while. In choosing one from personal experience,
I commit what many may call a positive sin of egotism. My
defence must rest on what I have said already. Style is the
expression in words of thought and emotion; each man's
thought and emotion differs from every other man's. I con-
fess to a growing belief that the best thing any one can do,
when occasion serves, is to tell us what he himself knows.
It may be of small value, but at worst it is not second-hand.
When Robert Browning died, then, I found running in my
head two lines from a poem of his I had read some years before—the "Grammarian's Funeral,"—

> "This is our master, famous, calm, and dead,
>   Borne on our shoulders."

I remembered of the poem only that it was a long funeral
chorus, if I may use the term, put into the mouths of the
pupils of an old Italian professor. At daybreak, one fifteenth-
century morning, they are bearing him up to his grave in one
of the hill-cities of Central Italy. I turned to the poem and
read it through; I was deeply interested from beginning to

end. I thought the poem, as I think it still, profoundly characteristic of the writer in that it is among the permanently
forcible pieces of our literature. On the other hand, when I
had finished the reading, I had very little more notion of
what the poem meant in detail than I had had before; again
I found it profoundly characteristic of the writer, in that on
a single reading it was about as far from clear as human
perversity could make it. Finally, in spite of the undoubted
fact that there was in it something which not only interested
but fascinated me, I found only one passage that at first
reading thoroughly pleased me: —

> "Sleep, crop and herd. Sleep, darkling thorp and croft,
> Safe from the weather!
> He, whom we convoy to his grave aloft,
> Singing together,
> He was a man born with thy face and throat,
> Lyric Apollo!"

And even the pleasure I found in the full-throated melody of
this refreshingly simple passage was marred by the thought
that before I could be sure of what a thorp is or a croft, I
should have to consult a dictionary. Elegance, then, save
for the splendidly sustained funereal rhythm, I found as
notable for its absence as clearness; herein, again the poem
was profoundly characteristic of the writer. But for all its
lack of clearness and elegance, the poem had a force I could
not resist; I read it over again and again. Each reading
made it clearer; each gain in clearness diminished in some
degree the annoyance I felt in its apparently deliberate perversity of diction; and now, after some dozens of readings,
I think I can understand at least nine lines out of every ten,
and I am sure that I find in the poem both an emotional stimulus that constantly strengthens, and a constantly growing
if permanently incomplete delight.

In all pieces of style as truly as in this "Grammarian's
Funeral," clearness, force, and elegance—or their absence—
may readily be detected. The question that naturally presents
itself now is how they are produced. To answer this we must
approach the subject afresh, and ask ourselves not what we

have experienced, but what we have seen. Clearly, we have
seen nothing but written or printed words,—black marks on
white paper. It is something inherent in these black marks
which has produced the knowledge or the ignorance or the
puzzle, the interest or the tedium, the pleasure or the annoyance, of which we are conscious. For the moment, then,
we must turn our attention to these written words, these
curious black marks, and satisfy ourselves, if we can, what
there is in them to produce such notable results.

In themselves, these black marks are nothing but black
marks more or less regular in appearance. Modern English
type and script are rather simple to the eye. Old English
and German are less so; less so still, Hebrew and Chinese.
But all alphabets present to the eye pretty obvious traces of
regularity; in a written or printed page the same mark will
occur over and over again. This is positively all we see,—
a number of marks grouped together and occasionally repeated. A glance at a mummy-case, an old-fashioned tea-
chest, a Hebrew Bible, will show us all that any eye can
ever see in any written or printed document. The outward
and visible body of style consists of a limited number of
marks which, for all any reader is apt to know, are purely
arbitrary.

Whoever knows an alphabet, however, as all of us know
the twenty-six letters that compose written English, sees in
these black marks, not the marks themselves, but the ideas
they stand for. In a rough way—a very rough way in English—
each of these marks is a symbol which stands for one of a
limited number of articulate sounds. The sounds for which
some of them stand—b, for example, r, k, s—are very well
fixed; the sounds for which others stand—c, notably, and
most of the vowels—are various. But in almost any given
case, a reasonably trained eye recognizes at a glance what
sound a given mark stands for. Now, so far as we can see,
there is no relation whatever between the symbol in question
and the sound,—not so much as there is between the black
marks on a sheet of music and the notes the musician pro-
duces in obedience to them, for these at least run up and
down the scale as the marks are higher or lower on the

written page. What gives to letters the significance which we all understand almost intuitively is simply and solely the tacit agreement of the people who have used them. The only reason why we should not spell schooner as a small boy late-ly spelled it—squner—is that the practice of a century or so agrees that it should be spelled otherwise; and that the practice of a number of centuries and languages agrees that in the compound letter qu, the u has no open vowel-sound. What makes us see in these black marks, then, the sounds the writers mean them to symbolize is exactly what prevents us from seeing in Chinese or Arabic writing anything more than the marks themselves: in the one case we are familiar with the practice on which those who use the letters are tacitly agreed; in the other we are not. Common consent, general practice, is what makes the English alphabet signify any-thing. In this fact lies the rather comical hopelessness of the efforts now and then made by innocent dogmatists, not possessed of despotic authority, to reform spelling; for spelling, like other things we shall consider in a moment, is a matter, not of law, but of practice. The question in a given instance is not what ought to be the case, but what is. And to the state of things which enables us to decide in spelling, as in other fashions, what the case is at any given moment, we give, for convenience's sake, the name "Good Use."

I have dwelt on this elementary phase of good use because the reason why the articulate sounds these black marks sym-bolize are anything more to us than meaningless noises is precisely the same as the reason why letters are anything more than meaningless marks. Language, as the very origin of the word shows,—it means almost exactly what we some-times express by its synonym tongue,—is originally spoken. Utterance, in the history of the human race, indefinitely precedes writing. But language itself consists at bottom only of a limited number of articulate sounds, mostly as arbi-trary to our ears as the marks that stand for them are to our eyes. Our own language, and perhaps a few others, we understand so intuitively that we are apt to forget how purely arbitrary they are; but we have only to listen to the talk of foreigners—even of Europeans, far more of grunting Indians or clicking Hottentots—to be reminded that the sounds we hear and utter are purely symbolic, and that we understand them only because we happen to know what the practice, the common consent, the good use, of those who use them has agreed that they shall stand for.

Perhaps the simplest way of realizing how all language is originally formed is just to recall how we come to know people by name. We meet for the first time a man of whom we know nothing except that he is clothed and to all appearances in his right mind. Somebody tells us that his name is John Jones; thereafter, when we wish to mention him, we utter the monosyllables—in themselves mere arbitrary sounds—John Jones. Pretty soon the syllables in question cease to be arbitrary sounds, and arouse in our minds the extremely specific idea of a human individual, washed, dressed, and amiably disposed,—eternally different too in certain aspects from any other human being on the planet. Or, to take a quite different example: Some years ago I happened to be in a small Sicilian town, infested by contagiously good-humored beggars. When they pressed about me inconveniently, I turned on them, and uttered, among other expressions unhappily not remarkable for politeness, the word skedaddle. Somehow it caught their fancy: "Skedaddo!" they shouted in chorus. When I next went out of doors, I was greeted with shouts of "Buon giorno, skedaddo!" The rascals had named me, and called me by the name for the remaining hours of my stay among them; and a Sicilian gentleman subsequently told me that very probably the word skedaddo might become, in the town in question, a permanent generic noun signifying a light-haired foreigner of excitable disposition.

Just as we name or nickname people, our ancestors have named and nicknamed the various ideas which in the course of their history they have had occasion to express. Nowadays there are in the world a great many different languages, many of which, now mutually unintelligible, may easily be traced to a common origin; from Latin, for example, have sprung French, Italian, Spanish, Portuguese. But the numerous changes whose accumulation has separated and distinguished these modern languages have all taken place by

means of local and increasing differences in use, —in consent
as to what a given sound shall mean. Thus, from Anglo-Saxon
and Norman-French has sprung the curious hybrid English
with which we are chiefly concerned, —the articulate sounds
by which the people of England and her dependencies have
been agreed, during the past four or five centuries, to express whatever thoughts and emotions they have known.

Now, the first question before any one who would use the
English language efficiently—as a vehicle by which thought
and emotion may be conveyed to somebody else—is what
words are at his disposal. It is clear that we must use the
words—the articulate sounds—to which the English-speaking
peoples of the present time agree to attach definite significance; and what these words are we can discover only by
such constant observation and care of what is going on about
us in the whole English-speaking world as a child or a foreigner would give to a language he was trying to learn. Dictionaries and grammars, to be sure, may codify what exists
at any given moment. Regarded as codes, they are invalua-
ble; but at best they are codes of common law, not legisla-
tive enactments. The only sanction behind them is that of
practice, of usage. Before we can use language with certainty we must understand that beneath all these codes lies the
great fact of common human consent. We must learn instinctively to feel this for ourselves, to appreciate it, to
judge it. In English, as in every other language, the final
test of what words we may use is inevitably the usage of
those who speak and write it; the test of what words we
should use is the usage of those who speak and write it best,
—in other words, good use.

To illustrate this, we may well consider the difference
that always exists between the words we ourselves speak and
those we write. Closely similar, written language and spoken are yet inevitably different. Whoever says habitually,
"He does not," or, "I will not," talks not like a human being,
but like a prig; whoever habitually writes, "He does n't,"
or, "I won't," writes with something like vulgarity. For
general purposes we speak the language of the people we address, with all its colloquialisms. In writing, which we use

to communicate thought and emotion to we know not whom
nor how many, we must carefully employ only such forms
as good use, in its broadest sense, sanctions.

We are now in a position to answer the question we asked
ourselves a little while ago. Why is it, we asked, that a certain number of apparently arbitrary black marks on white
pages should convey to us all the infinitely varied impressions—intellectual, emotional, aesthetic—that we find in
literature? Why is it that style—whose visible body is never
anything more or less than these black marks—should impress us primarily as something that possesses or lacks
Clearness, Force, and Elegance? Simply and solely because
the tacit agreement, the good use of many generations of
human beings, who at least linguistically are our ancestors,
has consented in the first place that certain articulate sounds
shall be fixed as symbols for certain distinct ideas, and in
the second place that certain arbitrary marks shall be fixed
as symbols for certain distinct sounds. Good use, and good
use alone, is the basis on which all style rests. A knowledge
of good use so familiar as to be practically instinctive is the
basis on which any writer who would be certain to write with
clearness, force, and elegance must ultimately rest his own
style. The limits of good use are wide and flexible; but finally they grow rigid. Whoever strays beyond them errs; whoever keeps within them may write, for various reasons,
ineffectively, but cannot be convicted of positive error. Every question of positive right and wrong in style is a question concerning nothing whatever but good use.

Good use, then, must be the basis of all good style. The
next thing to ask ourselves is how to recognize good use.
And here we are met by a fact that, more than any other I
know of, confuses most people who begin seriously to consider the matter in question. For various reasons, the chief
of which is that five centuries ago pretty much everything
worth reading was comprised in what survived of the literatures of Greece and Rome, the education of civilized Europeans and Americans is still based on a prolonged and not
always very fruitful study of classical Latin and Greek. Now,
what makes Latin or Greek letters stand for Latin or Greek

words, and what makes Latin or Greek words stand for the
thoughts and emotions which are not only Latin and Greek,
but broadly human too, is precisely what makes English letters and words stand for the thoughts and emotions that make
up our conscious lives; namely, that many thousands of human beings tacitly agreed what this double system of symbols should symbolize, and so that good use arose. But between the classical languages, which we call dead, and the
modern languages, whose life is more vigorous than the life
of any human being, there is a broad distinction, not very
often kept in mind. Good use, like all other vital things, not
only comes into being and flourishes, but it passes out of
being too; and Latin use and Greek passed out of being with
the nations whose political and intellectual lives they expressed. So completely are they things of the past, indeed,
that so far as I can learn from friends who have given their
lives to the classics, nobody to-day on earth has any real
knowledge of how Latin or Greek was pronounced. At Harvard College, and elsewhere, to be sure, they have sup-
planted the unquestionably barbarous English pronunciation
by one which they call probably ancient; but whether Pericles or Cicero could understand the most punctiliously
learned nineteenth-century professor is a question not to be
settled this side of Elysium. In short, though we know pretty
accurately what words classical letters symbolize, and what
thoughts and emotions are symbolized by classical words,
one part of the classical languages—the sound, the thing that
made them true languages or tongues—is as dead as Alexan-
der or Caesar. And along with the sound has perished the
vital principle of the languages,—the constantly changing use
which brought them from the rude jargons in which they began into the exquisitely finished forms in which their literatures preserve them. In other words, the classical languages, like other things that have passed out of this world,
are complete. Nothing but the occasional discovery of a
manuscript or an inscription can add a syllable to them;
nothing but the demonstration of a corruption or a forgery
can take a syllable away. Nothing, in all human probability,
can supply the place of that troublesome caret which used to

bother us so much in the old Latin grammars. Here lies the
distinction between the classical languages and the modern,
the dead and the living. Latin and Greek are complete; dictionaries and grammars can codify them with final authority.
English, on the other hand, like every living tongue, must
remain incomplete so long as it retains life enough to be
spoken and written by living men; and so dictionaries and
grammars can at most be mile-stones in its progress through
this world.

Now, of course the unlearned in matters of style look for
authority to the learned. And the learned, brought up from
childhood on the authority, in matters of classical style, of
Latin and Greek dictionaries and grammars, are accustomed
to display what little human frailty survives the process of
culture by attaching to dictionaries and grammars themselves an importance second only to that which good men
attach to Holy Writ. They do not stop to remember, or at all
events to remind us, that what makes Latin and Greek books
of reference so finally authoritative is not that they are
books of reference, but that the languages therein codified
have long since ceased to grow; and so that these tongues
can be codified with something which approaches perfection.

To be certain of what good use is in a living language,
then, we must have other things to rest our case on than the
fact that some maker of dictionaries or grammars has reg-
istered—and given chapter and verse for—the words or
phrases we would defend. There are other tests of good use
to which we must turn. The most notable, I think, are that
it must be Reputable, National, and Present,—Reputable as
distinguished from vulgar, slangy, eccentric; National as
distinguished from local or technical; Present as distinguished from obsolete or transient. In view of the fact that
every question of right or wrong in style must ultimately be
referred to good use, these three phases of good use are
worth separate attention.

Reputable use is the use of no single writer, however eminent; it is the common consent of the great body of writers
whose works, taken together, make up what we mean when
we seriously use the term English Literature,—a term which

of course includes any literature written in the English language, Scotch, Irish, American, Australian. The fact that
Shakspere uses a word, or Sir Walter Scott, or Burke, or
Washington Irving, or whoever happens to be writing earnestly in Melbourne or Sidney, does not make it reputable.
The fact that all five of these authorities use the word in the
same sense would go very far to establish the usage. On the
other hand, the fact that any number of newspaper reporters
agree in usage does not make the usage reputable. The style
of newspaper reporters is not without merit; it is very
rarely unreadable; but for all its virtue it is rarely a well
of English undefiled. And just here, I may say, lies perhaps
the most crying fault of contemporary style in general. For
better or worse, the fact remains that our grandfathers
used to read the Bible morning and night, and that we read
instead the morning and evening newspapers. Our spontaneous vocabularies differ from theirs accordingly,—not wholly
for the better. And when, now and then, somebody raises a
feeble voice in protest, the reporters, who as a class are
very human beings, grow much excited, forgetting that no
known system of logic can warrant the conclusion that because all good style is readable, all readable style is necessarily good.

But an example or two of style that is national and present,
but not reputable, and so not good, will make the matter
clearer than all the generalization in the world. In Mr. Mal-
lock's "New Republic," you may remember, is a tale of how
a fastidious gentleman refrained from offering himself to a
pretty girl because she asked him if he was partial to boiled
chicken. In any newspaper you may find a comfortable house
described as an "elegant residence" or a "costly home;"
and so on.

National use is the use of neither England, Ireland, Scot-
land, America, nor Australia; nor yet of any single body of
men, however learned. It is the use which is sanctioned by
the common consent of the whole English-speaking world.
Whoever uses technical words, or foreign, or local, violates
this rule of good use. The use of technical words, still more
the use of foreign, is commonly a conscious affectation,

which any sane man may avoid. The use of local terms is
often spontaneous; here lies the chief danger of falling into
a style not national.

A few examples of style that is reputable and present, but
not national, and so not good, will make the matter clear.
"Ecteronic appendages," I find in the first book of physiol-
ogy I open, "not found in man, make their appearance in
other animals." "I noticed a dirty gamin," writes a student;
and another, using a word now confined at Harvard College
to street urchins, describes the same small boy as a mucker.

Present use is best described, I think, in the familiar
lines of Pope: —

> "In words as fashions, the same rule will hold:
> Alike fantastic if too new or old.
> Be not the first by whom the new are tried,
> Nor yet the last to lay the old aside."

These lines mention a very suggestive analogy. Fashions
constantly change, nobody knows exactly why. But everybody
knows that a series of annual fashion-plates extending over
a century would show a very marked series of changes in the
outward aspect of the human form divine. Every theatre-
goer knows too that these changes are so marked that a play
written a generation ago—Bulwer's "Money," for example,
or even Robertson's "School"—cannot without a grotesque-
ness that would nullify its dramatic effect be produced with
such costumes as were worn by the original actors. Though
the more subtle fashion to which we have given the name
"good use" changes more slowly, it changes just as surely;
and to a certain degree it follows fashion itself. The most
curious example of this I have lately come across is in a
song familiar to most of us: —

> "Yankee Doodle came to town
> A-riding on a pony,
> He stuck a feather in his hat,
> And called him macaroni."

Now, why he should have described himself as a nutritious
article of diet popular in Southern Europe I could never

imagine until I happened to notice Sir Benjamin Backbite's impromptu verses in the "School for Scandal,"—a play produced just before the American Revolution: —

> "Sure, never were seen two such beautiful ponies;
> Other horses are clowns, but these macaronies.
> To give them this title I'm sure is not wrong,
> Their legs are so slim and their tails are so long."

Apparently the macaroni was a dandy in tights and very long coat-tails. The embattled farmers with feathers in their hats were derisively likened to him, just as a country fellow on a cart-horse is sometimes hailed to-day as a "dude on horseback." And a panorama of men's fashion-plates from Sheridan's time to ours would show a series of figures, each of which might have been described all along as an exquisite or a man of fashion; but for each of which, as it appears specifically different from the rest, a new and transient name arises: macaroni, for example, buck, dandy, swell, dude.

Perhaps, however, the most suggestive example of good use—reputable, national, and present—is a fact within the personal experience of every one of us. When we write letters, we begin them with the adjective dear. Now, the occasions when we mean by this word to express even the smallest degree of personal affection are so rare that at such moments we often feel called upon to change the word to dearest, or very dear, or darling. There is another form of address in all respects but one decidedly more expressive of what we really mean,—Friend. Yet none of us begins a letter "Friend Tompkins." And the only reason why none of us commits this unpardonable sin is that custom, fashion, good use, forbids. So nowadays we are no longer "Obedient, Humble Servants," but "Truly" or "Sincerely" or "Faithfully Yours,"—not because either phrase was ever literally true, but simply and solely because, nobody knows why, good use once sanctioned one form, and now sanctions the others.

I have dwelt thus long on good use because, as I have said more than once already, good use is inevitably the basis of all good style. Whoever strays from it is first "original,"

then eccentric, then obscure, then unintelligible. Whoever
writes a totally foreign language is of course unintelligible,
but unintelligible only because in every word he formulates,
and sometimes in every mark he puts down, he serenely
violates every rule of the reputable, national, and present
use that makes modern English the thing it is. But unless
I have sadly missed my purpose, I have shown you reason to
see that in the last sentence I used a word by no means felicitous. "Every rule," I wrote, "of good use;" but the very
essence of good use is that it is not a system of rules, but
a constantly shifting state of fact. Rules, dictionaries,
grammars, can help us to discover it, just as fashion-plates
and manuals of etiquette may help us to dress ourselves and
to behave properly at table. But in the one case, as in the
others, there is no more absolute rule than the one which
prudent people habitually exemplify; namely, that a wise
man should keep good company, and use good sense.

So far, in order to emphasize at once the laxity and the
tyranny of good use, I have been asking you to consider style
as a series of letters so joined together as to make words.
And I hope that our consideration of the subject has been
close enough to fix in our minds the fact that the chief reason why style impresses us as a thing possessed of very
subtle qualities is that human consent has agreed to associate with those palpably material facts, arbitrary sounds and
the arbitrary marks that stand for them, certain more or
less definite phases of that eternally immaterial reality to
which we give the name "thought." I shall ask you now, in
imagination, to turn once more to a printed page, —or better
still, to a printed book, —and ask yourselves whether we
have as yet seen all that is therein visible.

A number of black marks we found these words to be,
grouped together and occasionally repeated. A little closer
inspection will show us that, in any modern piece of printing
or writing, these groups of black marks to which we give the
name "words" are themselves grouped, by means of spaces
and of other black marks, which we call punctuation, in
masses which even to the most untrained eye are more or
less independent. In other words, anybody, whether he

understand English or not, can see that any piece of style consists not of an indefinite series of independent words, but of a series of words intelligently composed, —a word which means neither more nor less than <u>put together</u>. The Latin term, as a single word, is the more convenient. We need a name for the visible groups in which the words that make up style are arranged. The best and simplest word I know is <u>compositions</u>.

In a printed book or a properly written manuscript, we shall soon observe that more than one kind of composition is visible. The book or the manuscript itself is a complete composition; it is generally made up of a considerable num- ber of visibly distinct parts to which we give the name "chapters;" these in turn are made up of a number of some- what less distinct parts which we call "paragraphs;" these in turn of parts still less, but still visibly, distinct, which we call "sentences." Or, to state the matter conversely, all style consists of words, composed in sentences, composed in paragraphs, composed in larger groups to which we may for our purposes give the name "whole compositions."

The question which now presents itself to whoever has grasped the fact that good use, and good use alone, is what gives significance to the words of which all style primarily consists, takes a very definite form. Are compositions, like words, governed by good use? Or may we, in composing words, act with more independence than in choosing them? In that case, are there any general principles of composition by which we may to advantage govern our conduct?

The simplest way of answering this question, I think, is to answer it backward: in the first place, to inquire what gen- eral principles of composition might rationally be laid down if there were no such troublesome thing as good use to inter- fere with us; and then to inquire how far the action of these principles is balked in practice by good use.

And here we come to what has appeared to me the fault of almost every textbook of Rhetoric I have examined. These books consist chiefly of directions as to how one who would write should set about composing. Many of these directions are extremely sensible, many very suggestive. But in every case these directions are appallingly numerous. It took me some years to discern that all which have so far come to my notice could be grouped under one of three very simple heads, each of which might be phrased as a simple proposition. Various as they are, all these directions concern either what may be included in a given composition (a sentence, a paragraph, or a whole); or what I may call the outline, or perhaps better, the mass of the composition,—in other words, where the chief parts may most conveniently be placed; or finally, the internal arrangement of the composition in detail. In brief, I may phrase these three principles of composition as follows: (1) Every composition should group itself about one central idea; (2) The chief parts of every composition should be so placed as readily to catch the eye; (3) Finally, the relation of each part of a composition to its neighbors should be unmistakable. The first of these principles may conveniently be named the principle of Unity; the second, the principle of Mass; the third, the principle of Coherence. They are important enough to deserve examination in detail.

   I have said that all compositions should have unity,—in other words, that every composition should group itself about one central idea. The very terms in which I have phrased this principle suggest at once the chief fact that I have tried to keep before you in the earlier part of this chapter,—that words are after all nothing but arbitrary symbols standing for ideas. So really, when we come to consider the substance of any composition, we may better concern ourselves rather with what the words stand for than with the visible symbols themselves. If we once know what ideas we wish to group together, the task of finding words for them is immensely simplified; on the other hand, if in the act of composition—an act which is generally rather hasty—we have grouped together a number of words, the question of whether we shall leave them together, or strike out some, or add some, is generally to be settled by considering not what visible forms our composition has associated, but what ideas. Now, the principles on which we may properly group ideas together are as various as anything well can be. In the first place, as we have just seen, there are various kinds of

compositions,—sentences, paragraphs, and those larger
kinds which for convenience I have grouped under the single
head of wholes. Obviously there is in good style some reason why the unity of the sentence should be more limited
that of the paragraph, and the unity of the paragraph than
that of the whole. Yet, as our purposes in composing vary,
we may perfectly well devote to a single subject—George
Eliot, for example—a book, a chapter, a paragraph, or a
sentence. Any decently written life of George Eliot—Mr.
Cross's, let us say—has unity, in that it groups itself about
one central idea; namely, the notable writer in question.
Any history of English fiction in the nineteenth century—to
be sure, I do not at this moment recall one worth mentioning—would probably contain a chapter about George Eliot
which would possess unity for precisely the same reason.
So, in a general account of contemporary English literature,
we should be rather surprised not to find at least a paragraph devoted to George Eliot, and this paragraph would
have unity for precisely the same reason that caused us to
recognize it in the imaginary chapter, or in Mr. Cross's
book. And a very short article—a leader in a newspaper, for
example—which should deal with modern novels in general
would be more than apt to contain at least a sentence about
George Eliot, of which the unity would be demonstrable in
exactly the same way. In other words, the question of scale—
in many aspects important—has very little to do with the
question of unity. The question of unity is whether for our
purposes the ideas we have grouped together may rationally
be so grouped; if we can show that they may, we are safe.
Analogies are often helpful: we may liken the grouping of
ideas in compositions to the grouping of facts in statistics.
A group of statistics, such as the director of the Harvard
gymnasium calls anthropometic, may concern a single individual; again, a genealogy concerns, as the case may be,
a family, or a group of families related by blood or mar-
riage; a local history, such as we have hundreds of in New
England, properly concerns a considerable number of families who have lived at different times under the same political conditions; a State or a national census concerns the

entire population of State or nation, and groups it too in any
number of different ways. But each of these things has a
unity of its own; and to a certain degree each larger group
contains each smaller one. Here, I think, is the chief thing
to keep in mind: just as the sentence is a group of words,
the paragraph is a group of sentences, and the whole a group
of paragraphs. We should take care that each group has, for
our purpose, a unity of its own; and that the unity of each
larger group is of a kind that may properly be resolved into
the smaller unities of which it is composed.

In considering the question of unity, then, we consider
rather what the words stand for than the visible words themselves. In considering the second principle of composition,
—the principle of Mass,—I conceive the case to be different.
Style, you will remember, I defined as the expression of
thought and emotion in written words. Written words we saw
to be visible material symbols of that immaterial reality,
thought and emotion, which makes up our conscious lives.
What distinguishes written words from spoken, literature
from the colloquial language that precedes it, is that written
words address themselves to the eye and spoken words to
the ear. Though this fundamental physical fact has been neglected by the makers of textbooks, I know few more important. The principle of Mass, you will remember,—the principle which governs the outward form of every composition,
—is that the chief parts of every composition should be so
placed as readily to catch the eye. Now, what catches the
eye is obviously not the immaterial idea a word stands for,
but the material symbol of the idea,—the actual black marks
to which good use has in course of time come to attach such
subtile and varied significance. In these groups of visible
marks that compose style certain parts are more conspicuous than others. Broadly speaking, the most readily visible
parts of a given composition are the beginning and the end.
Run your eye over a printed page; you will find it arrested
by every period, more still by every one of those breaks
which mark the division of paragraphs. Compare a book not
broken into chapters—Defoe's "Plague" for example—with a
book in which the chapters are carefully distinguished; and

you will feel, on a conveniently large scale, the extreme
mechanical inconvenience of the former arrangement. On
the other hand, compare the ordinary version of the Bible—
broken into verses whose separation is based chiefly on the
fact that each by itself will make a tolerable text—with the
Revised Version, in most respects so deplorably inferior
as literature: in the former case, it is mechanically hard,
unless somebody is reading aloud to you, to make out which
break is important, which not; in the latter case, the task
is mechanically easy. Or again, remark a fact that is becoming in my literary studies comically general: familiar
quotations from celebrated books are almost always to be
found at the beginning or the end. "Music hath charms" are
the opening words of Congreve's "Mourning Bride." Don
Quixote fights with the windmill very early in the first volume; he dies with the remark that there are no birds in last
year's nests near the end of the last. Until I read "Don
Quixote" through, a few years ago, these two incidents were
the chief ones concerning him which general reading and
talking had fixed in my mind. Now, the fact that, for better
or worse, human readers notice the beginning and the end
of compositions a good deal more readily than the parts that
come between is the fact on which the principle of Mass is
based. A writer who is careful so to mass his compositions
as to put in places that catch the eye words which stand for
ideas that he wants us to keep in mind, will find his work
surprisingly more effective than that of a perhaps cleverer
man who puts down his words in the order in which they
occur to him.

The principle of Unity, we have seen, concerns itself
chiefly with the immaterial ideas for which the material
written words stand; the principle of Mass chiefly with the
written words themselves; the third principle of composition—the principle of Coherence—concerns itself, I think,
about equally with both. I phrased it, you will remember, in
the words that the relation of every part of a composition to
its neighbors should be unmistakable. In a given composition, for example, no word should appear without apparent
reason for being there,—in other words, no incongruous

idea should destroy the impression of unity. Again, to put
the matter differently, no written word should be so placed
that we cannot see at a glance how its presence affects the
words about it. Sometimes coherence is a question of the
actual order of words; sometimes, as in the clause I am at
this moment writing, of constructions; sometimes, as in the
clause I write now, it demands a pretty careful use of those
convenient parts of speech to which we give the name "con-
nectives." In that last clause, for example, the pronoun it,
referring to the word coherence, which was the subject of
the first clause in the sentence, made possible the change
of construction from "it is a question of" this or that to "it
demands" this or that. But perhaps the most important thing
to remember about this last principle of composition is its
name. Coherence is a much more felicitous name than Unity
or Mass. To "cohere" means to "stick together." A style
that sticks together is coherent; a style whose parts hang
loose is not.

We find, then, an answer to the first question we proposed
a little while ago: if there were no such troublesome thing
as good use to interfere with the free exercise of our inge-
nuity, we might clearly put together our compositions in
contented obedience to the principles of Unity, Mass, and
Coherence. It remains for us to inquire how far the action of
these principles is hampered in practice by good use.

Perhaps the simplest way of answering this inquiry is to
study an example of style frequently cited in the textbooks.
Among the various facts which have conspired to give unfavorable fame to the Emperor Nero is the general belief that
he killed his mother. In English we state this belief in these
words: Nero killed Agrippina. If asked to parse this sentence, we say that Nero is in the nominative case because
it is the subject of the verb killed; and that Agrippina is in
the objective case—or the accusative—because it is the object of the verb. But if Agrippina had been the slayer and
Nero the slain, Agrippina nominative and Nero objective, the
word Agrippina would still remain Agrippina; the word Nero
still Nero. In English the only way to change the meaning
would be to change the order of words, and to say, "Agrip-

pina killed Nero." In Latin, on the other hand, the accusative
case is different in form from the nominative; the original
sentence would be, "Nero interfecit Agrippinam." That convenient final m does Agrippina's business; the three words
may be arranged in any order we please. But if we wished
to say that Agrippina killed Nero, we should have to alter
the form of both names, and say "Neronem interfecit Agrippina." In this single example we can see as plainly as we
need, I think, the chief way in which good use interferes with
the free operation of the principles of composition. The English language has fewer inflections than almost any other
known to the civilized world; that is, each word has fewer
distinct forms to indicate its relations to the words about it.
All nouns have possessives and plurals; all verbs have
slightly different forms for the present and the past tense;
but this is about all. In English, then, the relation of word
to word is expressed not by the forms of the words, but
generally by their order; and any wide departure from the
normal order of a sentence—in brief, subject, verb, object—
is apt to alter or to destroy the meaning. "Nero interfecit
Agrippinam," "Agrippinam interfecit Nero," "Nero Agrippinam interfecit," all mean exactly the same thing; the difference in mass alters the emphasis, that is all. "Nero
killed Agrippina," on the other hand, means one thing;
"Agrippina killed Nero," means another; and what "Nero
Agrippina killed" may mean, nobody without a knowledge of
the facts can possibly decide.

What is true of this simplest of sentences is true in a general way of any sentence in the English language. Good use
has settled that the meaning of one great class of compositions in English—namely, of sentences—shall be indicated in
general, not by the forms of the words which compose them,
but by the order. Except within firmly defined limits, we
cannot alter the order of words in English without violating
good use; and in no language can we violate good use without
grave and often fatal injury to our meaning. "Nero Agrippina
killed," to revert to our example, is as completely ambiguous as any three words can be. While, on the one hand, then,
we who use uninflected English are free from the disturbing

array of grammatical rules and exceptions which so bothers us in Latin or in German, we are far less free than Romans or Germans to apply the principles of composition to the composing of sentences. The principle of Unity, to be sure, we may generally observe pretty carefully; but the principle of Mass is immensely interfered with by the fact that it is the order of words in a sentence that in general gives the sentence meaning; and so to a less degree is the principle of Coherence.

When we turn to the larger kinds of composition, however, we find the case different. As a matter of fact, the sentence is the only kind of composition that inevitably appears in spoken discourse. Until words are joined together, composed in sentences, there is, of course, no such thing as intelligible communication. The moment they are so joined, the organism of spoken language is complete. Paragraphs, on the other hand, do not appear in spoken discourse at all. And though, of course, in serious compositions the organic structure of the whole ought to be almost as palpable to hearers as to readers, the fact remains that in by far the greater part of oral discourse—the conversation, the chat, the bustle of daily life—there are no wholes at all. In other words, then, while oral usage—actual speech—is what the sentence is based on, the paragraph and the whole composition are based on written usage, which is commonly a great deal more thoughtful.

What is more, while the sentence is as old as language itself, the whole composition is hardly older than literature, and the modern paragraph is considerably younger than the art of printing. It follows, then, and a very slight study of the facts will prove the conclusion, that while in sentences good use very seriously interferes with the operation of the principles of composition, it interferes very little with their operation in paragraphs and in compositions of a larger kind. In other words, we are free to arrange sentences in paragraphs, and paragraphs in chapters, and chapters in books, pretty much as we think fit.

We are now, I think, in a position to sum up in a very few words the theory of style which I shall try to present to you.

Style, you will remember, I defined as the expression of thought and feeling in written words. Modern style—the style we read and write to-day—I believe to be the result of a constant though generally unconscious struggle between good use and the principles of composition. In words, of course good use is absolute; in sentences, though it relaxes its authority, it remains very powerful; in paragraphs its authority becomes very feeble; in whole compositions, it may roughly be said to coincide with the principles.

In the chapters that follow, I purpose first to examine as carefully as may be the outward and visible body of style. It is made up of what I may call four elements,—the prime element Words, composed in Sentences, composed in Paragraphs, composed in Whole Compositions. Each of these elements I shall examine in detail, inquiring first how far it is affected by the paramount authority of good use, and then how within the limits of good use it may be made, by means of the principles of composition or otherwise, to assume various forms and to perform various offices. Then, when we have studied the visible body of style, its material elements, as carefully as we can, I shall turn to the three qualities, Clearness, Force, and Elegance, and try to determine what it is in the elements by which each of them may be secured or lost.

A dull business this seems to many, yet after ten years' study I do not find it dull at all. I find it, rather, constantly more stimulating; and this because I grow more and more aware how in its essence this matter of composition is as far from a dull and lifeless business as earthly matters can be; how he who scribbles a dozen words, just as truly as he who writes an epic, performs—all unknowing—one of those feats that tell us why men have believed that God made man in His image. For he who scrawls ribaldry, just as truly as he who writes for all time, does that most wonderful of things,—gives a material body to some reality which till that moment was immaterial, executes, all unconscious of the power for which divine is none too grand a word, a lasting act of creative imagination.

Elegance

The last quality of style is far more subtile than either of the others. Any style that we can understand, we have found, is clear; and the secret of clearness lies in the denotation of our words and compositions. Any style that will hold the attention, we have found, is forcible; and not so obviously, but I hope almost as surely, we have determined that the secret of force lies in the connotation of our words and com- positions. But we come at last to a more elusive matter than force. What is it in style that may be trusted to please us; and what trait in the elements of style may be expected to secure it?

In my first chapter, I suggested to you both the name by which I shall describe the quality in question and the defini- tion I shall give it. Elegance is the distinguishing quality of a style that pleases the taste. By framing and repeating this definition, however, I do not mean that it satisfies me. On the contrary, both name and definition are among the least satisfactory things I have ventured to offer you. Yet, para- doxical as it may seem, this very fact has inclined me not to attempt to change them; for no single example could much better illustrate what I believe to be the real nature of the quality.

What we have in view, you see, is the aesthetic quality of style,—that subtile something in a work of literary art which makes us feel delight in the workmanship. Beauty, some call it; charm, others; others still, grace, ease, finish, mastery. Yet none of these terms, any more than the one I have chosen, speaks for itself. Most palpable, of course, in kinds of writing whose first object is to give pleasure,—in poetry, or in that finer kind of prose that we recognize as belonging to literature,—the quality I mean need not be wholly absent from even the most technical style or the most commonplace matter. We all feel it in the great poets; we all feel it in such prose as Addison's; in less certain form we all feel it in such modern prose as Mr. Matthew Arnold's, or Mr. Walter Pater's, just as we feel its absence in everyday journalism or in the astonishing vagaries of Carlyle or of Mr. Addington Symonds. But I think we do not all feel it in other places where nevertheless it exists; in technical treatises, for example, in every-day letters, in every case where human beings attempt the task of embodying in written words the elusive, immaterial reality of thought and emotion.

Our first task, then, is to realize what we mean; to fix in our minds the quality to which we are now trying to give a name. By so doing, we shall see why any name yet found for it must be unsatisfactory; and by so seeing we shall learn, I think, more about it than we can learn in any other simple way.

Perhaps the easiest way of approaching our task is for a moment to consider the name for it now before us. A moment ago I said that any one can feel the elegance of Addison's style. Nobody ever had much less fundamental liking for the somewhat priggish Whig who gave English literature the "Spectator" than that stoutest of Georgian Tories, Samuel Johnson. Yet Johnson's Life of Addison closes with these words: "Whoever wishes to attain an English style, familiar but not coarse, and elegant but not ostentatious, must give his days and nights to the volumes of Addison." The opinion thus expressed has become a tradition. To this day, Addisonian is a word not infrequently used to mean that a style has the finest grace. To a certain extent this is true: if a writer have in view such purposes as Addison's, little higher praise can be given him than that he approaches the standard of excellence that Addison fixed for the wits of Queen Anne's London. In another way, this Addisonian tradition has given rise to what I believe to be grave error. If to be Addisonian is to be excellent, people are apt to fancy, not to be

Addisonian is to be something not excellent at all. The logic,
when you stop to think, is obviously imperfect; but as a rule,
you do not stop to think. Now, the most salient trait of Addison's style is its politeness, its well-bred restraint, its
complete freedom from any manner of excess. An admirable
trait everybody must admit this, for a great many purposes;
but, to go no farther, to be at once Addisonian and passionate is simply impossible. And whoever should say that passionate writing cannot have the trait before us now—the quality that pleases the taste—as well as the intellectual quality
clearness, and the emotional quality force, would obviously
say something that would make his notion of the quality very
different from the notion I am trying to lay before you.

   To get a more comprehensive idea of just what this is, it
will be worth while to turn to four passages from English
poetry, in which four poets, each notable at a different period of our literature, have touched this matter. Among the
beautiful passages which make Marlowe's "Tamburlaine," to
whoever knows it well, something far more significant than
the surging sea of bombast for which it stands in tradition,
are these lines on beauty, —

> "If all the pens that ever poets held
> Had fed the feeling of their masters' thoughts,
> And every sweetness that inspired their hearts,
> Their minds, and muses on admired themes;
> If all the heavenly quintessence they still
> From the immortal flowers of poesy,
> Wherein, as in a mirror, we perceive
> The highest reaches of a human wit, —
> If these had made one poem's period,
> And all combined in beauty's worthiness,
> Yet should there hover in their restless heads,
> One thought, one grace, one wonder, at the least,
> Which into words no virtue can digest."

And this unspoken word is the final secret of beauty. Fifty
years later, in that England of Cavaliers and Puritans that
was in feeling centuries away from the passionate Renaissance of Elizabeth, John Ford, in his tragedy of the "Broken
Heart," wrote this song: —

"Can you paint a thought; or number
Every fancy in a slumber?
Can you count soft minutes roving
From a dial's point by moving?

. . . .

"No, oh no! yet you may
    Sooner do both that and this,
    This and that, and never miss,
Than by any praise display
    Beauty's beauty; such a glory
    As beyond all fate, all story,
        All arms, all arts,
        All loves, all hearts,
    Greater than those or they,
    Do, shall, and must obey."

In a poem as far from these in character as the limits of literature allow—in Pope's "Essay on Criticism"—are these
lines, which say the same thing: —

"Some beauties yet no precepts can declare,
For there's a happiness as well as care.
Music resembles Poetry; in each
Are nameless graces which no methods teach.

. . . .

"True wit is Nature to advantage dress'd,
What oft was thought, but ne'er so well express'd;
Something whose truth convinc'd at sight we find,
That gives us back the shadow of the mind."

And only a few years ago the most notable of our living
American poets, Mr. James Lowell, gave us these lines: —

"I have a fancy: how shall I bring it
Home to all mortals wherever they be?
Say it or sing it? Shoe it or wing it,
So it may outrun or outfly me,
Merest cocoon-web whence it broke free?

"Only one secret can save from disaster,

> Only one magic is that of the master.
> Set it to music; give it a tune,—
> Tune the brook sings you, tune the breeze brings you,
> Tune the wild columbines nod to in June!

> "This is the secret: so simple, you see!
> Easy as loving, easy as kissing,
> Easy as—well, let me ponder—as missing,
> Known, since the world was, by scarce two or three."

Each of these poets in his own way has said the same thing; and when we ask ourselves what this thing is, we find it something that in our own prosy way we have already tried to keep in mind. The work of any artist—and as surely as M. Jourdain spoke prose, every writer must be essentially an artist—is a far more subtle and wonderful thing than we are apt to realize. It is nothing less than an act of creative imagination, than giving to the eternally immaterial reality of thought a visible, material body of written words. As Wordsworth put it in the passage I cited from De Quincey, style is the "incarnation of thought;" and this thought which we would incarnate is an infinitely subtle, infinitely varied thing. And the means of incarnation that we mortals have is a very limited thing,—only a few thousand arbitrary sounds, to which good use, and nothing else, has given approximate meanings. At best the incarnation can be only a feeble shadow of the reality,—a symbol to which nothing but deep imaginative sympathy can give anything like the significance which the artist longed to pack within it. By irrevocable fate expression must be eternally, almost tragically, inadequate.

There is no single example of this more notable than the phase of fine art which I am disposed to think most characteristic of this last half of the nineteenth century: I mean the music-drama of Wagner. Any one can appreciate how great a poet Wagner was. In "Siegfried," for example, when the dragon lies sleeping on his hoard, Wotan comes to warn him of the approach of the hero who is to slay him; and from the depths of his cave comes the growling answer,—

"Ich lieg' und besitze.
Lass mich schlafen,"—

"I lie here, possessing. Let me sleep." In seven words Wagner has phrased the spirit that made the French Revolution
what it was; that among ourselves to-day seems to many so
terribly threatening to the prosperity of our own country.
But Wagner is not only a poet; most of you, I think, who
have let yourselves listen, must have felt the indefinable
power of the endlessly interwoven melody by which he seeks
to express in music, too, the thought and emotion for which
poetry alone is an inadequate vehicle. Perhaps you must go
to Baireuth to know the rest. But certainly at Baireuth,
where every engine of modern art was at his disposal, Wagner has brought all the other fine arts to his aid: architecture in the simple lines of the darkened theatre itself, where
the music of the instruments fills the air one knows not
whence; painting, in scenery, in costumes, in groupings of
heroic figures, where for once the pageantry of the stage is
treated as seriously as any great painting; even sculpture,
as when, through the whole celebration of the mystic sacra-
ment, Parsifal stands motionless as any figure cut from
marble. No one art of expression was enough for Wagner;
and it was at last his fortune to control them all. Yet when
all was done by this man, who seems to me the greatest of
modern artists; when at the point where each art by itself
had done its utmost, a fresh art came to do more still,—the
final reality (the real thought and emotion which all this
marvellous thing would express) is as far away as ever.
Even that wonderful "Parsifal," with all its fusion of the
arts, is another thing, and an infinitely lesser thing, than
the great simple truth which lies behind it: that the true
secret of wisdom is infinite sympathy with humanity, good
and evil.

In this vast, inevitable inadequacy of our means of expression lies the secret of the profound discouragement that must
often attend even the greatest of serious artists when he is
all in earnest. Shakspere himself phrases what I mean:—

"Wishing me like to one more rich in hope,
Featured like him, like him of wealth possest,
Desiring this man's art, and that man's scope,
With what I most enjoy contented least."

Whoever would work earnestly must learn, I believe, to
know this mood; to face, with courageous resignation, the
inevitable truth that underlies it; content with the thought,
in which lies no exhaustible stimulus, that, do what he may,
his ideal must always be beyond him, and so that there can
never be any moment of accomplishment when he may not
eagerly hope and strive to do better and better still.

We are far enough now, it seems, from Addisonian elegance; yet we are coming near to the place where we can
see why, perhaps unwisely, I have chosen the term elegance
to express that final quality in literary work which makes us
recognize its art as fine. This quality, we clearly see, is a
very wonderful thing,—a thing whose essence has eluded the
greatest masters as well as the dabblers; a thing which no
words we have can adequately phrase. And yet when we stop
to think once more, and ask ourselves by what means, in
works of literature, we become aware of this impalpable
quality, we find ourselves just where we have so often found
ourselves before. In the greatest poem, as truly as in the
most impudent advertisement that we laugh at in horse-cars,
all that meets the eye are the written words. It is something
in them, and only something in them, that makes all the
difference.

Is this thing a thing we can in any wise define? That is the
question now. Have words, alone or in composition, any
trait that is favorable to this exquisitely subtle quality to
which I have given this trivial name of elegance?

We have seen already that every word we use must in
greater or less degree possess two distinct traits,—denotation and connotation. It denotes the idea which good use
agrees that it shall stand for; it connotes the very various
and subtle thoughts and emotions which cluster about that
idea in the human mind, whose store of thought is so vastly

greater than its store of words with which to symbolize
thought. And the traits that words possess, compositions
must possess too; sentences, paragraphs, chapters, books,
put together the words which compose them, and all the
traits of these words. In all the elements of style, denotation
and connotation may alike be recognized. The secret of clearness, we saw, lies in denotation; the secret of force in connotation. But we have already seen that when all is done, the
expression of thought and feeling in written words can never
be complete. Do what we may, with denotation in mind and
connotation too, our style can at best be only something

"That gives us back the shadow of the mind."

No expression can be so perfect that a better cannot be im-
agined. In this truth, I believe, lies the final secret of the
quality I call elegance. The more exquisitely style is adapted
to the thought it symbolizes, the better we can make our
words and compositions denote and connote in other human
minds the meaning they denote and connote in ours, the
greater charm style will have, merely as a work of art. In
a single phrase, the secret of elegance lies in adaptation.

I said at the very beginning of this chapter, that I was dissatisfied with the name—elegance—which I have given this
aesthetic quality of style; and yet that I was induced to keep
it for the very reason that it dissatisfies me. Now, I think,
you can see why. We begin to understand, I hope, what the
quality is; and if you will stop to think, you will find, I believe, that our language contains no word which will begin at
once to denote and to connote all that we wish to express
when we name the quality. In such straits, I often think, we
may best choose a word whose literal meaning, when we
scan it closely, will remind us of what we really mean; and
the literal meaning of elegance comes nearer what we mean
now than that of any other word I have found. With all its
connotation of fashion and fastidiousness and over-nicety,
elegance means, when we stop to remember our Latin, the
quality that distinguishes anything that is carefully selected.
The words it comes from—ex and lego—mean literally to
pick out, to choose from among some great mass of things

the one thing that shall best serve our purpose; and this is precisely what the earnest writer would do who seeks constantly to adapt his style more and more exquisitely to his thought and emotion. In the very difficulty that meets us here, in the choice of a name, we can see, in concrete form, the nature of the quality we are considering, and the very remote approximation of style to thought with which the limits of human language so often compel us to rest satisfied.

To turn now to a few examples of the quality as it reveals itself in literature, we may best consider it in its finest form. In poetry everybody perceives it most clearly. Of course, the dialect of poetry differs from that of prose. To write prosy poetry, or to write prose full of words that belong to the vocabulary of poetry, is instantly to forget that the secret of elegance lies in the adaptation of style to thought. But the adaptation which gives its charm to the finest poetry is, after all, adaptation of means to end; and just such adaptation of style to meaning is what gives its charm to that fine prose whose purpose differs from that of poetry, and whose outward form must differ accordingly. Take a single word to begin with. For generations, English prose has discarded the pronoun thou and all its derivatives. No lover uses it to his sweetheart; nor could the phrase "thine eyes" stand for a moment in serious modern prose. But the moment we turn to song we find the phrase still acceptable: "Drink to me only with thine eyes," might have been written yesterday. Not very long ago, I saw a little poem, written at Harvard College, and in many respects charming. The first line of it, though, ran thus: —

"Thy eyes are mirrors of strange things."

Now, just as in Ben Jonson's line the style seems perfectly adapted to the thought, so in this line there is something lacking. A moment's study will show that it is only the letter n. "Thine eyes" has a sound which we recognize as charming; "thy eyes" has a clumsy repetition of sound which subtilely recalls the "ki-yi" of a small boy. Remote as this connotation is, it is enough to make the second line a far less exquisitely adapted one than the first. In poetry—and in

prose too—the mere question of sound, the mere choice of a
single letter, may make a passage or mar it. Transfer that
<u>n</u>, for example: suppose for a moment that Ben Jonson had
written, "Drink to me only with <u>thy eyes</u>," and that the modern poet had written, "<u>Thine eyes</u> are mirrors of strange
things;" and Ben Jonson's line is no longer certainly the
better. Again, take a single phrase, no longer from serious
literature, but from the work of a friend with whom I once
discussed it. He was writing, in tolerably impassioned
prose, a description of a landscape remarkable for a certain
softness of beauty. "No rock peeped forth," he wrote, "save
from a bed of verdure soft as a woman's breast." Putting
quite aside the question of felicity of figure, he found himself dissatisfied with that sentence, because there was in it
a connotation of voluptuousness foreign to his purpose. After
a while he changed one word, and then found he had said what
he meant to the best of his power. Instead of <u>woman</u> he wrote
<u>mother</u>: "No rock peeped forth save from a bed of verdure
soft as a mother's breast." The only change is in the choice
of a more specific word; but the whole connotation is altered,
and the style is as finely adapted to the thought as that man
could make it.

   Again, compare two passages of verse to which I have
called your attention before: the opening lines of Wordsworth's "Skylark," and those of Shelley's. You will find
them side by side in the "Golden Treasury." Here are Wordsworth's lines: —

   "Ethereal minstrel! pilgrim of the sky!
    Dost thou despise the earth, where cares abound?
    Or while the wings aspire, are heart and eye
    Both with thy nest upon the dewy ground?—
    Thy nest, which thou canst drop into at will,
    Those quivering wings composed, that music still."

And here are Shelley's lines: —

                "Hail to thee, blithe spirit!
                 Bird thou never wert,
                 That from heaven, or near it,

> Pourest thy full heart
> In profuse strains of unpremeditated art."

In the long words and the slow measure of Wordsworth's
first line—

> "Ethereal minstrel! pilgrim of the sky!"—

there is something that keeps the mind where the contempla-
tive poet would have it,—down on earth. In the short, ecstatic words of Shelley's first line—

> "Hail to thee, blithe spirit!"—

there is something that lifts the mind straight away from all
things earthly. Change a word in either of these, change
even a syllable or a letter, and something is lost.

Again, take, almost at random, one of Shakspere's descriptions: the beginning of the speech that tells how Ophelia
died: —

> "There is a <u>willow</u> grows <u>aslant</u> a <u>brook</u>
> That shows his <u>hoar</u> leaves in the <u>glassy</u> stream."

Try for yourselves, in seventeen words and twenty syllables,
to pack even half so much of a picture as is there; and you
will see for yourselves how marvellous those lines are in
their exquisitely simple adaptation to the purpose of the poet.
Then read the passage through; and when you have finished,
see for yourselves how this simple picture that begins it
sets the whole in a background of just such gentle, homely
nature as should best make us feel the loveliness of the
dying girl, and the mournfulness of her end. Or turn to Dante, and see how in the fifth canto of the "Inferno," where he
tells the story of Francesca, that wonderful simile of the
doves, full of suggestions of light and love and purity, sof-
tens and makes mournful the dreadful story of sin and expi-
ation that in lesser hands than his might have been merely
horrible. See too, if you will, the pathos of a single word
in the beginning of Francesca's speech: —

> "Siede la terra dove nata fui

Sulla marina, dove 'l Po discende
Per aver <u>pace</u> coi seguaci sui."

"The land where I was born lies by the shore,
There where the Po comes down into the sea,
To have at last <u>peace</u>, with his following streams."

No word but <u>peace</u> could so give the suggestion of all that
might have been, had these sinners kept from the sin which
has doomed them to the eternal torment of hell. I should not
stray from English, I suppose; English affords us examples
enough to last forever. But Dante happened to be the first
poet who spoke to me; and when I think of all that is best in
literature, I cannot help thinking of him.

We have seen enough of what this exquisite adaptation of
means to end is like. It is time to turn to another example,
where a real question arises. Is the passage that I shall now
recall to you exquisitely adapted to its purpose, or does it
fail to produce the effect the poet had in mind? I refer to the
last line but one of Mr. James Lowell's "Secret," which I
cited a little while ago: —

"This is the secret: so simple, you see!
Easy as loving, easy as kissing,
Easy as—well, let me ponder—as missing;
Known, since the world was, by scarce two or three."

Charming lines we must all find the first and the second and
the last; but how about the last but one? In the midst of the
simple melody about it, that conscious little phrase, "well,
let me ponder," startles us; it is a disagreeable discord.
At first we are annoyed; why on earth did he spoil a pretty
poem by such an ugly blemish? But look at the line again,
ask yourself what it means; and you will find that its very
purpose is to show how very easily we may fail to do what we
have in mind; it is: —

"Easy as—well, let me ponder—as missing."

Could four words more subtilely suggest just the kind of
failure that the line describes? And if this is what the poet

had in mind, could four words, after all, be much more exquisitely adapted to his purpose? It is like that line of Pope's,
who complains how, in bad verse, the measure drags: —

"And ten low words oft creep in one dull line."

But the art is more subtle than Pope's; you only feel its
effect; until you stop to analyze it, you do not see how the
effect is produced.

Few examples, I think, could bring us more directly to a
fact that critics of style are very apt to forget; and yet which
every one must fully realize before his criticism of style,
as style, can be certain. Style, I may remind you again, is
the expression of thought and feeling in written words. To a
critic of style, a given piece of style, then, presents a double problem, but a double problem of which the separate
parts are not clearly distinguished. First, he sees the written words which stand for the thought and feeling that were
in the writer's mind; secondly, he sees through those written words to the thought and the feeling which they incarnate.
Now, what he knows, until he begins to analyze, is merely
a general impression: he understands or fails to understand;
he is interested or bored; he is pleased or repelled. And a
careless critic confuses the two elements which may well be
present in these primary impressions; but, as I conceive
style, we must separate them rigorously. An artist, I believe, has the right to express whatever he will; what he
chooses to express may be a very hateful thing or a very
trivial, but if his expression be exquisitely adapted to his
purpose, we cannot deny that technically his art is fine, and
that if he displeases us ever so much in his purpose, he has
by the fineness of his art executed a work in which, as technical critics, we may honestly delight. In brief, I believe
that until we fully understand a writer's purpose, until we
really know both what he would denote and what he would
connote, we cannot safely object to any word or any composition on the ground of what I have called elegance.

Take, for example, two phrases, —"Them that was n't,"
and, "By thunder!" The former is as ungrammatical as
three words can well be; the latter is, to say the least, very

slangy. But see how those phrases come into these verses
by Mr. Henley: to get the full effect, I must quote the whole
little poem.

> "'Talk of pluck!' pursued the sailor,
> Set at euchre on his elbow,
> 'I was on the wharf at Charleston,
> Just ashore from off the runner.

> "'It was gray and dirty weather,
> And I heard a drum go rolling,
> Rub-a-dubbing in the distance,
> Awful, dour-like, and defiant.

> "'In and out among the cotton,
> Mud, and chains, and stores, and anchors,
> Tramped a squad of battered scarecrows,—
> Poor old Dixie's bottom dollar.

> "'Some had shoes, but all had rifles;
> Them that was n't bald, was beardless;
> And the drum was rolling Dixie,
> And they stepped to it like men, sir!

> "'Rags and tatters, belts and bayonets,
> On they swung, the drum a-rolling,
> Mum and sour. It looked like fighting,
> And they meant it too, by thunder!'"

I doubt if you can find a more skilful use of words. The old
blockade-runner, sick in hospital, gives this little glimpse
of what he saw in the Confederacy: it gives some of us a
glimpse of the Confederacy that we are not very used to.
Change a single one of those irregular terms of his. Instead
of, "Them that was n't bald was beardless," write, "Those
who were not bald were beardless;" instead of, "And they
meant it too, by thunder!" write, "And they were in deadly
earnest,"—and see how the picture begins to fade. The very
vulgarity of the phrases is perhaps what most of all so finely adapts the expression to the thought.

Again, take this passage from De Quincey's "Confessions;" it tells of his mood when he ran away from school,

and wondered whither he should go. Notice how the colloquial
vulgarity of one or two phrases expresses, in a way that
nothing else could express, the overwrought emotion he has
in mind.

"Amongst these attractions that drew me so strongly to
to the Lakes, there had also by that time arisen in this
lovely region the deep, deep magnet (as to me only in all
this world it then was) of William Wordsworth. Inevitably
this close connection of the poetry which most of all had
moved me with the particular region and scenery that most
of all had fastened upon my affections, and led captive my
imagination, was calculated, under ordinary circumstances, to impress upon my fluctuating deliberations a summary and decisive bias. But the very depth of the impressions which had been made upon me, either as regarded
the poetry or the scenery, was too solemn and (unaffect-
edly I may say it) too spiritual to clothe itself in any hasty
or chance movement as at all adequately expressing its
strength, or reflecting its hallowed character. If you,
reader, were a devout Mahometan, throwing gazes of
mystical awe daily towards Mecca, or were a Christian
devotee looking with the same rapt adoration to St. Peter's
at Rome or to El Kodah, the Holy City of Jerusalem (so
called even amongst the Arabs, who hate both Christian
and Jew), how painfully would it jar upon your sensibili-
ties, if some friend, sweeping past you upon a high-road,
with a train (according to the circumstances) of drome-
daries or of wheel carriages, should suddenly pull up,
and say, 'Come, old fellow, jump up alongside of me.
I'm off for the Red Sea, and here's a spare dromedary,'
or, 'off for Rome, and here's a well-cushioned barouche.'
Seasonable and convenient it might happen that the invitation were; but still it would shock you that a journey
which, with or without your consent, could not but assume
the character eventually of a saintly pilgrimage, should
arise and take its initial movement upon a casual summons,
or upon a vulgar opening of momentary convenience."

Still again, take what seemed when we were discussing
the elements of style almost inevitably bad,—such excessive

diffuseness as actually for the moment befogs meaning; and turn to "Henry the Fourth" or "Romeo and Juliet;" and see if anything else could so finely express what Shakspere had in mind when he conceived the characters of Mistress Quickly or of Juliet's nurse as the garrulous prolixity he puts into their mouths.

We must sympathetically understand a writer's purpose, you see, before we can sanely criticise his methods. In misunderstanding of this truth lies what I cannot but think the confusion of much everyday criticism. In literature, as in every other art, men have often wished to express things that might much better have been left unexpressed. The purpose of not a few admirable artists is so detestable that on grounds of morality and decency we may utterly condemn their work; but this fact does not, in my opinion, at all affect the value of their work as a work of art. I have in mind such things as the stories of M. Guy de Maupassant. The French are finer artists than we; but according to our standards, at all events, they are apt to apply their art to very abominable subjects. More than half the time M. de Maupassant's stories deal with matters that no decent man out of France would for a moment think worthy of his pains. The impression left on you by reading these stories is unpleasantly debasing,—at least, if you happen to have been born a respectable Yankee; but you will have to read far and wide before you can find stories in which every word and every turn of sentence is adapted to its purpose with more subtile skill. And some of the stories that are in themselves most hateful can give, and rightly, to the technical critic the keenest delight. As style, his style often seems perfect.

In English, on the other hand, this state of things is more frequently reversed. Far more commonly we find the motive of an English novel to our taste; naturally enough, for the genius of any literature is at bottom the broad human nature which marks the people who use the language in which that literature is phrased. But over and over again, in stories irreproachable or even edifying in motive, we find false touches that make them as subtilely disagreeable as if they dealt with most repellent things. I remember, a few years ago, picking up a novel in which a charming young woman

was engaged in sewing while a middle-aged gentleman sat by
smoking. Both were agreeable characters. But in the course
of the evening the young woman bit off her thread, and got a
piece of it stuck between her teeth; and the smoker, who had
been gnawing the end of his cigar, put the unpleasantly
fringed stump of it in a neighboring saucer. It is probable
that we have all seen charming women similarly inconven-
ienced by refractory threads, and very agreeable men whose
methods of thoughtless smoking were similarly remote from
winsome; but such sights have not enhanced in our minds
the impression of charm commonly produced by the individuals in question. Indeed, if we wish to keep the charm in
mind, we have a polite, if not deliberate habit of forgetting
the unpleasant little traits which, if we choose to look for
them, would mar the charm of anybody; and if we are writing stories in which we wish the reader's sympathy to go
with our characters, we should be careful not to make the
characters do anything disgusting. Not, I may repeat, because even very disgusting matters may not be deliberately
introduced in any work of art; but because our purpose for
the moment is not to excite disgust. Heroines, then, should
not get thread stuck between their teeth,—simply because
such a proceeding is essentially unpleasant; for the same
reason, we should wink at the fact that agreeable elderly
gentlemen sometimes masticate the ends of their cigars.
A style which introduces such traits in such characters is
exactly what M. de Maupassant's style commonly is not,—
admirably unadapted to the purpose in hand.

Actions that are out of character, indeed, are conveniently broad types of what I mean by inelegance. In everybody's
life there are endless details which, for artistic purposes,
are out of character. No man is great to his body-servant,
you remember; nor anybody so contemptible as not to have
many engaging qualities. A mediaeval soldier, like Othello,
would in all probability occasionally amuse himself by sing-
ing comically ribald songs; and Scotch gentlemen of the
period of Macbeth would, very likely, in moments of relax-
ation, take part in national dances. But for Shakspere's
purpose these wholly natural traits would have been out of

character; they would have attracted attention to phases of life which for the moment we are not properly called on to observe. On the whole, then, we may be content that Othello does not lead a drinking chorus, and that Macbeth does not gladden the gallery with a Highland fling; not because the real Othello or Macbeth would not have done such things serenely, but because if they did such things on the boards, they were by no means such satisfactory protagonists in tragedy. In short, if Shakspere had made them act out of character, he would have missed the quality we have agreed to call elegance.

There is one trick of style to which I have referred before, which is commonly resorted to from a mistaken notion of literary taste, and which is responsible for much of the minor inelegance that disfigures our literature. I mean euphemism,—the naming of a disagreeable idea by a word not in itself disagreeable. There are times in life, of course, when we have to mention disagreeable ideas; at such times we may well ask ourselves whether we may not best mask them a little. But generally, I think, the better plan is to ask ourselves whether we may not best of all leave them unmentioned. There are few safer habits than calling things by their real names; in that case we do not mention hateful things needlessly. On the other hand, if we habitually palliate hateful ideas, we begin before long to lose our sense of their hatefulness. As a result, one hears a great deal more than one need of such phenomena as accompany the experience of a landsman in a rough sea, or as make starched linen unbeautiful in July. And to take an example, where the real idea is not disgusting, but solemn, think for yourselves how habitual euphemism degrades the great fact of death. We all know what "to die" means; it means something we all have to face, and that we all face with some degree of dread. Tender-hearted people resort to metaphor: "to pass away," they say, or, "to fall asleep." Untender people take up the euphemistic metaphor: "to pass on," they say, or, "to kick the bucket." And a little while ago I saw in a newspaper that some unhappy creature who had taken his life had "executed a determination to become a gloomy corpse."

Grosser indecency, I think, not even the vilest of our vilest
news-mongers could invent. And all this comes from deliberate neglect of the real secret of elegance, —of constant,
earnest effort to adapt our means to our end, our style to
the thought and emotion it must express.

We have seen enough, I think, to understand now that nothing but constant, earnest effort can result in that habitual
adaptation of means to end which must mark the style of a
master. We have seen enough besides to understand that
there is no little truth in the vulgar conception of elegance
in style, which holds as a standard such a writer as Addison.
It is true that we have in English very few writers whose
style is more exquisitely than his adapted to the purpose for
which it is used. It is also true that Addison very rarely has
in view any purpose not in itself agreeable. There is in the
man, with all his obvious limits, a certain sustained urbanity of temper that has made him for nearly two centuries
the acknowledged model of literary breeding. But if literature could express nothing but polite breeding, it were an
unspeakably less potent thing than many of us rejoice to find
it; and the real secret of Addison's literary excellence is
not his urbanity of temper, but the fact that, given his temper, his style expresses it almost to perfection.

There is in Addison's style, however, one subtle trait
which it shares with any style, no matter how different in
aspect and effect, which possesses the quality we have
agreed to name elegance. This is the ease of habitual mastery. You all remember the old saw which I have quoted to
you already: Ars celare artem ("The finest art seems artless"). To a great degree, I think, any style which we may
ultimately regard as a model, adapted to its purpose as exquisitely as human power can adapt it, possesses this trait
of ease. In much style that is clear as crystal the trait is
absent. In reading George Eliot's novels, for example, one
is constantly sensible of the effort that very notable writer
is making. In much style so forcible that you care little
whether it be clear or not, the trait is equally wanting. In
Carlyle, for example, or in Browning, you may look far before you find it. And sometimes, as in most of the prose of

Landor, you may find it fatally divorced from force, if not
from clearness. But the ideal style is a style that is clear, —
that cannot be misunderstood; that is forcible, —that holds
the attention; and that is elegant, —that is so exquisitely
adapted to its purpose that you are conscious of its elegance
only by subtilely feeling the wonderful ease of habitual mastery.

Such habitual mastery of style is what we must strive for
if we would give our work this final quality of elegance. The
question before us, then, is how we may strive for it. In a
very little while, I think, we may get some manner of answer. Style, we must always remember, is the expression
of thought and feeling in written words. To express thought
and feeling with the ease of mastery, we must in the first
place train our hands. The master's hand is the hand that is
always at command. In some degree, then, that daily work
which we saw so great a factor in the securing of force will
serve our purpose here too. Whoever will let no day pass
without its record, nor any record be other than the best he
can make, will do much; but he will not do all. He must
train, too, with equal constancy his power of perception.

One phase of perception, concerning which I have as yet
said nothing, becomes of real importance here. I mean perception of what is fine in literary art. It is not hard for one
who has very little such perception to write clearly, nor
very hard for him to write with a great degree of force. But
it is not often, I think, that one can learn to give one's style
the final quality which comes from the most exquisite possible adaptation of style to thought, unless one has trained
his power of appreciating and enjoying that quality in the
works of the masters. Trained it, I say deliberately. With
some of us it is inborn; with some it is so dormant that
nothing but strenuous work can arouse it. But even those
who possess it most will not waste the hours they give to
earnestly developing it. One is sometimes inclined to think
that native love for art is a fatal gift, preventing him who
has it from ever being sure of what is really good; and those
who do not possess this native love for art may surely, by
earnest work, arouse in themselves perceptions of which

without the work they would hardly deem themselves capable.

There have been endless discussions of what poetry is;
and no definition of it that was ever framed has proved adequate. Each new critic makes his new one, and no better one
than the last. But this at least we may say: that poetry is
the finest form of literary art. And the secret of its fineness
lies in an adaptation of word—and even of the most subtile
sound—to meaning that comes as near perfection as human
power can bring it. Like all fine art, poetry can give to human beings a kind of pleasure more exquisite, more lasting,
purer than can come from anything but fine art. And this
pleasure any sane man can by and by begin to feel. I say this
with conviction because as a teacher I have so often seen
boys, to whom poetry seemed merely a clumsy statement of
ideas in lines that broke off before they reached the edge of
the page, teach themselves, by deliberately resolving to find
the charm that other people had found there, slowly to know
that keenest of delights which comes when at last they can
begin to feel that what they read is, above and beyond its
meaning and its interest, a thing of lasting beauty. And I am
sure that no other earnest work will bring half so sure and
lasting a benefit to whoever would finally master the art of
letters as will come to him from a mastery of what poetry
means.

I do not mean, of course, that every man should fancy
himself a poet, or that any but poets should seriously try to
express their thought or emotion in the terms of poetry. Yet
it is a notable fact that there are few masters of prose, at
least in our own literature, who have not at some time tried
their hand at verse. What they learn by the effort is oftenest,
perhaps, that poetry is not for them; that what they say must
be said in what seems to so many the less sublime vehicle
of prose. But in the very process of learning this, they have
learned, too, if not the secret, at least the charm, that
makes the finest of literary art the marvellous thing it is.
Beyond the perception of life that we saw the forcible writer
must seek, beyond the perception of human nature which
should make him know the human beings he addresses, beyond the perception of what words suggest or connote, as

well as of what they mean, the writer who would attain the
certainty of mastery must train himself in that finest of perception that delights in the great works of the masters.

Something of this every one who thinks of these matters we
have been discussing perceives for himself. It is some gleam
of this perception, perhaps, which makes almost every one
who longs to write well try his hand—by no means well as a
rule—at poetry. It is some gleam of this perception that
makes so many, equally earnest and more sanely aware of
their limitations, saturate themselves in conventional culture and then try piteously to express themselves in a way
that shall speak to fellow human beings. The masters can
write poems; the masters can enjoy the masterpieces: this
they see, and striving to write and to enjoy, they fancy they
are rising toward the point of mastery. The truth, though,
as we have seen long ago, is that whoever would write with
thorough mastery must write in a style that has not only the
aesthetic quality we have just been considering, but that has
too the emotional quality and the intellectual as well. And
these qualities, I believe, must be striven for in the order
in which we have considered them. First of all, be clear:
address the average human being, remembering not what is
commonplace in him, but what is human. Then be forcible:
do not content yourself with merely addressing him, but do
your utmost to hold his attention. Finally, when these things
are done, let your style have all the grace, the finish, the
charm, that your finest care can give it,—remembering that
no style is finally good until along with clearness and force
it possesses too the quality we have named elegance. In
other words, when you choose and compose the elements of
your style, let your first thought concern their denotation;
your second, their connotation; and only when these are
secure, let yourself begin that ceaseless effort whose end
shall be a finer and finer adaptation of style to meaning.

Finer and finer, I have said purposely. Often as I have
repeated it, I cannot repeat too often that we are dealing now
with something that can never be perfectly accomplished.
There have been great writers, blind teachers tell us; look
at them, reverence them, imitate them. When you equal

them or approach them, your own work will be great. This
mood—the mood of so many of our teachers and guides—
seems to me a phase of that deep tendency in human nature
to glorify the past, to worship at the shrines of heroic ancestors, to look far back in primeval times for traces of the
golden age. Great things have been done, and good, in life
and in art; and these great things are the most precious
treasures that have come to us from the humanity that is
gone before. But what makes the great works of expression
that have come down to us so precious is not that they are
themselves supreme, but that they are the best images which
human beings, akin to us in all but the genius which makes
them sometimes seem more akin to divinity, have yet been
able to make of the supreme truths of thought and emotion
which each knows for himself in that great, endless world of
immaterial reality. We every-day men cannot see far. Our
thoughts and passions are petty things at best; and when we
are brought face to face with the thoughts and the passions of
the masters, which seem by the side of ours so vast and glorious, we are apt to forget that the noblest expression of the
noblest art is as petty a thing beside the great, infinite expanse of truth that the masters strive to express, as is our
work beside the little truth which is all that reveals itself to
our eyes.

Far enough all this may seem from the technical matters
with which we have concerned ourselves; and yet without
something of this in mind I could never have faced the dreary
work of professional teaching that has almost insensibly become the work of my life. Year after year I must plod
through ream upon ream of manuscript that college students
write in an effort to learn how to make themselves writers.
Bewildering, depressing, maddening, debasing, I should
have found this work years ago, but for the growing conviction, which strengthens as the years go by, that the meanest
of these works, if we will only let ourselves see it truly, is
a very marvellous thing. Careless, thoughtless, reckless as
these boys so often are, the most careless, the most thoughtless, the most reckless of all, has put before me an act of
that creative imagination for which, as I have said to you

before, one can find no lesser word than divine. All unknowing, and with the endless limitations of weakness and perversity, he has looked for himself into that great world of
immaterial reality which, just as he knows it, no other human being can ever know; and with these strange, lifeless
conventions we call words he has made some image of what
he has known in that world which is all his own; and that
image begins by and by to arouse within me some conception
of what life has meant to him.

Petty enough this thing that life has meant to these thoughtless boys must often seem; yet it is an unspeakably greater
thing than the lifeless words in which they have striven to
set it forth. And as year after year I have striven to understand what these lame and blundering words and sentences
mean, to penetrate the symbol, to grasp the thought, to tell
the makers of these feeble elements of style how they may
better the work that seems so worthless, I have found myself year after year more and more aware that what they
have done in their little way is what the masters have done
in the way that we like to call great. More and more I have
come to know that the realities which lie behind the symbols
that make the greatest works great are things as far beyond
the mere symbols themselves as the thoughtless thoughts of
these college boys are beyond the symbols their pens so
carelessly scrawl. And year by year there has come to me,
amid this work that seems so dreary, the growing knowledge
that beyond the ken of the students, and beyond the ken of
the greatest of our masters too, lie unending, infinite realms
of truth. And these no human power can ever exhaust; here
to the end of time human beings may constantly seek farther
and farther, with endless hopes of more to come; and here
these endless stretches of truth not yet known, and truth
perhaps never to be known to human beings, make the work
of the greatest of the masters seem almost as small a thing
as the work of the pettiest of the pupils. For what either has
revealed is but some unspeakably little fragment of infinite
eternities.

Technical, dull, lifeless, as all these things I have been
prosing about must seem to whoever has not studied them

deeply; dull and lifeless, I fear, as I have made them seem
to many of you,—they are things that lead us by and by into
a conviction of the truths of idealism that to some minds
could never come so strongly by any other means. And idealism, I believe, is a truth that cannot be shaken. What we
read is but a symbol of the living thought behind it; what we
see and know in life are but symbols of some greater, deeper, infinitely more real truth beyond them all, that only in
these material forms can be revealed to such beings as we,
who are living here on earth. Whatever leads us to such
thoughts as this is a thing that leads us to thoughts that make
us wiser, better men.

It is this that makes me more and more feel that the work
so many of us are trying to do at Harvard College, the work
of which I have tried to give you some account, the work of
any earnest teacher of this subject—composition—that seems
to most men so dull, is a work that may rightly claim a
place in any system of education, no matter how high it hold
its head. If teacher or pupil keep himself down to the symbol
alone, he sinks hopelessly into the depths of pedantry. But
if teacher or pupil keep himself alive to the truth that what
he is striving to accomplish is no less a thing than an act of
creative imagination; if he learn to know that in his own little way he is trying to do just such a thing as the greatest of
the masters have done before him; if through the symbol his
eye learn to seek and to know the infinite reality of truth that
lies beyond,—he will find that even though technical mastery
never come, he will learn more and more the infinite, mysterious significance of that human life that each of us is living for himself. The old systems strove to bring us to such
wisdom by reverent study—and sometimes by cruelly irrev-
erent mangling—of the greatest works of the masters. There
are minds, and not a few, that can come thither only by such
means; but there are other minds, and not a few, I think,
who can come thither better by such humbler means as ours:
by striving each for himself to do his best. By and by he
must come to know how little a thing that is by the side of
what he longed to do; and by and by he will find that thus he
has come to learn how vast a thing beside the little that the

masters have accomplished is the thing for which they have striven. So, by one road as by the other, men may come at last face to face with what most of all wise men love to face, —with the infinite realities that lie, and must forever lie, beyond human ken.

William Shakspere

We have now reached the last stage of our study. We have
glanced at the facts of Shakspere's life; we have briefly considered the condition of English Literature when his work
began; and, with what detail has proved possible, we have
considered, in conjecturally chronological order, all the
works commonly ascribed to him. The few remaining works
which are probably more or less his—Edward III., the Two
Noble Kinsmen, and a few lyrics—are not generally included
in the standard editions. Less accessible, then, than what
we have considered, they are also less interesting; nor do
they contain anything which should alter our conclusions.
Our conclusions, however, may well be affected by another
matter at which we have glanced,—the English literature, in
general, which came into existence between 1587 and 1612,
during which interval, in some order or other, the works of
Shakspere were certainly produced. We are ready, then,
finally to review our impressions.

In looking back over our course, perhaps nothing is more
notable than its limits. We are so far from having covered
the whole subject of Shakspere, that we have neglected parts
of it important enough to make our neglect seem almost a
confession of ignorance. Not to speak of endless details, we
have hardly touched on the range or the quality of his genius;
we have thought little about the subtleties of his art; we have
hardly glanced at the scope and the character of his philosophy; nor yet have we discussed at all the surprising range
of his learning. And so on. The truth is that the subject of
Shakspere is inexhaustible. Whoever would deal with it,

must perforce neglect much of it. At any moment, then, those phases may best be neglected which happen at that moment to have been best discussed elsewhere.

Such a phase, clearly, is Shakspere's genius. In the fine arts, we remember, a man of genius is he who in perception and in expression alike, in thought and in phrase, instinctively so does his work that his work remains significant after the conditions which actually produced it are past. The work of any man of genius, then, is susceptible of endless comment and interpretation, varying as the generations of posterity vary from his and from one another. Such interpretative comment is always suggestive. The most notable example of it concerning Shakspere may perhaps be found in the writings of Coleridge. Foreign alike to Shakspere's time and to our own, the mood of Coleridge was not long ago vitally contemporary. While to-day what Coleridge says about Shakspere often seems queerly erratic, it must always be interesting, both as an important phase of human thought, and as lasting evidence of how Shakspere's genius presented itself to one who came near being a man of genius himself. In some such manner the genius of Shakspere, like any other, must present itself, with ever fresh significance, to men of our own time and of times to come. Like Nature herself, the work of the great artists must always possess a fresh significance for every generation which comes to it with fresh eyes. As we have seen, however, this significance is generally implicit. It is there because, by the very laws of his nature, the artist worked with instinctive fidelity to the greater laws which govern actual life. In a course of study like ours, then, whose object is chiefly to see the artist as he may have seen himself, we may well neglect those aspects of his work which are visible only after the lapse of centuries. On these, as the centuries pass, there will always be emphasis enough. The danger is not that Shakspere's genius will be forgotten; but that, in admiration for the aspects in which, from time to time, that genius defines itself, people may fatally forget the truth that Shakspere's work really emanated from a living man.

Again, there is a great deal of criticism about the art of

Shakspere,—discussion as to how conscious it was, how
deliberate, how essentially fine. One still hears much debate
as to whether the free, romantic form of his dramas be a
nobler thing or a meaner than the more rigid form of the
classics, and of their modern imitations. Such discussion is
interesting; and so far as it deals with the precise artistic
methods of Shakspere might well have found place in our
study. Here and there, indeed, as space permitted, we have
touched on it,—most notably, perhaps, in showing how the
finished form of the <u>Midsummer Night's Dream</u> grew at once
from old motives and from old and crude conventions. So
far, however, as such discussion deals with general matters,—questioning, for example, whether classic art or romantic be the finer,—it is foreign to our purpose, and in
some aspects akin to the less famous discussion as to whether shad or custard be the greater delicacy. For our purposes, we may be content with knowing that Shakspere, an
Elizabethan playwright, was as much bound by the conditions
of his time to write in the Elizabethan manner as was Soph-
ocles of Athens to compose his tragedies after the manner of
the Greeks. Whoever, then, would finally or intelligently
criticise the art of Shakspere must first master, as hardly
anybody has yet mastered, the conditions of Shakspere's
theatre. Much of the extant criticism of Shakspere's art resembles that of Gothic cathedrals which prevailed when
pseudo-classic architecture was all the fashion; much of
what remains resembles that criticism of the same Gothic
churches which refers the origin of their aisles and arches
to the trunks and boughs of forest alleys. Partly for want of
space, then, partly for want of sufficient knowledge as yet,
we have studied Shakspere's art only so far as was necessary to make clear the general conditions of his time.

   Concerning Shakspere's philosophy,—his deliberate
teaching,—the state of affairs is much like that concerning
his genius. Earnest students innumerable have read between
his lines endless lessons, some of which are doubtless very
wise and valuable. Just how far he meant to put them there,
however, is another question. We have seen enough of Elizabethan Literature to recognize that much of its aphorism is

nothing intentionally more serious than a fresh combination
of language. In the very prevalence of its aphorism, however, we must have recognized a symptom at once of a general appetite for proverbial philosophy, and of that generally
ripe state of practical experience which at intervals in history gives more or less final expression to a state of life
about to pass away. The aphoristic wisdom of Elizabethan
Literature, so far as it is more than verbal, broadly expresses the experience of mediaeval England. To this aphorism
Shakspere added much. Very probably, though, what he
added was no system of philosophy; it was rather a series
of superbly final phrases, now and again combining to produce a complete artistic impression, —such as the pessimism
of Macbeth, or the profound idealism of the Tempest, —which
to him would have seemed rather emotional than dogmatic.
In one sense every artist is a philosopher; but as philosophy
is commonly understood, artists are apt to be unconscious
philosophers, —philosophers rather by the inevitable law of
their nature than by any deliberate intention; and, whatever
else we have done, we have never allowed ourselves to forget that from beginning to end Shakspere was an artist.

Another matter, much discussed nowadays, we have hardly glanced at. Nothing more surprises such readers of
Shakspere as are not practical men of letters than the man's
apparent learning. To one used to writing, the phenomenon
is less surprising. To translate technical matters from a
book merely glanced at, into such finished terms as the un-
initiated suppose to imply years of study and research, is
within anybody's power. Whoever will take a few Elizabethan books, —North's Plutarch, for example, Paynter's
Palace of Pleasure, Foxe's Martyrs, Holinshed, and Coke
on Littleton, —and, with the help of stray passages from all,
translate some narrative from one of them into blank-verse
dialogue, will produce an effect of erudition which shall profoundly impress not only his readers but himself. Whoever
has a few compendious works at hand and knows how to use
them, in fact, can make himself seem a miracle of learning
to whoever does not know his secret. In Elizabethan England
almost all books were compendious; so was the common

talk of all intelligent men,—for learning was not yet specialized. Given these facts, and given the exceptionally concrete
habit of thought and phrase native to Shakspere, and Shakspere's learning is no longer a marvel, except to those who
insist on finding it so.

To pass from matters neglected to a matter purposely re-
served, nothing is more notable to a student of Elizabethan
Literature than the fact that Elizabethan Literature presents
a remarkably typical example of artistic evolution. Art, of
any kind, in nations, in schools, even in individuals, pro-
gresses by a rhythmical law of its own. At certain epochs
the arts of expression are lifelessly conventional. Born to
these conventions, often feeble and impotent, the nation, the
school, or the individual destined to be great, will begin,
like those who preceded, by simple imitation, differing from
the older conventions only in a certain added vigor. By and
by, the force which we have called creative imagination will
develop, with a strange, mysterious strength of its own,
seemingly almost inspired. Throbbing with this imaginative
impulse, the nation, the school, or the individual artist will
begin no longer to imitate, but instead, to innovate, with an
enthusiasm for the moment as unconscious of limits to come
as it is disdainful of the old, conventional limits which it has
transcended. After a while, the limits to come will slowly
define themselves. No creative or imaginative impulse can
stray too far. The power of words, of lines and colors, of
melody and harmony, is never infinite. If slavish fidelity to
conventions be lifeless, utter disregard of conventions tends
to the still more fatal end of chaotic, inarticulate confusion.
One may break fetter after fetter; but one's feet must still
be planted on the earth. One may move with all the freedom
which the laws of nature allow; but if one try to soar into
air or ether, one is more lost even than if one count one's
footsteps. So to nations, to schools, to individuals alike a
growing sense of limitation must come. There are things
which may be achieved; there are vastly more things and
greater which remain fatally beyond human power. Experience, then, begins to check the wilder impulses of creative
innovation. Imagination is controlled by a growing sense of

fact. Finally, this sense of fact, this consciousness of environment, grows stronger and stronger, until at length all
innovating impulse is repressed and strangled. Again art
lapses into a convention not to be disturbed until, perhaps
after generations, fresh creative impulse shall burst its
bonds again.

As elsewhere in nature, so in art, creative impulse is a
strange, unruly thing, tending constantly to variation from
the older types, but not necessarily to improvement. While
the general principles just stated are constantly true everywhere, their result is often abortive, often, too, eccentric
or decadent. At rare moments, however, creative impulse
surges for a while in a direction which carries art irresistibly onward to greater and better expressions than men have
known before. Such impulses as this the centuries find marvellous. When a great creative impulse has come, when the
shackles of old convention are broken, when the sense of
the new limits is developed at once so far as to tell instinctively what may be accomplished, and not so overwhelmingly
as to crush imagination with the fatal knowledge of all which
is beyond human power, then, for a little while, any art is
great. The moment of ultimate greatness comes when a true
creative impulse is firmly controlled, but not yet checked,
by a rational sense of fact.

These general phenomena are nowhere more concretely
shown than in the growth, development, and decay of English
Literature during the period which we call Elizabethan.
Really beginning before the reign of Elizabeth, this literary
evolution really survived her, lasting indeed until the unhappy times of Charles I. The central figure of the period during which it took place, however, was undoubtedly the great
queen, who, above any other English sovereign, was once
the central fact of national life. The literature, then, which
we may assume to have begun with Wyatt and to have ended
with Shirley, may safely enough be named Elizabethan. In
this literature the earlier work—such as that of Wyatt, of
Surrey, of Roger Ascham, of Foxe, of Paynter—was chiefly
notable for its eager breaking away from old conventions.
In substance and in form alike its chief motive was to present

to English readers other and better things than English readers had known before. Its method was to imitate the thought
or the manner of greater or more polished peoples or times.
Then came a fresh group of writers, —Sidney, Lyly, Spenser,
Hooker, and the earlier dramatists. All alike, these bold,
spirited linguistic innovators were busy chiefly in proving,
with constantly freshening impulse, what the newly found
English language might do. Then came Marlowe and Shakspere, and the great Elizabethan drama, —the one thing which
at that moment the language and the race might best accomplish. Then, very swiftly, came the decline, when such men
as Bacon and Drayton, and Davies, and Chapman, and lesser
ones, —actually contemporary with the greatest, but tending
rather toward limitation than toward innovation, —began to
use the tamed language for purposes more and more special.
The old impulse was a thing of the past.

Such generalizations must seem nebulous. A glance at a
half-forgotten, but still great work of the period, may perhaps define them. During the reign of Queen Elizabeth no
Englishman lived a more complete life than Sir Walter Ralegh. Country gentleman, student, soldier, sailor, adven-
turer, courtier, favorite and spoilsman, colonizer, fighter,
landlord, agriculturist, poet, patron of letters, state pris-
oner, explorer, conqueror, politician, statesman, conspir-
ator, chemist, scholar, historian, self-seeker, and ultimately a martyr to patriotism, he acquired through the
latter half of Elizabeth's reign the most comprehensive
experience ever known to an Englishman. Almost with the
accession of King James his prosperity came to an end. He
was imprisoned in the Tower, where for above ten years he
busied himself with writing his great History of the World.
To this task he brought a rare equipment; for not only did he
nobly conceive history as the visible record of God's dealing
with mankind, but he had actually experienced more wide
variety of such matters as make history than has any other
Englishman before or since. With above ten years of enforced leisure and concentration, with the best scholarship
of the time to help him collect material, with a very beautiful stately English style of his own, he set about his task.

In 1614, as much of his work as he ever finished was published. The History of the World has so long been obsolete that except for its name it is almost forgotten. It is traditionally supposed to be queer and fantastic, with occasional fine bits of rhetoric. Really, it is among the most nobly planned books in the world. History, as we have seen, Ralegh conceived to be the visible record of God's dealing with men. Its value, then, lay chiefly in the fact that to whoever should study it seriously and reverently, it taught truths not elsewhere accessible concerning the nature and the will of God. In the language of his time this meant what to-day would be meant by a philosophic historian, who should find in his subject not merely stirring narrative or plain record of fact, but the visible teachings of human experience, which, properly understood, should govern future conduct. Not only was Ralegh's effort a grandly philosophic one, too, but, as we have seen, he brought to its accomplishment an almost unique equipment. Besides all this, the man had a wonderfully cool, clear, rational head; his mind was among the most prudently and judiciously critical in all historical literature. Yet, as we have seen, his great History has proved of so little value that people nowadays mostly suppose it to be merely quaint.

The reason for this failure clearly defines just what the chief limit of Elizabethan Literature was bound to be. Human nature has always open to it a wealth of experience which may indefinitely develop individuals; and in the time of Elizabeth the possible range of individual experience was probably wider than at any other period of history. Whoever would write, like Ralegh, however, in a profoundly philosophic spirit, needs more experience to work with than can ever come to any individual. No individual can master the material world, even of his own day; still less can he extend his experience beyond the limits of his own life. To deal with history, then, on such a scale as Ralegh planned, a man must have recourse to endless records which, to avail him, must have been subjected to generations of patient scientific criticism; and in Ralegh's time—in Elizabethan England—there were no records which he could safely trust. In history,

in science, in all things alike, the gathering of valid material was still to make. All that was ready for anything like
final expression, then, was on the one hand the actual experience of individuals, and on the other a plain assertion of
some method by which, in generations to come, serious
study might safely be guided.

In the ripeness of Elizabethan Literature, both of these
things were finally expressed. Whatever its error of detail,
the philosophical writing of Bacon has done more than any
other work of modern times to guide in the road which they
have travelled the thought and the scholarship of the future.
More notably still, the Elizabethan Drama—whatever its
artistic peculiarities, or faults, or vagaries—expressed with
a power and a range never surpassed the infinitely varied
possibility and intensity of individual experience. Of these
two final achievements the drama, if not the more lasting in
its effects, was for the moment the more complete. Nothing
less than the lapse of centuries could have demonstrated the
value of Bacon's philosophy. By the very nature of things,
on the other hand, the power of a great dramatic literature
must be evident to the public which first welcomes it. With
an approach to truth, then, we may say that Elizabethan
Literature reduces itself finally to the Elizabethan Drama.

In the work of Shakspere we have studied this drama
somewhat minutely. Incidentally, too, we glanced at the
state in which Shakspere found the stage, and also at the
work of his greatest predecessor and early contemporary,—
Marlowe. Before Shakspere had really begun to show what
power was in him, Marlowe was dead. Since Marlowe's
time, we have considered the drama only as it appears in
Shakspere. More clearly to define his position, we may now
to advantage glance at another dramatist who seems, like
Marlowe, greater than most of his contemporaries.

This is John Webster. While Mr. Fleay[1] shows reason to
believe that Webster collaborated with Drayton and Middleton and others as early as 1602, there seems no doubt that
his first independent work was the White Devil,—the play,
published in 1612, which he expressly hopes shall be read
in the light of Chapman's work, and Jonson's, and Beaumont

and Fletcher's, and Shakspere's, and Dekker's, and Heywood's. Just as the work of Marlowe typifies what the stage was like when Shakspere's writing began, then, the <u>White Devil</u>,—a fair type of Webster's power,—coming after Shakspere's work was done, may be taken as an example of what the stage was like when Shakspere's writing ceased.

The story of the <u>White Devil</u> is virtually historical; what is more, it was almost contemporary. The events therein detailed occurred, about 1585, in that Italy which to Elizabethans was much what the Second Empire in France was to the Americans of thirty years ago—at once their model of civilization, the chief source of their culture, and at the same time the sink wherein they learned, along with much polite accomplishment, to what depths of depravity human nature may fall. The story, in short, bore to Webster's audience such relation as might be borne to a modern audience by a play which should deal with the career of Louis Philippe's Duc de Choiseul-Praslin, or with that of Louis Napoleon's Countess Castiglione. Webster, to be sure, took his artist's privilege, and altered certain characters for dramatic effect: Camillo, the injured husband, for example, he made a wittol, and Isabella, the murdered wife, a highly respectable person,—which was far from the actual case. On the whole, however, he preserved enough fact to claim the protection of historical authority.

As he tells the story, Vittoria Corombona, the daughter of a poor Venetian family, is married to Camillo, a Roman numskull. Her brother, Flamineo, an utterly corrupt soldier of fortune, induces her not unwillingly to become the mistress of the Duke of Brachiano. This infatuated voluptuary finally determines to marry her; whereupon he has his faithful wife, Isabella, poisoned, and meanwhile Flamineo manages to make Camillo break his neck. Francisco de Medicis, brother of the murdered Isabella, and the Cardinal Monticelso suspect foul play, and have Vittoria arrested on a charge of murdering her husband, Camillo. Although the crime cannot be proved, sufficient evidence is adduced to send Vittoria to a Roman Bridewell. Francisco, meanwhile, has privately convinced himself that the real murderer of

Isabella was Brachiano. In pursuance of revenge, then, he takes advantage of the confusion attending the election of Monticelso to the papacy,[2] and enables Brachiano to steal Vittoria from prison, and to carry her, with all her family, to Padua. For this impious escapade, the fugitives are excommunicated. Francisco, still bent on vengeance, follows them in disguise, accompanied, among other ruffians, by a certain Count Lodovico, who had hopelessly loved the murdered Duchess. At a tournament, they managed to poison Brachiano's helmet. As he lies dying in agony, Lodovico, disguised as a priest, pours into his ears, under color of extreme unction, all the curses his revengeful brain can devise. Then, while Flamineo and Vittoria are quarrelling over what Brachiano has left, Lodovico breaks in and kills them— only to be killed in turn by Francisco, who would cover his tracks.

The first thing which impresses one in the treatment of this morbidly horrible story is that, within the now established traditions of dramatic form, it is studiously realistic. The characters throughout are considered as living human beings. The atmosphere is so veracious that the play can teach us, almost historically, what Sixteenth Century Italy was like. This Italy—the country which produced Machiavelli —was remarkable for such bewildering complexity as always pervades an over-ripe period of society. Of this complexity, Webster, with his realistic purpose, was so profoundly aware that throughout the play, despite all his power of imagination, you feel him constantly hampered by a sense of how much he had to tell. Great as he was, in short, his subject and his vehicle combined almost to master him. Every scene, every character, every speech, every phrase, seems deliberately studied; every line shows painful thought; yet for all these pains the play remains in total effect rather a tremendous sketch than a finished work of art. At first sight, with all its complexity of detail, it is puzzling. As you study it, you begin to feel its power more and more, until, compared with any other power except Shakspere's own, it seems almost supreme. Constantly, however, you feel that at an earlier period in the drama such power might have

exerted itself not with painful effort, but with spontaneous
ease. As matters stand, though the construction of scenes
and the development of character prove Webster a great
dramatist, and though phrase after phrase prove him a great
poet, you feel him paralyzed by a crushing sense of his limitations. A wonderful stroke of character stands by itself,
then comes a startling situation, then an aphorism, then a
simile, then some admirable interjected anecdote; and so
on. Nothing is finally fused, however; you feel none of that
glowing heat of spontaneous imagination which, unchecked by
adequate sense of fact, kept still half-inarticulate the aspiring poetry of Marlowe. If one would know what the force of
creative imagination is like which awakens a great school of
art, one cannot do better than turn to Marlowe; if one would
realize the sense of limitation in which a great school of art
finally declines, one cannot do better than turn to Webster.

Between them stands Shakspere, actually contemporary
with both, and throughout his best period, fusing the chief
merits of each. Between them, too, in artistic evolution, if
not always in actual dates, comes the great group of ripe
dramatists with whom, during the most vigorous period of
his work as well as during its laborious decline, Shakspere
competed for public favor. We can glance at them only very
hastily; but a hasty glance is worth our while. Ben Jonson
was the greatest master of eccentric "humour"—a trait always dear to the English—who ever wrote for the English
stage; probably, too, he was the most consummate master
of mere stage-business. Marston, though coarse, was an
admirable writer of sensational tragedy. Dekker was unique
for a joyous, off-hand spontaneity of feeling and of phrase.
Middleton, but for a fatal coldness of personal temper,
might almost have rivalled Shakspere in the handling of character, tragic and comic alike. Heywood, untroubled by such
traditions of courtly grandeur as made Shakspere, to the
end, habitually head his dramatis personae by the figure of
a sovereign, was thorough master of romantic sentiment.
Chapman, if inarticulate, was a constantly impressive and
weighty moralizer. Tourneur was almost modern in his impious recklessness. Beaumont and Fletcher, though palpably

decadent, were superb masters of fascinatingly sentimental,
always mellifluous, constantly interesting romance. Nowadays, of course, any one can see that neither these nor any
of their fellows can compare, for range or power, with
Shakspere. None of them, nor indeed any Elizabethan but
Shakspere, was contemporary at once with Marlowe and with
Webster. One and all, however, have merits which, by any
contemporary standards, might well have been confused with
his. Generally spontaneous, their work has continual flashes
of insight; it is often very beautifully phrased; and it is
rarely overburdened with anything which should fatigue or
repel a popular audience. In the full flush of their power,
these men had popular merits, as well as merits which have
proved lasting. From the outset, too, their merits were
patent.

In several ways, however, these later men differed both
from the earlier group which preceded Shakspere, and less
palpably from Shakspere himself. As we saw in the beginning, the first Elizabethan playwrights were closely connected with the actual stage, at a time when the stage was socially disreputable. They were men of fine poetic gifts and
of tolerable education; but they were the Bohemians of a
society which admitted no distinction between reputable life
and such professional crime as is lastingly pictured in the
tavern scenes of Henry IV. The later playwrights, on the
other hand, were men of higher rank and of far more reputable habit. Beaumont, for example, was the son of a judge;
Fletcher was the son of a bishop; Webster's father was a
London citizen of the better sort; and so on. In their own
private life the traditional Mermaid Tavern, which foreshad-
owed the clubs and the coffee-houses of the Eighteenth Century, took the place of such squalid surroundings as saw the
end of Marlowe and of Greene. Many of these men, too,
were merely poets or dramatic authors; they were not
actors. The stage, in short, was growing into such better
repute as was bound to come with the increasingly definite
organization of society. A true Bohemia was coming into existence.

The work of these more reputable men, at the same time,

was less reputable than that of their predecessors. As the stage grew established, it grew more and more licentious. The work of Marlowe needs little expurgation; that of Beaumont and Fletcher, for all its grace and beauty, is full of abominations. As will often be the case with any school of art, the beginnings of the Elizabethan drama had a simple, spontaneous purity which vanished when the development of the school made over-refinement of effort, take the place of such broadly general motives as underlay the work of Greene and Peele and Marlowe.

Another distinction has been admirably defined by Mr. Fleay:[3] —

> "I may perhaps at this point note how greatly the playwrights who were also actors excelled the gentlemen authors . . . We have first on the actor-poet list Shakspere, more than enough to counterpoise all the rest; then Jonson, the second greatest name in our annals; then Heywood, Field, Rowley, Armin, Monday. On the other side are great names also: Beaumont, Fletcher, Webster, Massinger, Shirley, Chapman, and many others, all great as poets, but none (except Massinger perhaps) equal to even the lesser men in the other list in that undefinable quality which separates the acting play from the drama for closet reading; the quality which makes Goldsmith and Sheridan successful, but the want of which condemns Henry Taylor, Browning, and Shelley to remain the delight, not of the crowd, but of the solitary student. My opinion in this matter is no doubt open to much qualification, but there is in connexion with it one fact beyond dispute, viz., all actor-poets of any great note began their theatrical careers before the accession of James."

These brief notes must suffice to define the historical position of Shakspere as the central figure, and the most broadly typical, in the evolution of perhaps the most broadly typical school of art in modern literature. Quite apart from its lasting literary value, apart, too, from its unique personal quality, the work of Shakspere has new interest to modern students as a complete individual example of how fine art

emerges from an archaic convention, fuses imagination with
growing sense of fact, and declines into a more mature convention where the sense of fact represses and finally stifles
the force of creative imagination.

To repeat in detail the summaries of his work already
made were tedious. It is enough merely to glance at the four
periods into which we divided his career. The first—from
1587 to 1593 or thereabouts—we called experimental. He
contented himself with widely versatile imitation, revealing
two personal qualities: a habit of mind by which, to a degree
unique in English Literature, words and concepts were identical; and later, a power of enlivening the conventional figures of his original sources by no end of little touches
derived from observation of life. Throughout this first period, however, his work never so differed from that of his
contemporaries as to be free from the palpable archaism
amid which a great school of art begins.

During the second period of his career—from 1593 to
1600—the force of his imagination, first revealing itself in
the artistic completeness of the Midsummer Night's Dream
and almost simultaneously in the vivid characterization of
Romeo and Juliet, pervaded and altered whatever he touched.
His command of language almost constantly strengthened,
until—as throughout his career—one felt half insensibly that
while his native habit of mind, fusing phrases and concepts,
never altered, he tended constantly to consider thoughts
more and words less. Meanwhile his power of enlivening
character by the results of observation so persisted and
strengthened that at last—as in the case of Falstaff—his
characters began to have almost independent existence. At
the same time, with all this power of creating character and
of uttering ultimate phrases, he displayed more and more
palpably a sluggishness, if not an actual weakness, of invention. He repeated, to a degree unapproached by any other
writer of his time, whatever device had proved theatrically
effective,—confusion of identity, for example, and later
self-deception. Apart from these traits, this second, purely
artistic period revealed little. He created a small army of
living individuals, he displayed a constant artistic impulse,

but he revealed no profound personal sense of fact. During
this period, then, his own peculiar power of imagination and
of artistic impulse was at work almost unchecked. The most
marked peculiarity of his power, however,—that it was confined to such matters of detail as character, phrase, or atmosphere,—meant that his natural sense of fact was strong.
The growing vitality of his personages indicated meanwhile
a superb fusion of imagination with this sense of fact.

During the third period of his artistic career—from 1600
to 1608—we found again this superb fusion of his own peculiar creative power and his own strong sense of fact. During
this period, however, we found something far more significant than the merely artistic impulse which had preceded.
Up to this time his plays had expressed nothing deeper than
the touch of irony which underlies Much Ado About Nothing.
Now, in place of the old versatility first of experiment and
then of concentration, we found a constant, crescent expression of such emotion as should come only from profound
spiritual experience. He began to use his thoroughly mastered vehicle for the dramatic expression of such motives
as we had seen to underly his wonderfully finished Sonnets.
In these motives we observed first a profound and increasing
sense of irony, of fate, of the helplessness of human beings
in the midst of their crushing environment. Then came, with
endless variations, a profound sense of the evil which must
always spring from the mysterious fact of sex. Finally,
perhaps as a result of these two causes, came a state of
mind so over-wrought that, had it not been balanced by his
supreme artistic sanity, it might almost have lapsed into
madness. At the height of this period, when he produced his
four great tragedies, his imagination was working with its
fiercest power, and his sense of fact meanwhile controlled
it with ultimate firmness.

One by one, the profound traits of this period began to
disappear. With Macbeth we saw the end of the morbid ex-
citement of mind; with Antony and Cleopatra we bade farewell to the evil of woman; with Coriolanus, where at length
eccentricity or "humour" began to replace inevitable charac-
acter, came the last complete expression of despairing irony.

In other words, the power of his imagination, perhaps exhausted by the very intensity of its exercise, began to weaken under the pressure of a crushing sense of fact.

In Timon and Pericles we found a moment of artistic transition. The spontaneous power was gone. All that remained of the old Shakspere was the marvellous command of language, palpable even in his earliest work, and crescent with him to the end.

Finally, in the fourth and last period of his career—which extended at most from 1609 to 1612—we found a colossal series of technical experiments, where, with all his unequalled mastery of art, and with a serenely ideal philosophy, he was struggling, in vain, to enliven with something like the old spontaneous imaginative power, the crushing sense of fact which was fatally closing in not only on him, but on the school of literature to which he belongs. The more one studies Shakspere's work as a whole, the more complete becomes its typical historic significance.

This typical quality, however, is not the trait which has made it survive. Just now the study of literary evolution happens to be the fashion, or at least to appeal to the temper of the day. The temper in question is new and probably transient. Shakspere was a supreme figure long before it existed; he will remain such long after it has taken its place among the curiosities of the past. What makes him perennial is that, above any other modern poet, he was a man of genius,—one who in perception and in expression alike, in thought and in phrase, instinctively so did his work that it remains significant long after the conditions which actually produced it have vanished. In our admiration for this genius, for this constantly fresh significance, we are apt to forget all else, and in our forgetfulness to be lost in stammering wonder.

Nowadays the form which this wonder most aptly takes is, perhaps, first amazement, then incredulity, then frank doubt as to whether all this wonderful poetry could conceivably have been produced by a middle-class Englishman, the record of whose life is so calmly commonplace. Such doubt can no more be dispelled by any process of argument than

can religious scepticism. Like religious scepticism, too,
such doubt has small effect on anything but the temper of
people who are not disposed to share it. To the doubters,
such views as have been set forth in this study may perhaps
seem pathetically erroneous. To believers, on the other
hand, certain obvious coincidences between these views and
the recorded facts may perhaps seem fortifying if not con-
vincing.

In the first place, of course, we must assume that William
Shakspere happened to be what many another man of humble
origin has been before and since, —a man of genius. In the
second place, as we saw perhaps most clearly when we
studied the Sonnets, the man's temperament, for all his
genius, was strongly individual, —different from that of any
contemporary, or indeed of anybody else at all. In the third
place, as our whole course of study has shown us, his artistic development from beginning to end was perfectly normal.
In the fourth place, his two most marked traits as an artist
are both unmistakable and persistent: from beginning to end
he displayed a habit of mind which made less distinction than
is generally conceivable between words and the concepts for
which words stand; and his imaginative power, in many
aspects unlimited, always exerted itself chiefly in matters
of detail, —most of all in the creation of uniquely individual
characters. In mere invention, in what is vulgarly called
originality and what really means instinctive straying from
fact, he was weaker than hundreds of lesser men.

Given these facts, there is a marked correspondence between the conjectural chronology of his work and the recorded facts of his life. What little is known of him up to the time
of Greene's allusion in 1592 indicates that, in country and in
city alike, he had during the first twenty-eight years of his
life rather unusual opportunities for varied experience; and
a distinct motive for making the most of his chances to better his condition. The experience of these experimental
years began to bear fruit with the Midsummer Night's Dream.
At the time to which we assigned the Merchant of Venice and
Henry IV., the process of fruition had gone far enough to
establish him as for the moment the ablest dramatic writer

in England. Here, on the one hand, the records show him
beginning to re-establish his family at Stratford; and a little
later Meres's allusion proves, what any one might have inferred, that he had actually won professional recognition.
With the exceptional publication of 1600 came the climax of
his career. Later we found him no longer merely an artist,
but a poet deeply stirred by such emotions as should normally have come to him had the conjectural story of the Sonnets
been substantially true. Meanwhile he produced the great
tragedies; and all the time, with the growing prosperity
which such work should have involved, he kept strengthening
the position of his family in their country home. About 1609
came the break in his creative power, at a moment when
professional competition was stronger than it had ever been
before. After that, the actual records show him no longer
connected with professional life, but retiring more and more
into the comfortable ease of a country gentleman. And so
came the end.

   At first glance, of course, the two records still look in-
compatible. They have in common, however, a trait which
to many minds may well seem the most profoundly characteristic of all. Throughout Shakspere's career his imagination, for all its power, was concentrated on matters of detail. He created a greater number and variety of living
characters than any other writer in modern literature. He
made innumerable final phrases. Ever and again, by patient
and repeated experiment with familiar motives, he combined
old materials in constantly fresh and lastingly beautiful artistic effects. To a degree hardly paralleled, however, he
was free from vagaries. Throughout his career, one may
almost say, what he really and constantly did was this: instead of soaring into the clouds or the ether, he looked
calmly about him, took account of what material was at hand,
and with the utmost possible economy of invention decided
what might be done with it and disposed of it accordingly.
Among imaginative artists he is unique for practical prudence.

   In the conduct of his life, as the records reveal it, precisely the same trait is manifest. The problem before him,

as a man, in 1587, was one which most men find insoluble.
The son of a ruined country tradesman, and saddled with a
wife and three children, his business at twenty-three was so
to conduct his life that he might end it not as a laborer but
as a gentleman. After five-and-twenty years of steady work
this end had been accomplished.

Grossly material it is the fashion to call such aspiration
and such success as this. No doubt there is much to warrant
such a contemptuous slur on self-made men. Personally
such people are often unlovely, scarred and seamed by the
struggles of a contest for which their critics are more than
often too feeble. Even though the self-made man of petty
commerce seem a prosaic fact, however, the real trait
which has raised him above his fellows is a trait which his
critics as a rule so lack that they honestly fail to appreciate
its existence. What the successful tradesman has really
done is to perform a feat of constructive imagination every
whit as marvellous, if not so beautiful, as the work of any
artist or poet. Facing the actual world as he sees it, all
against him, he has made in his mind, perhaps unwittingly,
an image of some state of things not yet in existence: a popular demand for some new commodity, it may be, or a sud-
den shift of values. Acting on this perception, to which less
imaginative people are blind, he has outstripped others in
the race for fortune. To put the matter perhaps extravagant-
ly, what vulgar criticism would call grossly material success really involves a feat of creative imagination in certain
aspects more wonderful than any other known to human experience; for while the creative artist is bound only to imitate the divine imagination which controls the universe, the
man who achieves practical success is bound so to share
that divine imagination as for a while even to share, too,
the prophetic foresight of divinity.

Such a material achievement as Shakspere's, then, involves an imaginative feat quite as wonderful, if not so rare,
as the imaginative feat involved in the creation of Shakspere's works. Granting this, as all who honestly appreciate it surely must, we may see in the peculiar concreteness
of Shakspere's artistic imagination a trait which instead of

contradicting the record of his life goes as far as any one
fact can go to confirm it. Applied to the stage by which he
was forced to make his way, his peculiar imaginative power
produced the marvellous characters and phrases which make
his work almost a part and parcel of the divine creation.
Applied to the material facts of life, this same concrete imagination so controlled and grouped and composed and mastered them that a life-time of honest work resulted in just
such achievement as throughout English history has been the
general ideal of honest, simple-hearted Englishmen.

Life and work alike, then, if we will but look at them together, tell the same story. Both begin simply, carelessly,
trivially. Both pass through a period of growing impulse and
aspiration. To both alike—if for a moment we may pass from
records and take for granted that, whatever the actual story
of the Sonnets, the Sonnets are spiritually true—come fierce
buffets. Both alike, after years of struggle and conquest,
fade into peace.

Notes

1. [Original footnote:] Chronicle of the English Drama,
II, 268.

2. [Original footnote:] Historically the man whom Webster calls Monticelso was named Montalto, and was made
pope by the name of Sixtus V. Webster makes him take the
name of Paul IV.—historically that of a Caraffa. This licentious treatment of historic fact is typically Elizabethan.

3. [Original footnote:] Chronicle History of the London
Stage, p. 167.

A Literary History
of America: Introduction

Literature, like its most excellent phase, poetry, has never
been satisfactorily defined. In essence it is too subtle, too
elusive, too vital, to be confined within the limits of phrase.
Yet everybody vaguely knows what it is. Everybody knows
that human life, in its endless, commonplace, unfathomable
complexity, impresses human beings in ways which vary not
only with individuals, but with the generations and the nations. Somewhere in the oldest English writings there is an
allegory which has never faded. Of a night, it tells us, a
little group was gathered about the fireside in a hall where
the flicker of flame cast light on some and threw others into
shadow, but none into shadow so deep as the darkness without. And into the window from the midst of the night flew a
swallow lured by the light; but unable by reason of his wildness to linger among men, he sped across the hall and so out
again into the dark, and was seen no more. To this day, as
much as when the old poet first saw or fancied it, the swallow's flight remains an image of earthly life. From whence
we know not, we come into the wavering light and gusty
warmth of this world; but here the law of our being forbids
that we remain. A little we may see, fancying that we understand,—the hall, the lords and the servants, the chimney
and the feast; more we may feel,—the light and the warmth,
the safety and the danger, the hope and the dread. Then we
must forth again, into the voiceless, unseen eternities. But
the fleeting moments of life, like the swallow's flight once

more, are not quite voiceless; as surely as he may twitter
in the ears of men, so men themselves may give sign to one
another of what they think they know, and of what they know
they feel. More too; men have learned to record these signs,
so that long after they are departed, others may guess what
their life meant. These records are often set forth in terms
which may be used only by those of rarely special gift and
training, —the terms of architecture and sculpture, of painting and music; but oftener and more freely they are phrased
in the terms which all men learn somehow to use, —the
terms of language. Some of these records, and most, are of
so little moment that they are soon neglected and forgotten;
others, like the fancied story of the swallow, linger through
the ages. It is to these that we give the name of literature.
Literature is the lasting expression in words of the meaning
of life.

Any definition is the clearer for examples. To make sure
of ours, then, we may well recall a few names which undoubtedly illustrate it. The Psalms are literature, so is the
Iliad, so are the Epistles of Saint Paul, so is the Aeneid,
and the Divine Comedy, and Don Quixote, and Hamlet. These
few names are enough to remind us not only of what literature is, but also of the fact which most distinguishes it from
other arts of expression. The lines and colours which embody architecture, sculpture, and painting, can be understood by anybody with eyes. Though to people like ourselves,
who have grown up amid the plastic traditions of classical
antiquity and the Italian Renaissance, an Egyptian painting
or a Japanese print looks odd, it remains, even to us, comprehensible. The Psalms, on the other hand, were written
in Hebrew, the Iliad and the Epistles in dialects of Greek,
the Aeneid was written in Latin, the Divine Comedy in Italian,
Don Quixote in Spanish, and Hamlet in Elizabethan English;
except through the unsatisfactory medium of translation one
and all must be sealed books to those who do not know the
languages native to the men who phrased them. World-old
legends, after all, are the wisest; the men who fled from
Babel could each see in the deserted tower a monument of
impious aspiration, but this thought of each was sealed from

the rest by the confusion of tongues. So to this day literature is of all fine arts the most ineradicably national.

Here again we come to a word so simple and so frequent that an important phase of its meaning is often overlooked. Nationality is generally conceived to be a question of race, of descent, of blood; and yet in human experience there is a circumstance perhaps more potent in binding men together than any physical tie. That old legend of Babel tells the story. The confusion of tongues broke every bond of common kinship; the races which should hold together through the centuries sprang afresh from men who newly spoke and newly thought and newly felt in terms of common language. For these languages which we speak grow more deeply than anything else to be a part of our mental habit who use them. It is in terms of language that we think even about the commonplaces of life,—what we shall eat, what we shall wear, whom we shall care for; in terms of language too, and in no others, we formulate the ideals which consciously, and perhaps still more unconsciously, guide our conduct and our aspirations. In a strange, subtle way each language grows to associate with itself the ideals and the aspirations and the fate of those peoples with whose life it is inextricably intermingled.

Languages grow and live and die in accordance with laws of their own, not perfectly understood, which need not now detain us. This English of ours, with which alone we are immediately concerned, may be taken as typical. Originating, one can hardly say precisely when or how, from the union and confusion of older tongues, it has struggled through the infantile diseases of dialect, each of which has left some trace, until long ago it not only had become the sole means of expression for millions of people, but also had assumed the literary form which now makes its literature in some respects the most considerable of modern times. Whatever else, this literature is the most spontaneous, the least formal and conscious, the most instinctively creative, the most free from the rankness and the debility of extreme culture, and so seemingly the most normal. Its earliest forms were artless; songs and sayings began to stray from oral tradition into written record, laws were sometimes phrased and

chronicles made in the robust young terms which carried
meaning to unlearned folks as well as to those versed in
more polite tongues. By and by came forms of literature
which at least comparatively were artistic, influenced by an
impulse of writers and of readers too towards expression
for expression's sake. The earliest of these which has lasted
in general literary memory reached its height in the work of
Chaucer. After his time came a century or more of civil
disturbance, when Englishmen were too busy with wars of
the Roses and the like for further progress in the arts of
peace. Then, with the new national integrity which grew under the Tudors, came a fresh and stronger literary impulse,
unsurpassed in vigorous spontaneity.

In 1575 there was hardly such a thing as modern English
literature; in 1625 that great body of English literature
which we call Elizabethan was complete. Fifty years had
given us not only incomparable lyric verse and the final version of the Bible, but the work too of Spenser, of Shakspere
and the other great dramatists, of Hooker, of Ralegh, of
Bacon, and of all their fellows. Among these, of course,
Shakspere stands supreme, just as Chaucer stood among his
contemporaries whose names are now forgotten by all but
special scholars; and one feature of Shakspere's supremacy
is that his literary career was normal. Whoever has followed it from his experimental beginning, through the ripeness to which he brought comedy, history, and tragedy alike,
to its placid close amid the growing languor of freshly established tradition, will have learned something more than
even the great name of Shakspere includes, —he will have had
a glimpse of the natural law which not only governed the
course of Shakspere himself and of Elizabethan literature,
but has governed in the past and will govern in the future the
growth, development, and decline of all literature and of all
fine art whatsoever. Lasting literature has its birth when a
creative impulse, which we may call imaginative, moves
men to break the shackles of tradition, making things which
have not been before; sooner or later this impulse is checked
by a growing sense of the inexorable limits of fact and of
language; and then creative imagination sinks into some new

tradition, to be broken only when, in time to come, the vital force of imagination shall revive.

As English literature has grown into maturity, the working of this law throughout its course has become evident. The first impulse, we have seen, gave us the work of Chaucer; the second, which came only after generations, gave us the Elizabethan lyrics and dramas, Spenser and Shakspere, and the final form of the English Bible. This last is probably the greatest masterpiece of translation in the world; it has exercised on the thought and the language of English-speaking people an influence which cannot be overestimated. As a translation, however, it rather indicates how eager Elizabethan Englishmen were to know the splendours of world-old literature, than reveals a spontaneous impulse towards native expression. Apart from this supreme work, the fully developed literature of the Elizabethan period took on the whole the form of poetry; that of the eighteenth century, on the other hand, took on the whole the form of prose; and as English prose literature has developed, no phase of it has developed more highly than its fiction. Vaguely general though this statement be, it is perhaps enough to indicate an important general tendency. The first form in which the normal literature of any language develops is instinctively poetic; prose comes later; and prose fiction, that intricate combination of poetic impulse with prosaic form, comes later still. In 1625 English literature was fully developed only in the forms of lyric and dramatic poetry.

It was about this time that the America with which we shall be concerned came into existence. It began with a number of mutually independent settlements, each of which grew into something like political integrity. When the Constitution of the United States was adopted, somewhat more than a hundred years ago, the sentiment of local sovereignty in the separate States was accordingly too strong to allow the federal power to assume an independent name. As the power thus founded developed into one of the most considerable in modern history, its citizens found themselves driven by this unique fact of national namelessness to a custom which, if misunderstood, is often held presumptuous; they called

themselves Americans, a name geographically proper to all
natives of the Western Hemisphere, from Canada to Pata-
gonia. By this time the custom thus historically established
has given to the name "America" the sense in which we generally use it. The America with whose literary history we
are to be concerned is only that part of the American continent which is dominated by the English-speaking people now
subject to the government of the United States.

A literary history of America, then, should concern itself
with such lasting expressions in words of the meaning of life
as this people has uttered during its three centuries of growingly independent existence; or, in simpler terms, with what
America has contributed to the literature of the English language.

Accidents of chronology though the centuries of any era
must be, they prove in such study as ours convenient divi-
sions of time, at once easy to remember and characteristically distinct. In the history of America, at least, each century has traits of its own. In 1600 there was no such thing as
English-speaking America; in 1700 all but one of the colonies which have developed into the United States were finally
established, and the English conquest of the middle colonies
founded by the Dutch or the Swedes was virtually complete.
In 1700 every one of the American colonies was loyally subject to the government of King William III.; in 1800 there
remained throughout them no vestige of British authority. In
1800, the last complete year of the presidency of John Adams, the United States were still an experiment in government of which the result remained in doubt; the year 1900
has found them, whatever else, a power which seems as
established and as important as any in the world. Clearly
these three centuries of American history are at least as
distinct as three generations in any race.

Again, though the political crises which decided the distinct features of these centuries were far from coincident
with the centuries themselves, the typical American character of the seventeenth century differed from that of the
eighteenth, and that of the eighteenth from that of the nineteenth, as distinctly as the historical limits of these centu-

ries differed one from the other. In the seventeenth century
the typical American, a man of English-speaking race, seemed
to himself an immigrant hardly at home in the remote regions where his exiled life was perforce to be passed. In the
eighteenth century the typical American, still English at
heart, was so far in descent from the immigration that almost unawares his personal ties with the mother country had
been broken. By tradition, perhaps, he knew from what part
of the old world his ancestors had come, but that old home
itself had probably both lost all such traditions of those ancestors and ceased to feel even curiosity about their descendants. For better or worse, this new America had become the only real home of its natives. In the nineteenth
century the typical American, politically as well as personally independent of the old world, and English only so far as
the traditions inseparable from ancestral law and language
must keep him so, has often felt or fancied himself less at
one with contemporary Englishmen than with Europeans of
other and essentially foreign blood.

Yet, English or not, we Americans are English-speaking
still; and English-speaking we must always remain. An accident of language and nothing more, this fact may seem to
many. To those who think more deeply it can hardly fail to
mean that for better or worse the ideals which underlie our
blundering conscious life must always be the ideals which
underlie the conscious life of the mother country, and which
for centuries have rectified and purified her blunders. Morally and religiously these ideals are immortally consecrated
in King James's version of the Bible; legally and politically
these ideals are grouped in that great legal system which,
in distinction from the Canon Law or the Civil, may broadly
be called the Common Law of England. What these ideals
are, every one bred in the traditions of our ancestral language instinctively knows; but such knowledge is hard to
phrase. Perhaps we come as near as may be to truth when
we say that in their moral aspect the ideals which underlie
our language are comprised in a profound conviction that,
whatever our station or our shortcomings, each of us is
bound to do right; and that in their legal aspect these ideals

may similarly be summarised in the statement that we are
bound on earth to maintain our rights. But the rights con-
templated by our ancestral law are no abstract ones; they
are those which the gradually varying custom and experience
of the centuries have proved in actual exercise to be safely
favourable to the public and private welfare of men like ourselves.

Vague and general as all this may seem, it has lately
come to possess significance hardly paralleled since at the
beginning of our Christian era the imperial power, the law
and the language, of Rome dominated what was then the
world. Our law and our language, our ideals and our vital
energies, which had their earliest origin in England, are at
this moment struggling for world-existence with what else
in ideals, in law, and in language have developed themselves
otherwise in modern time. Yet for a century or more the two
great English-speaking races, the native English and that of
independent America, have been so disunited that each has
often seemed to the other more hostile than many an alien.
There are no feuds fiercer than the feuds of kindred. As we
pursue our study, we shall perhaps see how this breach between the two branches of our race has grown. In brief,
from the first settlement of Virginia until the moment when
the guns of Admiral Dewey brought America unawares but
fatally face to face with the problem of Asiatic empire, there
has never been an instant when to native Englishmen and to
English-speaking Americans the great political problems
have presented themselves in the same terms. To-day at last
there is little difference. To-day, then, the disunion of sympathy which for a century and more has kept Americans
apart from the native English takes on world-wide significance.

An important phase of our study must accordingly be that
which attempts to trace and to understand the changes in the
native character of the Americans and of the English, which
so long resulted in disunion of national sentiment. We can
scrutinise them, however, only as they appear in literary
history,' and mostly in that of America. For our chief business concerns only the question of what contributions Amer-

ica has made, during its three centuries, to the literature
of the English language.

Recurring to our rough, convenient division of native
Americans into the three types which correspond to these
three centuries of American history, we can instantly perceive that only the last, the Americans of the nineteenth century, have produced literature of any importance. The novelists and the historians, the essayists and the poets, whose
names come to mind when American literature is mentioned,
have all flourished since 1800. The greater part of our study,
then, must concern the century just at an end. For all that,
the two earlier centuries were not sterile; rather indeed the
amount of native American writing which each produced is
surprising. What is more, the American writings of the
eighteenth century differed from those of the seventeenth
quite as distinctly as did the American history or the American character. Of both centuries, meanwhile, two things
are true: neither in itself presents much literary variety,
and most of what was published in each has already been
forgotten. Our task, then, is becoming plainer; it is to
glance at the literary history of America during the seventeenth century and the eighteenth, and to study, with what
detail proves possible, that literary history during the past
hundred years.

From all this, too, an obvious method of proceeding begins to define itself. Taking each century in turn, we may
conveniently begin by reminding ourselves briefly of what it
contributed to the history and to the literature of England.
With this in mind we may better understand a similar but
more minute study of America during each of the three periods in question. When we come to the last and most important of these, the nineteenth century, we may find ourselves
a little troubled by the fact that so much of it is almost contemporary with ourselves. Contemporary life is never quite
ripe for history; facts cannot at once range themselves in
true perspective; and when these facts are living men and
women, there is a touch of inhumanity in writing of them as
if we had already had the misfortune to lose them. In these
straits one decision seems unavoidable, —so far as our study

concerns individuals, we must confine it to those who are no longer living. Unhappily the list has so swollen that these should prove quite enough for our main purpose. For this, we should constantly remember, is chiefly to discern what, if anything, America has so far contributed to the literature of our ancestral English language.

Nathaniel Hawthorne

In our study of the New England Renaissance we have glanced at Emerson, whom we may call its prophet; at Whittier, who so admirably phrased its aspirations for reform; at Longfellow, its academic poet; at Lowell, its humanist; and at Holmes, its rationalist. The period produced but one other literary figure of equal eminence with these, —Nathaniel Hawthorne, above and beyond the others an artist.

His origin was different from that of his contemporaries whom we have lately considered. Emerson and Longfellow and Lowell and Holmes were all born into the social class which at their time was dominant in New England; and Whittier sprang from sturdy country yeomen. Hawthorne came from a family eminent in early colonial days, but long lapsed into that sort of obscurity which modern cant would call social degeneracy. His father, a ship captain of the period when New England commerce was most vigorous, died in Guiana when Hawthorne was only four years old; and the boy, who had been born at Salem in 1804, grew up there in his mother's care, singularly solitary. His youthful experience was confined to Salem, then a more important town than now, but already showing symptoms of decline. He made at least one prolonged visit in search of health to the woods of Maine. To this day wild and then wilder still, these forests early made familiar to him the atmosphere of our ancestral wilderness. In 1821 he went to Bowdoin College. There he was a student with Longfellow, and of Franklin Pierce, afterwards President of the United States. His friendship with the latter was close and lifelong. In 1825, they took their degrees at Bowdoin.

For the ensuing fourteen years Hawthorne lived with his mother at Salem, so quietly that his existence was hardly known to the townsfolk of that gossipy little Yankee seaport. He spent much time indoors, constantly writing but neither successful nor generally recognised as an author. He took long solitary walks, and his personal appearance is said to have been romantic and picturesque. In 1839 he was appointed a clerk in the Boston Custom House; in 1841 the spoils system turned him out of office, and for a few months he was at Brook Farm. The next year he married, and from then until 1846 he lived at Concord, writing and by this time pleasantly recognised as a writer of short stories. From 1846 to 1849 he was Surveyor in the Custom House of Salem. During the ensuing four years, when he resided at various places in Massachusetts, he produced his three most characteristic long books,—the "Scarlet Letter," the "House of the Seven Gables," and the "Blithedale Romance,"—as well as his two volumes of mythological stories for children, the "Wonder-book" and "Tanglewood Tales." In 1853, his friend, President Pierce, made him Consul at Liverpool. He remained abroad until 1860, passing some time during his later stay there in Italy. From this experience resulted the "Marble Faun." In 1860, he came home and returned to Concord, where he lived thenceforth. He died in the White Mountains, on the 18th of May, 1864.

Chronologically, then, Hawthorne's position in New England literature seems earlier than that of his contemporaries at whom we have glanced. He was only a year younger than Emerson, he was three years older than Longfellow and Whittier, five years older than Holmes, and fifteen years older than Lowell. He died thirty-six years ago; and Emerson and Longfellow survived until 1882, Lowell till 1891, Whittier till 1892, and Holmes till 1895. Though Hawthorne, however, was the first to die of this little company, he had been a fellow-writer with them during the thirty years when the full literary career of all had declared itself. In the time which followed Hawthorne's death, the survivors wrote and published copiously; but none produced anything which much altered the reputation he had achieved while Hawthorne was

still alive. So far as character goes, in short, the literature
of renascent New England was virtually complete in 1864.

Under such circumstances chronology becomes accidental.
The order in which to consider contemporaries is a question
simply of their relative character. We had good reason,
then, for reserving Hawthorne till the last; for above all the
rest, as we have already remarked, he was an artist. This
term is so general that we may well linger on it for a moment. A little story of the Yankee country may help define
our meaning. Not long ago a sportsman, who had started out
in a dory along with a native fisherman, found himself be-
calmed at night off the New Hampshire coast. Observing that
the fisherman, who had sat quiet for a little while, was star-
ing at the North Star, he asked what he was thinking about.
"I was thinkin'," drawled out the Yankee, "how fur off you'd
hev to be to get that south of you." Whereupon he shook himself and fell to his oars. That momentary experience, you
see, had awakened in a Yankee countryman something like
imaginative emotion. He spoke it out, and then forgot it; but
just for a moment he had felt the impulse of artistic spirit,
and had found relief in an expression imaginative enough to
be memorable. Some such experience as this everybody
knows sometimes, many people often; and occasionally there
are born into the world natures so sensitive to impressions
that they find almost every day overcharged with emotions
from which they can find relief only in attempts at expression. Generally such expression is of only momentary value.
Now and again, however, some human being proves endowed
not only with sensitiveness to impulse but with mastery of
expression as well. Such a man, whatever his art, is an
artist; and such was Hawthorne.

It chances that fate has posthumously treated him with exceptional irony. The general solitude of his life was partly
due to a fastidious reticence which made him shrink from
personal revelation. This trait was not inherited by his children; so since his death we have had more publications from
his note-books, and more records of his private life than is
the case with anybody else in American literary history.
Among these posthumous records none are more character-

istic or valuable than the first which appeared. The "Passages from American Note Books," published in 1868, extend over many years, mostly before Hawthorne's sojourn abroad. For our purposes they are perhaps the most significant of all his work. They show him in various parts of the New England country, freshly impressed almost every day with some aspect of life which aroused in him concrete reaction. He actually published tales enough to establish more than one literary reputation. These note-books show how few fragments of his wealthy imaginative impulse he ever coined into finished literary form. They reveal, too, another characteristic fact. Though Hawthorne wrote hardly any formal verse, though his natural impulse to expression rarely if ever took metrical form, he was a genuine poet. His only vehicle of expression was language, and to him language meant not only words but rhythm too. Even in these memoranda, then, which he never expected to stray beyond his note-books, you feel the constant touch of one whose meaning is so subtle that its most careless expression must fall into delicately careful phrasing.

Such a temperament would inevitably have declared itself anywhere. Some critics, then, have lamented the accident which confined Hawthorne's experience for almost fifty years to isolated, aesthetically starved New England. In this opinion there is considerable justice. The extreme localism of Hawthorne's life, until his maturity was passing into age, may very likely have made world literature poorer. The "Marble Faun" is our only indication of what he might have done if his sensitive youth had been exposed to the unfathomably human influence of Europe. Yet, whatever our loss, we can hardly regret an accident so fortunate to the literature of New England.

This Hawthorne, whose artistic temperament would have been remarkable anywhere, chanced to be born in an old Yankee seaport, just at its zenith. It was soon to be stricken by the Embargo, and swiftly to be surpassed by a more prosperous neighbour. When he knew it best, it was like some iridescent old sea-shell, whose denizens are dead and gone, but whose hollows still faintly vibrate with the voices

of the illimitable waters. From this passing, ancestral
Salem he visited those woods of Maine which were still so
primeval as to recall the shadowy forests whose mystery
confronted the immigrant Puritans. Then he lived for a while
in Boston, just when Transcendentalism was most in the air;
and he had a glimpse of Brook Farm; and he passed more
than one year in the Old Manse at Concord; and finally he
strayed among the hills of Berkshire. Until he finally set
sail for England, however, he had never known any earthly
region which had not traditionally been dominated by the
spirit of the Puritans; nor any which in his own time was not
alive, so far as life was in it, with the spirit of the New
England Renaissance.

In considering this period, we have hitherto dwelt only on
its most obvious aspect. Like any revelation of new life, it
seemed to open the prospect of an illimitably excellent
future. Amid such buoyant hopes people think little of the
past, tending indeed to regard it like some night of darkness
to which at last the dawn has brought an end. They forget the
infinite mysteries of the night, its terrors and its dreamy
beauties, and the courage of those who throughout its trem-
ulous course have watched and prayed. So when the dawn
comes they forget that the birth of day is the death of night.
Thus the men of our New England Renaissance forgot that
their new, enfranchised life and literature meant the final
passing of that elder New England so hopefully founded by
the Puritan fathers. As our Renaissance has passed its
swift zenith, and begun itself to recede into dimming memory, we can see more plainly than of old this tragic aspect
of its earthly course. The world in which Hawthorne lived
and wrote was not only a world where new ideals were
springing into life; it was a world, too, where the old ideals
were suffering their agony.

Of all our men of letters Hawthorne was most sensitive to
this phase of the time when they flourished together. He was
not, like Emerson, a prophet striving to glean truths from
unexplored fields of eternity; he was not, like Whittier, a
patient limner of simple nature, or a passionate advocate of
moral reform; he was not, like Longfellow or Lowell, a

loving student of world literature, moved by erudition to the
expression of what meaning he had found in the records of a
wonderful foreign past; he was not, like Holmes, a combat-
ant who, with all the vivacity of lifelong wit and all the method of scientific training, rationally attacked the chimeras of
his time; he was an artist, who lived for nearly fifty years
only in his native country, daily stirred to attempt expression of what our Yankee life meant. Of all our men of letters
he was the most indigenous; of all, the least imitative.

By hastily comparing his work, then, with some which was
produced in England during the same years, we may perhaps
define our notion of what the peculiar trait of American letters has been. His first collection of "Twice Told Tales"
appeared in 1837; in England, where the Queen had just
come to the throne, Dickens published "Oliver Twist," and
Thackeray the "Yellowplush Papers." The second series of
"Twice Told Tales" came in 1842, when Bulwer published
"Zanoni," and Dickens his "American Notes," and Macaulay
his "Lays." In 1846, when Hawthorne published the "Mosses
from an Old Manse," Dickens published "Dombey and Son."
In 1850, the year of the "Scarlet Letter," came Mrs. Browning's "Sonnets from the Portuguese," and Carlyle's "Latter
Day Pamphlets," and Tennyson's "In Memoriam;" in 1851,
along with the "House of the Seven Gables," came "Casa
Guidi Windows" and the "Stones of Venice;" in 1852, with
the "Blithedale Romance," came Dickens's "Bleak House,"
and Charles Reade's "Peg Woffington," and Thackeray's
"Henry Esmond;" in 1853, along with "Tanglewood Tales,"
came Kingsley's "Hypatia," Bulwer's "My Novel," and
Miss Yonge's "Heir of Redclyffe;" and in the year of the
"Marble Faun," 1860, came the "Woman in White," the
"Mill on the Floss," the "Cloister and the Hearth," and the
last volume of "Modern Painters." The list already grows
tediously long for our purpose. Like Irving and Poe, the two
Americans who preceded him as literary artists, Hawthorne
proves, the moment you compare him with the contemporary
writers of England, to be gifted or hampered with a pervasive sense of form which one is half disposed to call classic.

Yet that term "classic," applied even to Irving, and still

more to Poe or Hawthorne, must seem paradoxical if one
has sympathetically read them. Such terms as "romantic"
and "classic" of course are inexactly bewildering; but for
general purposes one would not go far wrong who should include under the term "classic" that sort of human impulse
which reached its highest form in the fine arts of Greece,
and under the term "romantic" that which most nearly approached realization in the art and the literature of mediaeval Europe. The essence of classic art is perhaps that the
artist realises the limits of his conception, and within those
limits endeavours to make his expression completely beautiful. The essence of the romantic spirit is that the artist,
whatever his conception, is always aware of the infinite
mysteries which lie beyond it. Mr. Cabot, in his biography
of Emerson, described Transcendentalism as an outbreak of
romanticism. The romantic spirit is almost always tran-
scendental.

Now, even the stories of Irving are pervaded with one kind
of romantic temper,—that which delights in the splendours
of a vanished past, and in the mysteries of supernatural
fancy. Something more deeply romantic underlies the inarticulate work of Brockden Brown, and still more the poems
and the tales of Poe. Both Brown and Poe had a deep sense
of what horror may lurk in the mysteries which always lie
beyond human ken. Even Brown, however, and surely Poe
conceived these melodramatically. Brown can sometimes
thrill you; and Poe often; but when you wake again to normal
placidity, you find in your nostrils some lingering trace of
such fumes as fill theatres where red lights have been burn-
ing. In common with Irving and Poe, Hawthorne had an instinctive tendency to something like classic precision of
form. In common with them he possessed, too, a constant
sensitiveness to the mysteries of romantic sentiment; but
the romanticism of Hawthorne differs from that of either Poe
or Irving as distinctly as it differs from that of Brockden
Brown. In Hawthorne's there is no trace of artificiality.
Beyond human life he feels not only the fact of mystery; he
feels the mysteries which are truly there.

In the mere fact of romantic temper, then, Hawthorne is

broadly American, typically native to this new world which
has been so starved of antiquity. In the fact that his romantic
spirit is fundamentally true he proves individual, and more
at one than our other artists with the deepest spirit of his
peculiar country. The darkly passionate idealism of the Puritans had involved a tendency towards conceptions, which
when they reached artistic form must be romantic. The
phase of mystery on which the grim dogmas of these past
generations incessantly dwelt lies in the world-old facts,
which nothing shall ever much abate, of evil and sin and suffering. Now Hawthorne had passed so far beyond Puritan
dogma that in mature life he could rarely be persuaded to
attend a religious service. His temper, indeed, when not
concerned with the forms of artistic expression, was impatient of all formality. Just as truly, however, as his nature
was that of a born artist, it could never shake off the temperamental earnestness of the Puritan. Throughout his work,
then, he is most characteristic when in endlessly varied
form he expresses that constant, haunting sense of ancestral
sin in which his Puritan forefathers found endless warrant
for their doctrines of depravity and of eternal retribution.
With the Puritans, of course, this sense of sin was a conviction of fact; they believed in the Devil, whose essential
wickedness, lurking within every human heart, is bound if
we lack divine help to sweep us into deserved and lasting
torment. Hawthorne, on the other hand, felt all this only as
a matter of emotional experience. To him Puritanism was no
longer a motive of life; in final ripeness it had become a
motive of art. When any human impulse has thus ripened, we
may generally conclude it historically a thing of the past.

Another aspect of this deep sense of sin and mystery
shows us that it involves morbid development of conscience.
Conscience in its artistic form Hawthorne displays throughout; and though artistic conscience be very different from
moral, the two have in common an aspiration toward beauty.
For all its perversities of outward form, the impulse of the
moral conscience is really toward beauty of conduct; artistic
conscience, often evident in works morally far from edifying, is a constant, strenuous impulse toward beauty of

expression. In America this latter trait has generally
seemed more frequent than in England; one feels it even in
Brockden Brown, one feels it strongly in Irving and Poe,
one feels it in the delicately sentimental lines of Bryant, and
one feels it now and again through most of the expression of
renascent New England. Whatever American writers have
achieved, they have constantly tried to do their best. Hawthorne, we have seen, surpassed his countrymen in the gen-
uineness of his artistic impulse; he surpassed them, too, in
the tormenting strenuousness of his artistic conscience. In
his choice of words and, above all, in the delicacy of his
very subtle rhythm, he seems never to have relaxed his effort to write as beautifully as he could. He displays the ancestral conscience of New England, then, in finally exquisite
form.

Of course the man has limits. Comparing his work with
the contemporary work of England, one is aware of its clas-
sically careful form, of its profoundly romantic sentiment,
and of its admirable artistic conscience. One grows aware,
at the same time, of its unmistakable rusticity; in turns of
thought as well as of phrase one feels monotony, provincialism, a certain thinness. Throughout, one feels again that
tendency to shrink from things of the flesh which to some
foreign minds makes all American writing seem either
emasculate or hypocritical. It is reported of Hawthorne, indeed,—who first saw Europe, we should remember, when he
was nearly fifty years old,—that he could never reconcile his
taste to the superbly unconscious nudities of masterly sculpture and painting. Here is an incalculable limit; and he has
plenty more. One and all of these limits, however, prove,
like his merits, to be deeply characteristic of the New England which surrounded his life.

It is hard to sum up the impression which such a writer
makes. He was ideal, of course, in temper; he was intro-
spective, with all the self-searching instinct of his ancestry;
he was solitary; he was permeated with a sense of the mysteries of life and sin; and by pondering over them he tended
to exaggerate them more and more. In a dozen aspects,
then, he seems typically Puritan. His artistic conscience,

however, as alert as that of any pagan, impelled him constantly to realise in his work those forms of beauty which
should most beautifully embody the ideals of his incessantly
creative imagination. Thus he grew to be of all our writers
the least imitative, the most surely individual. The circumstances of his life combined with the sensitiveness of his
nature to make his individuality indigenous. Beyond any one
else, then, he expresses the deepest temper of that New England race which brought him forth, and which now, at least in
the phases we have known, seems vanishing from the earth.

Walt Whitman

Walt Whitman was older than one is apt to remember. He was born on Long Island in 1819, and he died in 1892. His life, then, was almost exactly contemporary with Lowell's. No two lives could have been much more different in condition. Lowell, the son of a minister, closely related to the best people of New England, lived all his life amid the gentlest academic and social influences in America. Whitman was the son of a carpenter and builder on the outskirts of Brooklyn; the only New England man of letters equally humble in origin was Whittier.

The contrast between Whitman and Whittier, however, is almost as marked as that between Whitman and Lowell. Whittier, the child of Quaker farmers in the Yankee country, grew up and lived almost all his life amid guileless influences. Whitman, born of the artisan class in a region close to the most considerable and corrupt centre of population on his native continent, had a rather vagrant youth and manhood. At times he was a printer, at times a school-master, at times editor of stray country newspapers, and by and by he took up his father's trade of carpenter and builder, erecting a number of small houses in his unlovely native region. Meanwhile he had rambled about the country and into Canada, in much the temper of those wanderers whom we now call tramps; but in general until past thirty years old, he was apt to be within scent of the East River. The New York of which his erratic habits thus made the lower aspects so familiar to him was passing, in the last days of the Knickerbocker School, into its metropolitan existence. The first edition of Whitman's "Leaves of Grass" appeared in 1855, the year which produced the "Knickerbocker Gallery."

During the Civil War he served devotedly as an army nurse. After the war, until 1873, he held some small government clerkships at Washington. In 1873 a paralytic stroke brought his active life to an end; for his last twenty years he lived an invalid at a little house in Camden, New Jersey.

Until 1855, when the first edition of "Leaves of Grass" appeared in a thin folio, some of which he set up with his own hands, Whitman had not declared himself as a man of letters. From that time to the end he was constantly publishing his eccentric poetry, which from time to time he collected in increasing bulk under the old title. He published, too, some stray volumes of prose, —"Democratic Vistas," and the like. Prose and poetry alike seem permeated with a conviction that he had a mission to express and to extend the spirit of democracy, which he believed characteristic of his country. To himself, then, he seemed the inspired prophet of an America which he asserted to be above all things else the land of the people; few men have ever cherished a purpose more literally popular. His fate has been ironic. Though even in his lifetime he became conspicuous, it is doubtful whether any man of letters in his country ever appealed less to the masses. He was a prophet of democracy, if you like; but the public to which his prophecy made its way was at once limited, fastidiously overcultivated, and apt to be of foreign birth.

Beyond question Whitman had remarkable individuality and power. Equally beyond question he was among the most eccentric individuals who ever put pen to paper. The natural result of this has been that his admirers have admired him intensely; while whoever has found his work repellent has found it irritating. Particularly abroad, however, he has attracted much critical attention; and many critics have been disposed to maintain that his amorphous prophecies of democracy are deeply characteristic of America. The United States, they point out, are professedly the most democratic country in the world; Whitman is professedly the most democratic of American writers; consequently he must be the most typical.

The abstract ideal of democracy has never been better
summed up than in the well-known watchwords of republican
France: Liberty, Equality, Fraternity. Disguised and distorted though these words may have been by a century of
French Revolutionary excess, there is no denying that they
stand for ideals essentially noble and inspiring. What is
more, these ideals, which everywhere underlie the revolutionary spirit, have consciously influenced the nineteenth
century on both sides of the Atlantic. In the progress of
American democracy, however, one of these ideals has been
more strenuously kept in mind than the other two. American
democracy did not spring from abstract philosophising; it
had its origin in the old conceptions of liberty and rights as
maintained by the Common Law of England. Though no commonplace, then, has been more familiar to American ears
than the glittering generality which maintains all men to be
born equal, the practical enthusiasm of American democracy has been chiefly excited by the ideal of liberty. The
theoretical democracy of Europe, on the other hand, has
tended rather to emphasise the ideal of fraternity, which
seems incidentally to include a sound thrashing for any
brother who fails to feel fraternal; and still more this European democracy has tended increasingly to emphasise the
dogma of human equality. Though this doubtless beautiful
ideal eloquently appeals to many generous natures, it seems
hardly to accord with the teachings either of natural law or
of any recorded experience. Nothing, it maintains, ought
really to be held intrinsically better than anything else. In
plain words, the ideal of equality, carried to its extreme,
asserts all superiority, all excellence, to be a phase of evil.

Now, Walt Whitman's gospel of democracy certainly included liberty and laid strong emphasis on fraternity. He
liked to hail his fellow-citizens by the wild, queer name of
"camerados," which, for some obscure reason of his own,
he preferred to "comrades." The ideal which most appealed
to him, however, was that of equality. Though he would
hardly have assented to such orthodox terms, his creed
seems to have been that, as God made everything, one thing
is just as good as another. There are aspects in which such
a proposition seems analogous to one which should maintain

a bronze cent to be every whit as good as a gold eagle because both are issued by the same government from the
same mint. At best, however, analogies are misleading ar-
guments; and people who share Whitman's ideal are apt to
disregard as superstitious any argument, however impressive, which should threaten to modify their faith in equality.
It is a superstition, they would maintain, that some ways of
doing things are decent and some not; one way is really just
as good as another. It is a superstition that kings, nobles,
and gentlemen are in any aspect lovelier than the mob. It is
a superstition that men of learning are intellectually better
than the untutored. It is a superstition which would hold a
man who can make a chair unable consequently to make a
constitution. It is a superstition that virtuous women are in-
herently better than street-walkers. It is a superstition that
law is better than anarchy. There are things, to be sure,
which are not superstitions. Evil and baseness and ugliness
are real facts, to be supremely denounced and hated; and
incidentally, we must admit, few arraignments of the vulgarity and materialism which have developed in the United
States are more pitiless than those which appear in Whitman's "Democratic Vistas." The cause of these hurtful
things, however, he is satisfied to find in the traces of our
ancestral and superstitious devotion to outworn ideals of excellence. We can all find salvation in the new, life-saving
ideal of equality. Let America accept this ideal, and these
faults will vanish into that limbo of the past to which he
would gladly consign all superstitions. Among these, he logically, though reluctantly, includes a great part of the poetry
of Shakspere; for Shakspere, undoubtedly a poet, was a poet
of inequality, who represented the people as a mob. For all
his genius, then, Shakspere was an apostle of the devil, another lying prophet of the superstition of excellence.

Even though excellence be a wicked and tyrannical ideal,
however, democratic prophecy does not forbid the whole
world equally to improve. Equalisation need not mean the
reducing of all that is admirable to the level of what is base.
It may just as well mean the raising of much that is base towards the height of what is admirable. The superstition

which has worked most sordid evil is that which denies human equality. Retract the denial, then; let human beings be equal, and the force which has most distorted mankind shall cease working. Then all alike may finally rise, side by side, into an equality superior to what has gone before. The prophets of equality are so stirred by dreams of the future that they half forget the horrors of present or past; and among prophets of equality Walt Whitman has the paradoxical merit of eminence.

Now, this dogma of equality clearly involves a trait which has not yet been generally characteristic of American thought or letters, —a complete confusion of values. In the early days of Renaissance in New England, to be sure, Emerson and the rest, dazzled by the splendours of that new world of art and literature which was at last thrown open, made small distinction between those aspects of it which are excellent and those which are only stimulating. At the same time they adhered as firmly as the Puritans themselves to the ideal of excellence; and among the things with which they were really familiar they pretty shrewdly distinguished those which were most valuable, either on earth or in heaven. With Walt Whitman, on the other hand, everything is confused.

Take, for example, a passage from his "Song of Myself," which contains some of his best-known phrases: —

"A child said What is the grass? fetching it to me with
    full hands;
  How could I answer the child? I do not know what it is any
    more than he.

"I guess it must be the flag of my disposition, out of hope-
    ful green stuff woven.

"Or I guess it is the handkerchief of the Lord,
  A scented gift and remembrancer designedly dropt,
  Bearing the owner's name someway in the corners, that
    we may see and remark, and say Whose?

"Or I guess the grass is itself a child, the produced babe
    of vegetation.

"Or I guess it is a uniform hieroglyphic,

And it means, Sprouting alike in broad zones and narrow
  zones.
Growing among black folds as among white,
Kanuck, Tuckahoe, Congressman, Cuff, I give them the
  same, I receive them the same.

"And now it seems to me the beautiful uncut hair of graves.

"Tenderly will I use you, curling grass,
  It may be you transpire from the breasts of young men,
  It may be if I had known them I would have loved them,
  It may be you are from old people, or from offspring
    taken soon out of their mothers' laps,
  And here you are the mothers' laps.

"The grass is very dark to be from the white heads of old
    mothers,
  Darker than the colourless beards of old men,
  Dark to come from under the faint red roofs of mouths.

"O I perceive after all so many uttering tongues,
  And I perceive they do not come from the roofs of mouths
    for nothing.

"I wish I could translate the hints about the dead young
    men and women,
  And the hints about the old men and mothers, and the
    offspring taken soon out of their laps.

"What do you think has become of the young and old men?
  And what do you think has become of the women and
    children?

"They are alive and well somewhere,
  The smallest sprout shows there is really no death,
  And if ever there was it had forward life, and does not
    wait at the end to arrest it,
  And ceas'd the moment life appear'd.

"All goes onward and outward, nothing collapses,
  And to die is different from what any one supposed, and
    luckier."

Here is perhaps his best-known phrase, "the beautiful uncut hair of graves." Here are other good phrases, like "the
faint red roofs of mouths." Here, too, is undoubtedly tender
feeling. Here, into the bargain, is such rubbish as "I guess
it is the handkerchief of the Lord,"—who incidentally uses
perfumery,—and such jargon as "Kanuck, Tuckahoe, Congressman, Cuff." In an inextricable hodge-podge you find at
once beautiful phrases and silly gabble, tender imagination
and insolent commonplace,—pretty much everything, in
short, but humour. In America this literary anarchy, this
complete confusion of values, is especially eccentric; for
America has generally displayed instinctive common-sense,
and common-sense implies some notion of what things are
worth. One begins to see why Whitman has been so much
more eagerly welcomed abroad than at home. His conception
of equality, utterly ignoring values, is not that of American
democracy, but rather that of European. His democracy, in
short, is the least native which has ever found voice in his
country. The saving grace of American democracy has been
a tacit recognition that excellence is admirable.

In temper, then, Walt Whitman seems less American than
any other of our conspicuous writers. It does not follow that
in some aspects he is not very American indeed. Almost as
certainly as Hawthorne, though very differently, he had the
true artistic temperament; life moved him to moods which
could find relief only in expression. Such a temperament
would have expressed itself anywhere; and Whitman's would
probably have found the most congenial material for expression in those European regions which have been most disturbed by French Revolutionary excess. He chanced, however, to be born, and to attain the maturity which he awaited
before he began to publish, in unmingled American surroundings. As obviously as Hawthorne's experience was confined
to New England, Whitman's was confined to that of the lower
classes in those regions which were developing into modern
New York.

Whoever remembers the growth of this region will remember what sometimes seemed the ugliest thing to the eye, the
most overwhelmingly oppressive to any instinct of taste, the

most sordidly hopeless atmosphere possible to human experience. Now, Whitman, we remember, came to his maturity
within scent of the East River; and certainly the East River,
separating New York and Brooklyn, was at that time the spot
of spots where life seemed most material, most grindingly
distant from ideal beauty. Yet the contemplation of this very
East River evoked from Whitman the poem which sometimes
seems his most nearly beautiful. Here is the last stanza of
this "Crossing Brooklyn Ferry": —

> "Flow on, river! flow with the flood-tide, and ebb with
>   the ebb-tide!
> Frolic on, crested and scallop-edg'd waves!
> Gorgeous clouds of the sunset! drench with your splen-
>   dour me, or the men and women generations after me!
> Cross from shore to shore, countless crowds of passen-
>   gers!
> Stand up, tall masts of Mannahatta! stand up, beautiful
>   hills of Brooklyn!
> Throb, baffled and curious brain! throw out questions and
>   answers!
> Suspend here and everywhere, eternal float of solution!
> Gaze, loving and thirsting eyes, in the house or street
>   or public assembly!
> Sound out, voices of young men! loudly and musically
>   call me by my nighest name!
> Live, old life! play the part that looks back on the actor
>   or actress!
> Play the old rôle, the rôle that is great or small accord-
>   ing as one makes it!
> Consider, you who peruse me, whether I may not in
>   unknown ways be looking upon you;
> Be firm, rail over the river, to support those who lean
>   idly, yet haste with the hasting current;
> Fly on, sea-birds! fly sideways, or wheel in large
>   circles high in the air;
> Receive the summer sky, you water, and faithfully hold it
>   till all the downcast eyes have time to take it from you!
> Diverge, fine spokes of light, from the shape of my head,
>   or anyone's head, in the sunlit water!

Come on, ships from the lower bay! pass up or down,
    white-sail'd schooners, sloops, lighters!
Flaunt away, flags of all nations! be duly lowered at
    sunset!
Burn high your fires, foundry chimneys! cast black
    shadows at nightfall! cast red and yellow light over the
    tops of the houses!
Appearances, now or henceforth, indicate what you are;
You necessary film, continue to envelope the soul,
About my body for me, and your body for you, be hung
    our divinest aromas,
Thrive, cities,—bring your freight, bring your shows,
    ample and sufficient rivers,
Expand, being than which none else is perhaps more
    spiritual,
Keep your places, objects than which none else is more
    lasting.

"You have waited, you always wait, you dumb, beautiful
    ministers,
We receive you with free sense at last, and are insatiate
    henceforward,
Not you any more shall be able to foil us, or withhold
    yourselves from us,
We use you and do not cast you aside—we plant you per-
    manently within us,
We fathom you not—we love you—there is perfection in
    you also,
You furnish your parts toward eternity,
Great or small you furnish your parts toward the soul."

The eight preceding stanzas are very like this,—confused,
inarticulate, and surging in a mad kind of rhythm which
sounds as if hexameters were trying to bubble through sewage. For all these faults, Whitman has here accomplished a
wonder. Despite his eccentric insolence both of phrase and
of temper you feel that in a region where another eye would
have seen only unspeakable vileness, he has found impulses
which prove it, like every other region on earth, a fragment

of the divine eternities. The glories and beauties of the universe are really perceptible everywhere; and into what seemed utterly sordid Whitman has breathed ennobling imaginative fervour. Cultured and academic folk are disposed to shrink from what they call base, to ignore it, to sneer at it; looking closer, Whitman tells us that even amid base things you cannot wander so far as to lose sight of the heavens, with all their fountains of glorious emotion.

But what is this emotion? Just here Whitman seems to stop. With singular vividness, and with the unstinted sympathy of his fervent faith in equality, he tells what he sees. Though often his jargon is amorphously meaningless, his words are now and again so apt as to approach that inevitable union of thought and phrase which makes lasting poetry. When he has reported what he sees, however, utterly confusing its values, he has nothing more to say about it. At most he leaves you with a sense of new realities concerning which you must do your thinking for yourself.

Sometimes, of course, he was more articulate. The Civil War stirred him to his depths; and he drew of its byways such little pictures as "Ethiopia Saluting the Colours":—

"Who are you dusky woman, so ancient, hardly human,
  With your wooly-white and turban'd head, and bare bony
    feet?
  Why rising by the roadside here, do you the colours
    greet?

"('T is while our army lines Carolina's sands and pines,
  Forth from thy hovel door thou Ethiopia com'st to me,
  As under doughty Sherman I march toward the sea.)

"Me master years a hundred since from my parents
    sunder'd,
  A little child, they caught me as the savage beast is
    caught,
  Then hither me across the sea the cruel slaver brought.

"No further does she say, but lingering all the day,
  Her high-borne turban'd head she wags, and rolls her
    darkling eye

And courtesies to the regiments, the guidons moving by.

"What is it fateful woman, so blear, hardly human?
Why wag your head with turban bound, yellow, red and
    green?
Are the things so strange and marvellous you see or
    have seen?"

In Lincoln he found his ideal hero; and his verse on Lincoln's death is probably his best: —

"O Captain! my Captain! our fearful trip is done,
The ship has weathered every rack, the prize we sought
    is won,
The port is near, the bells I hear, the people all exulting,
While follow eyes the steady keel, the vessel grim and
    daring;
        But O heart! heart! heart!
            O the bleeding drops of red,
                Where on the deck my Captain lies,
                    Fallen cold and dead.

"O Captain! my Captain! rise up and hear the bells;
Rise up—for you the flag is flung—for you the bugle
    trills,
For you bouquets and ribbon'd wreaths—for you the
    shores a-crowding,
For you they call, the swaying mass, their eager faces
    turning;
        Here Captain! dear father!
            This arm beneath your head!
                It is some dream that on the deck,
                    You've fallen cold and dead.

"My Captain does not answer, his lips are pale and still,
My father does not feel my arm, he has no pulse nor will,
The ship is anchored safe and sound, its voyage closed
    and done,
From fearful trip the victor ship comes in with object
    won;

> Exult O shores, and ring O bells!
>   But I with mournful tread,
>   Walk the deck my Captain lies,
>   Fallen cold and dead."

Even in bits like this, however, which come so much nearer form than is usual with Whitman, one feels his perverse
rudeness of style. Such eccentricity of manner is bound to
affect different tempers in different ways. One kind of reader, naturally eager for individuality and fresh glimpses of
truth, is disposed to identify oddity and originality. Another
kind of reader distrusts literary eccentricity as instinctively
as polite people distrust bad manners. In both of these instinctive reactions from such a method of address as Whitman's there is an element of truth. Beyond doubt, eccentric
masters of the fine arts give rise to perverse eccentricity
in imitators. Browning and Carlyle, to go no further, have
bred in brains feebler than their own much nonsensical
spawn; and so has Walt Whitman. But some artists of great
power prove naturally unable to express themselves properly.
Their trouble is like a muscular distortion which should
compel lameness, or a vocal malformation which should
make utterance hoarse or shrill. So there have been great
men, and there will be more, whom fate compels either to
express themselves uncouthly or else to stay dumb. Such a
man, great or not, Whitman seems to have been. Such men,
greater than he, were Carlyle and Browning. The critical
temper which would hold them perverse, instead of unfortu-
nate, is mistaken.

On the other hand, that different critical temper which
would welcome their perversities as newly revealed evi-
dences of genius is quite as mistaken in another way. If any
general law may be inferred from the history of fine arts, it
is that any persistent school of expression must be articulate.
In any art, of course, vital expression must be spontaneous;
academic training, dogmatic routine, has never originated
much that is worth while. The nobler works of art, however,
which have maintained themselves as permanent parts of the
great structure of human expression, have form. Their

lasting vitality comes partly from the fact that their makers
have spontaneously obeyed natural laws which may be gen-
eralised into academic principles. The development of human
expression seems like the growth of a tree. The same vital
force which sends the trunk heavenward, puts forth branches,
and from these in turn sends forth twigs and leaves; but the
further they stray from the root, the weaker they prove. The
trunk lives, and the greater branches; year by year, the lesser twigs and leaves wither. Now, eccentricity of manner,
however unavoidable, is apt to indicate that art has strayed
dangerously far from its vital origin. Oddity is no part of
solid artistic development; however beautiful or impressive,
it is rather an excrescent outgrowth, bound to prove abortive, and at the same time to sap life from a parent stock
which without it might grow more loftily and strongly.

Walt Whitman's style is of this excrescent, abortive kind.
Like Carlyle's or Browning's, it is something which nobody
else can imitate with impunity; and so, like theirs, it is a
style which in the history of literature suggests a familiar
phase of decline. That it was inevitable you will feel if you
compare "Ethiopia Saluting the Colours" or "My Captain"
with the unchecked perversities of Whitman's verse in general. The "Song of Myself," or "Crossing Brooklyn Ferry,"
which we may take as generally representative of his work,
are so recklessly misshapen that you cannot tell whether
their author was able to write with amenity. When you find
him, however, as in those lesser pieces, attempting technical form, you at once feel that his eccentricity is a misfortune, for which he is no more to blame than a lame man for
limping, or a deaf and dumb for expressing emotion by inarticulate cries. The alternative would have been silence; and
Whitman was enough of a man to make one glad that he never
dreamed of it.

In this decadent eccentricity of Whitman's style there is
again something foreign to the spirit of this country. American men of letters have generally had deep artistic conscience. This trait has resulted, for one thing, in making the
short story, an essentially organic form of composition, as
characteristic of American literature as the straggling,

inorganic three-volume novel is of English. Now and again,
to be sure, American men of letters have chosen to express
themselves in quite another manner. They have tried to re-
produce the native dialects of the American people. This
impulse has resulted in at least one masterpiece, that amazing Odyssey of the Mississippi to which Mark Twain gave the
fantastic name of "Huckleberry Finn." As we remarked of
the "Biglow Papers," however, this "dialect" literature of
America often proves on analysis more elaborately studied
than orthodox work by the same writers. Neither the "Biglow
Papers" nor "Huckleberry Finn" could have been produced
without an artistic conscience as strenuous as Irving's, or
Poe's, or Hawthorne's. The vagaries of Walt Whitman, on
the other hand, are as far from literary conscience as the
animals which he somewhere celebrates are from unhappi-
ness or respectability. Whitman's style, then, is as little
characteristic of America as his temper is of traditional
American democracy. One can see why the decadent taste of
modern Europe has welcomed him so much more ardently
than he has ever been welcomed at home; in temper and in
style he was an exotic member of that sterile brotherhood
which eagerly greeted him abroad. In America his oddities
were more eccentric than they would have been anywhere
else.

On the other hand, there is an aspect in which he seems
not only native but even promising. During the years when
his observation was keenest, and his temper most alert, he
lived in the environment from which our future America
seems most likely to spring. He was born and grew up, he
worked and lived, where on either side of the East River the
old American towns of New York and Brooklyn were developing into the metropolis which is still too young to possess
ripe traditions. In full maturity he devoted himself to army
nursing,—the least picturesque or glorious, and the most
humanely heroic, service which he could have rendered his
country during its agony of civil war. In that Civil War the
elder America perished; the new America which then arose
is not yet mature enough for artistic record. Whitman's
earthly experience, then, came throughout in chaotic times,

when our past had faded and our future had not yet sprung into being. Bewildering confusion, fused by the accident of his lifetime into the seeming unity of a momentary whole, was the only aspect of human existence which could be afforded him by the native country which he so truly loved. For want of other surroundings he was content to seek the meaning of life amid New York slums and dingy suburban country, in the crossing of Brooklyn Ferry, or in the hospitals which strove to alleviate the drums and tramplings of civil war. His lifelong eagerness to find in life the stuff of which poetry is made has brought him, after all, the reward he would most have cared for. In one aspect he is thoroughly American. The spirit of his work is that of world-old anarchy; its form has all the perverse oddity of world-old abortive decadence; but the substance of which his poems are made—their imagery as distinguished from their form or their spirit—comes wholly from our native country.

In this aspect, then, though probably in no other, he may, after all, throw light on the future of literature in America. As has been said before, "He is uncouth, inarticulate, whatever you please that is least orthodox; yet, after all, he can make you feel for the moment how even the ferry-boats plying from New York to Brooklyn are fragments of God's eternities. Those of us who love the past are far from sharing his confidence in the future. Surely, however, that is no reason for denying the miracle that he has wrought by idealising the East River. The man who has done this is the only one who points out the stuff of which perhaps the new American literature of the future may in time be made."

A Literary History of America: Conclusion

The literary history of America is the story, under new conditions, of those ideals which a common language has compelled America, almost unawares, to share with England. Elusive though they be, ideals are the souls of the nations which cherish them, —the living spirits which waken nationality into being, and which often preserve its memory long after its life has ebbed away. Denied by the impatience which will not seek them where they smoulder beneath the cinders of cant, derided by the near-sighted wisdom which is content with the world-old commonplace of how practice must always swerve from precept, they mysteriously, resurgently persist.

The ideals which for three hundred years America and England have cherished, alike yet apart, are ideals of morality and of government, —of right and of rights. Whoever has lived his conscious life in the terms of our language, so saturated with the temper and the phrases both of the English Bible and of English Law, has perforce learned that, however he may stray, he cannot escape the duty which bids us do right and maintain our rights. General as these phrases must seem, —common at first glance to the serious moments of all men everywhere, —they have, for us of English-speaking race, a meaning peculiarly our own. Though Englishmen have prated enough and to spare, and though Americans have declaimed about human rights more nebulously still, the rights for which Englishmen and Americans alike have been

eager to fight and to die are no prismatic fancies gleaming
through clouds of conflicting logic and metaphor; they are
that living body of customs and duties and privileges, which
a process very like physical growth has made the vital condition of our national existence. Through immemorial experience, the rights which we most jealously cherish have
proved themselves safely favourable at once to prosperity
and to righteousness.

Threatened throughout history, both from without and from
within, these rights can be preserved by nothing short of
eternal vigilance. In this we have been faithful, until our
deepest ideal of public duty, which marks Englishmen and
Americans apart from others, and side by side, has long ago
defined itself. The vitally growing rights bequeathed us by
our fathers, we must protect, not only from invasion or ag-
gression attempted by other races than ours, but also from
the internal ravages both of reaction and of revolution. In
loyalty to this conception of duty, the nobler minds of England and of America have always been at one.

Yet to careless eyes the two countries have long seemed
parted by a chasm wider even than the turbulent and foggy
Atlantic. Wide it has surely been, but never so vague as to
interpose between them the shoreless gulf of sundered principle. The differences which have kept England and America
so long distinct have arisen from no more fatal cause than
unwitting and temporary conflicts of their common law. The
origin of both countries, as we know them to-day, was the
England of Queen Elizabeth, with all its spontaneity, all its
enthusiasm, all its untired versatility. From this origin
England has sped faster and further than America. Throughout two full centuries, then, America and England have
faithfully, honestly quarrelled as to just what rights and liberties were truly sanctioned by the law which has remained
common to both.

How their native tempers began to diverge we have already
seen. During the seventeenth century, England proceeded
from its spontaneous, enthusiastic Elizabethan versatility,
through the convulsions of the Civil Wars, to Cromwell's
Commonwealth; and from the Commonwealth, through the

baseness of the Restoration and the renewing health of the
Glorious Revolution, to that state of parliamentary government which, in vitally altering form, still persists. English
literature meanwhile proceeded from the age of Shakspere,
through the age of Milton, to the age of Dryden. During this
same seventeenth century,—the century of American immigration,—the course of American history was interrupted by
no such convulsion as the wars and tumults which destroyed
Elizabethan England. American character, then, which from
the beginning possessed its still persistent power of absorbing immigration, preserved much of the spontaneity, the
enthusiasm, and the versatility transported hither from the
mother country when Virginia and New England were founded.
So far as literature went, meantime, seventeenth-century
America expressed itself only in occasional historical records, and in a deluge of Calvinistic theology. Though long
since abated, these first outpourings of New England have
left indelible traces. Partly to them, and still more to the
devout source from which they welled, is due the instinctive
devotion of America to such ideals of absolute right and truth
as were inherent in the passionate idealism of the Puritans.

It was here that America most distinctly parted from the
mother country. In England, the Puritan Commonwealth,
with its nobly futile aspiration toward absolute right, so en-
twined itself about the life of Cromwell that when he died it
fell. In America a similar commonwealth, already deeply
rooted when Cromwell was still a sturdy country gentleman
of St. Ives, flourished fruitful long after his relics had been
cast out of Westminster Abbey. Generation by generation,
the immemorial custom of America, wherein America has
steadily discerned the features of its ancestral rights and
liberties, grew insensibly to sanction more abstract ideals
than ever long persisted in England.

Whoever will thus interpret the seventeenth century need
be at little pains to understand the century which followed.
The political events of this eighteenth century—the century
of American independence—forced England into prolonged
international isolation; and this, combined with reactionary
desire for domestic order, bred in British character that

insular conservatism still typified by the portly, repellent
integrity of John Bull. English literature meanwhile proceeded from the Addisonian urbanity of Queen Anne's time,
through the ponderous Johnsonian formality which satisfied
the subjects of George II., to the masterly publicism of
Burke and the contagious popularity of Burns.

Eighteenth-century America was politically free from the
conditions which so highly developed the peculiar eccentric-
ities of England. There is no wonder, then, that American
character still retained the spontaneity, the enthusiasm, and
the versatility of the elder days when it had shared these
traits with the English. Nor is there any wonder that Americans went on traditionally cherishing the fervent idealism of
the immigrant Puritans, wherein for a while the ancestral
English ideals of right and of rights had fused. Unwittingly
lingering in its pristine state, the native character of America became less and less like the character which historical
forces were irresistibly moulding in the mother country. The
traditional law of America—the immemorial rights, the customs and the liberties, of a newly conscious people eagerly
responsive to the allurements of absolute truth—seemed on
its surface less and less like the more dogged and rigid system which was becoming the traditional law of England. When
disputes arose, the spirit of old Babel was reawakened. Despite their common language, neither of the kindred peoples,
separated not only by the wastes of the ocean but also by the
forgotten lapse of five generations, could rightly understand
the other. Dispute waxed fruitlessly high. The inevitable
result was the American Revolution.

The same causes which wrought this imperial disunion had
tended to alter the literary character of America. American
theology had already evaporated in metaphysical abstraction;
its place, as the principal phase of American expression,
had been taken by politics. Of this, no doubt, the animating
ideal was not so much that of morality as that of law; the
writings of eighteenth-century America have less concern
with right than with rights. Yet America would not have been
America unless these ancestral ideals had remained blended.
A yearning for absolute truth, an unbroken faith in abstract

ideals, is what makes distinctly national the political utterances of the American Revolution. The love of abstract right
which pervades them sprang straight from that aspiration
toward absolute truth which had animated the grim idealism
of the Puritans.

So came the nineteenth century,—the century of American
nationality, when, for all their community of language and of
ideals, England and America have believed themselves mutually foreign. English history has proceeded from the extreme isolation which ended at Waterloo, through the consti-
tutional revolution of the Reform Bill to the present reign.
What the future may decide to have been the chief features
of this Victorian epoch, it is still too soon to assert; yet,
whatever else, the future can hardly fail to remember how,
throughout these sixty and more years, England has continually developed in two seemingly divergent ways. At home,
on the one hand, it has so tended toward democracy that
already the political power of the English masses probably
exceeds that of the American. In its world relations, on the
other hand, England has become imperial to a degree un-
dreamed of when Queen Victoria ascended the throne. Wherever the influence of England extends to-day, democracy and
empire go hand in hand.

Throughout this nineteenth century, America has had the
Western Hemisphere almost to itself. This it has dominated
with increasing material power, believing all the while that
it could keep free from entanglement with other regions of
the earth. From this youthful dream it has at last been rude-
ly awakened. In the dawning of a new century, it finds itself—
like England, at once democratic and imperial—inevitably
confronted with world conflict; either its ideals must prevail,
or they must perish. After three centuries of separation,
then, England and America are once more side by side. With
them, in union, lies the hope of imperial democracy.

It is only during the nineteenth century—the century of
American nationality—that America has brought forth literature. First appearing in the Middle States, this soon developed more seriously in New England, whose mental life, so
active at first, had lain comparatively dormant for almost a

hundred years. These two phases of American literary expression, the only ones which may as yet be regarded as
complete, have been the chief subject of our study. On the
impression which they have left with us must rest our estimate of what the literature produced in America has hitherto
signified.

To define this impression, we may helpfully glance back
at what the nineteenth century added to the literature of England. First came the poetry of Wordsworth and Coleridge
and Shelley and Keats and Byron, —a poetry, for all its individual variety, aflame with the spirit of world-revolution.
Then, just after Waterloo, came those bravely ideal retrospective romances which have immortalised the name of
Scott. He died in 1832, the year of the Reform Bill. The later
literature of England has expressed the meanings of life discerned and felt by men whose mature years have fallen within the democratic and imperial reign of Queen Victoria. This
literature includes the great modern novelists, —Dickens and
Thackeray and George Eliot, with their host of contemporaries and followers; it includes the poetry of Tennyson, and
of the Brownings, and of more; it includes a wealth of serious prose, the work of Macaulay, of Carlyle, of Ruskin, of
Newman, of Matthew Arnold, and of numberless others; it
includes the studied and fastidious refinement of Stevenson;
it still happily includes the scope and power of writers now
living.

In the nineteenth century English literature began with a
passionate outburst of aspiring romantic poetry; it passed
into an era of retrospective romantic prose; it proceeded to
a stage where, for all the merit of persistent poetry, the
chief fact seems to have been fiction dealing mostly with
contemporary life; its serious prose, all the while, tended
more and more to dwell on the problems of the times; and
these surely underlie the utterances of its latest masters.
The more one considers what the century has added to English literature, the more one marvels at its riches. Yet all
the while one grows aware of something which, if not a loss,
is at least a change. Throughout the century, English letters
have slowly lapsed away from the grace of personal distinction.

The literature of nineteenth-century England, like its history, expresses an irresistible advance of democracy.

Political democracy, no doubt, declared itself earlier and more outspokenly in America than in England. So far as literature is concerned, on the other hand, the first thirty years of the nineteenth century excited from America much less democratic utterances than came from the revolutionary poets of the mother country. If you doubt this, compare Brockden Brown with Wordsworth, Irving with Coleridge, Cooper with Shelley, Bryant with Byron. What that earlier literature of the Middle States chiefly certifies of American character is the trait which so far has most surely controlled the progress of the United States: whatever our vagaries of occasional speech, we Americans are at heart disposed, with good old English common-sense, to follow those lines of conduct which practice has proved safe and which prudence has pronounced admirable. The earlier literature of the Middle States has another trait which seems nationally characteristic: its sensitiveness of artistic conscience shows Americans generally to be more alive to artistic duty than Englishmen have often been. The first literary utterances of inexperienced America were marked by no wildness or vagary; they showed, rather, an almost timid loyalty to the traditions of excellence.

A few years later came what so far seems the nearest approach of America to lasting literature,—the final utterances of New England during the years of its Renaissance, which, broadly speaking, were contemporary with the first half of the reign of Queen Victoria. The new life had begun, of course, somewhat earlier. It had first shown itself in the awakening of New England oratory and scholarship, and in the ardour which stirred Unitarianism to break the fetters of Calvinistic dogma. Scholarship bore fruit in the later works of the New England historians. Unitarianism tended, through Transcendentalism, to militant, disintegrating reform. Amid these freshening intellectual surroundings appeared some men whose names seem destined at least for a while to live in the records of literature. The chief of these were Emerson and Whittier and Longfellow and Lowell and Holmes and Hawthorne. If you will compare them with the writers who in their time were most eminent in England, —with Dickens, Thackeray, and George Eliot, with Tennyson and the Brownings, with Carlyle and Ruskin, with Newman and Matthew Arnold, —you can hardly help feeling a difference, palpable even though indistinct, undeniable even though hard to define.

One phase of this difference soon grows clear. Though the writers of renascent New England were generally better in prose than in poetry, —and thus resembled their English contemporaries, —their spirit was rather like that which had animated the fervent English poetry of a generation before. One and all of them, accepting the revolutionary doctrine that human nature is not evil but good, confidently hoped that illimitable development was at hand for a humanity finally freed from the shackles of outworn custom. In this faith and hope, the men of the New England Renaissance were sustained by a fact never true of any other civilised society than that from which they sprung. For more than two hundred years, national inexperience had protected American character from such distortion as the pressure of dense population always twists into human nature. With a justified enthusiasm, then, the literary leaders of New England, full of the earnest idealism inseparable from their Puritan ancestry, and finally escaped from the dogmas which had reviled humanity, fervently proclaimed democracy. And here, at first, their temper seems to linger a little behind that of the mother country. The undimmed confidence of their faith in human nature is like that which was beginning to fade from English literature before the death of Scott.

Yet these New England writers were no mere exotic survivors of the days when English Romanticism was fervid. They were all true Americans; and this they could not have been without an almost rustic limitation of worldly knowledge, without a shrewd sense of fact which should at once correct the errors of such ignorance and check the vagaries of their idealism, or without exacting artistic conscience. Their devotion to the ideals of right and of rights came straight from ancestral England. Their spontaneous aptitude for idealism, their enthusiastic love for abstractions and for absolute truth, they had derived, too, from the Elizabethan Puritans

whose traits they had hereditarily preserved. What most
surely marked them apart was the quality of their eager faith
in democracy. To them this was no untested dream; it was
rather a truth confirmed by the national inexperience of their
still uncrowded country. Hence sprang the phase of their
democratic temper which still seems most precious and most
pregnant.

The spirit of European democracy has been dominated by
blind devotion to an enforced equality. In many American
utterances you may doubtless find thoughtless assertion of
the same dogma. Yet if you will ponder on the course of
American history, and still more if you will learn intimately
to know those more eminent American men of letters who
remain the living teachers of our growing country, you must
grow to feel that American democracy has a wiser temper,
still its own. The national ideal of America has never yet
denied or even repressed the countless variety of human
worth and power. It has urged only that men should enjoy
liberty within the range of law. It has resisted both lingering
and innovating tyranny; but all the while it has kept faithful to
the principle that, so far as public safety may permit, each
of us has an inalienable right to strive for excellence. In the
presence of approved excellence it has remained humble.

The history of such future as we can now discern must be
that of a growing world-democracy. The most threatening
future danger, then, is often held to lurk in those dogged
systems of authority which still strive to strangle humane
aspiration. No doubt these are dangerous, yet sometimes
there must seem even deeper danger in that crescent phase
of democracy itself which hates and condemns excellence. If
in the conflicts to come, democracy shall overpower excellence, or if excellence, seeking refuge in freshly imperious
assertion of authority, shall prove democracy another futile
dream, the ways before us are dark. The more one dreads
such darkness, the more gleams of counsel and help one may
find in the simple, hopeful literature of inexperienced, renascent New England. There, for a while, the warring ideals of
democracy and of excellence were once reconciled, dwelling
confidently together in some earthly semblance of peace.

Edgar Allan Poe

Mr. President, Ladies and Gentlemen:

On the 19th of January, 1809, Edgar Allan Poe was born in Boston. The fact, to be sure, has been disputed; for the scanty and defective vital records of that period make no mention of it. It remains, however, certain. Almost exactly a hundred years later, my friend, Mr. Walter Watkins, impelled by occasional statements that Poe was born elsewhere, collected, from the Boston newspapers of 1808 and 1809, notices of all the plays in which the parents of Poe appeared during that season. These demonstrate that Mrs. Poe withdrew from the stage about Christmas time, 1808, and reappeared only on February 9th, 1809, when one of the newspapers congratulated her on her happy recovery from her confinement. This is apparently the most nearly contemporary record of Poe's birth. The researches of Mr. Watkins did not end here. All record of Poe's birthplace was supposed to have been lost; and indeed there is little likelihood that Poe himself ever knew just where it was. By examining the tax lists for 1808 and 1809, Mr. Watkins discovered that David Poe, the father of the poet, was taxed that year as resident in a house owned by one Henry Haviland, who had bought the property, a few years before, from a Mr. Haskins—a kinsman, I believe, of the mother of Ralph Waldo Emerson. The house was pulled down some fifty years ago, but Mr. Watkins has ascertained from the records that it was situated at what is now No. 62 Carver Street. In 1809, this was a respectable, though not a fashionable, part of the city. There Poe was born.

The circumstances of his career were restless; on the
whole, they were solitary. Throughout his forty years of
mortal sunlight and shadow he was never quite in accord with
his surroundings. He was never tried by either of the tests
for which ambition chiefly longs—the gravely happy test of
wide responsibility, or the stimulatingly happy test of dominant success. Troublous from beginning to end his earthly
life seems; to him this world could not often have smiled
contagiously sympathetic. So much is clear; and a little
more is clear as well. When he sought sympathy, or found
semblance of it, and thus for a little while could feel trouble
assuaged, he could find it most nearly among those generous
phases of Southern spirit which surrounded the happier years
of his youth. There was little trace of it, for him, in the still
half-Puritan atmosphere of that New England where he
chanced, a stranger, to see the light.

So it was with deep and reverent sense of your Southern
generosity that I received your grave and friendly summons
to join with you here and now. Here, in this sanctuary of
Virginia tradition, you have not scrupled to call me from the
heart of New England, to pay tribute not only for myself, and
for my own people, but tribute in the name of us all, to the
memory of Poe. If one could only feel sure of performing
such a task worthily, no task, of duty or of privilege, could
be more solemnly happy. For none could more wonderfully
imply how Virginians and the people of New England—each
still themselves—have so outlived their long spiritual mis-
understandings of one another that with all our hearts we can
gladly join together, as fellow countrymen, in celebrating
the memory of one recognised everywhere as the fellow-
countryman of us all.

Everywhere is a nowise hyperbolic word to describe the
extent of Poe's constantly extending fame, sixty years after
they laid him in his grave. His name is not only eminent in
the literary history of Virginia, or of New York, or of
America; it has proved itself among the very few of those
native to America which have commanded and have justified
admiration throughout the civilised world. Even this does
not tell the whole story. So far as we can now discern, he

has securely risen above the mists of time and the fogs of
accident. His work may appeal to you or leave you deaf; you
may adulate it or scrutinise it, as you will; you may dispute
as long and as fruitlessly as you please concerning its positive significance or the magnitude of its greatness. The one
thing which you cannot do—the thing for which the moment is
forever past—is to neglect it. Forever past, as well, all
loyal Americans must gladly find the moment—if indeed
there ever was a moment—when any of us could even for an
instant regret it. There is no longer room for any manner of
question that the writings of Poe are among the still few
claims which America can as yet urge unchallenged in proof
that our country has enriched permanent literature. Even
with no other reason than this, loyal Americans must already
unite in cherishing his memory.

So true, so obvious, this must seem to-day that we are
prone, in accepting it, to forget the marvel of it, as we forget the marvels of Nature—of sunrise, of sleep, of birth, of
memory itself. The marvel of it, in truth, is none the less
reverend because, like these, we need never find it miraculous. Happily for us all—happily for all the world—Poe is
not an isolated, sporadic phenomenon in our national history.
He was an American of the Nineteenth Century. If we ponder
never so little on those commonplace words, we shall find
them charged with stirring truth. To summarise the life of
any nation, there is no better way than to turn to the succes-
sive centuries of its history, and to ask yourself, with no
delay of slow or painful study, what names and what memories, unborn at the beginning of these epochs, were in per-
petual existence when they ended. When we thus consider our
United States of America, the spiritual splendour of the
Nineteenth Century glows amazing.

That Nineteenth Century, as we all gravely know, was by
no means a period of national concord. Rather, far and wide,
it was a period when the old order was fatally passing, yield-
ing place to new. Thus inevitably, throughout our country, it
was a period of honest and noble passion running to the inspiring height of spiritual tragedy. For no tragedy can be
more superbly inspiring than that of epochs when earnestly

devoted human beings, spiritually at one in loyalty to what
they believe the changeless ideals of truth and of righteousness, are torn asunder by outbreaks of such tremendous historic forces as make the mechanical forces of Nature seem
only thin parables, imaging the vaster forces still which we
vainly fancy to be immaterial. It is not until times like these
begin to fade and subside into the irrevocable certainty of the
past that we can begin to perceive the essential unity of their
grandeur. Nothing less than such supreme ordeal of conflict
can finally prove the quality and the measure of heroes; and
in the stress and strain, no human vision can truly discern
them all; but once proved deathless, the heroes stand side
by side, immortally brethren. So, by and by, we come won-
drously to perceive that we may honour our own heroes most
worthily—most in the spirit which they truly embodied; most,
I believe, as they themselves would finally bid us, if our
ears could still catch the accents of their voices—when we
honour with them their brethren who, in the passing years of
passion, seemed for a while their foes.

When we of America thus contemplate the Nineteenth Century, we cannot fail to rejoice in the memories it has left us.
They are so many, so full of inspiration, so various in all
but the steadfastness with which they withstand the deadening
test of the years, that it would be distracting, and even in-
vidious, to call the roll of our worthies at a moment like
this. What more truly and deeply concerns us is an evident
historical fact, generally true of all the human careers on
which our heroic memories of the Nineteenth Century rest
unshaken. Among those careers almost all—North and South,
East and West—won, in their own time, distinguished public
recognition. What I have in mind we may best realise, perhaps, if for a moment we imagine ourselves in some Nineteenth Century congregation of our countrymen, similar to
this where we are gathered together. Fancy, for instance,
the companies assembled to welcome Lafayette, far and wide,
during his last visit to our nation which he had helped call
into being. Among the American dignitaries then in their
maturity, and still remembered by others than their own
descendants, almost every one would already have been well

and widely known. A local stranger in any such assemblage,
to whom his host should point out the more distinguished
personages there present, would generally have found their
names not only memorable but familiar, just as we should
find them still. What would thus have been the case in 1824
would have stayed so, too, five and twenty years later. The
heroes of our olden time were mostly gladdened by the consciousness of recognised and acknowledged eminence.

Now, in contrast with them, let us try to imagine a figure
which might perhaps have attracted the eye in some such
American assemblage sixty-five years ago. Glancing about,
you might very likely have observed a slight, alert man,
with rather lank, dark hair, and deep, restless eyes. His
aspect might hauntingly have attracted you, and set you to
wondering whether he was young or old. On the whole you
might probably have felt that he looked distrustful, defiant if
not almost repellent, certainly not ingratiating or engagingly
sympathetic. Yet there would have hovered about him an impalpable atmosphere of fascination, which would have attracted your gaze back to him again and again; and each new
scrutiny would have increased your impression that here
was some one solitary, apart, not to be confused with the
rest. He would hardly have been among the more notable
personages, on the platform or at the high table. You might
well have wondered whether anybody could tell you his name;
and if, in answer to a question, your neighbour had believed
that this was Edgar Allan Poe, you might very probably have
thought the name unimportant. You would, perhaps, have had
a general impression that he had written for a good many
magazines, and the like, —that he had produced stories, and
verses, and criticism, —but the chances are that you would
not clearly have distinguished him unless as one of that affluent company of literati who illustrated the '40's, and who
are remembered now only because their names occur in
essays preserved among Poe's collected works. Almost certainly he would hardly have impressed you as memorable.
His rather inconspicuous solitude would not have seemed remarkable. Very likely, if you were a stranger thereabouts,
you would have paid little more attention to his presence, but

would rather have proceeded to inquire who else, of more solid quality, was then and there worth looking at.

All this might well have happened little more than sixty years ago; and though to some of us sixty years may still seem to stretch long, they are far from transcending the period of human memory. It would be by no means extraordinary if in this very company, here present, there were some who can remember the year 1845, or the election of President Taylor. Beyond question, every one of us has known, with something like contemporary intimacy, friends and relatives, only a little older than ourselves in seeming, to whom those years remained as vivid as you and I shall find the administration of President Roosevelt. That olden time, in fact, when amid such congregations as this, anywhere throughout America, the presence of Poe would hardly have been observed, has not quite faded from living recollection. At this moment, nevertheless, there is no need to explain anywhere why we are come together here, from far and wide, to honour his memory. Not only all of us here assembled, not only all Virginia, and all New York, and all New England, and all our American countrymen beside, but the whole civilised world would instantly and eagerly recognise the certainty of his eminence. What he was, while still enmeshed in the perplexity of earthly circumstance, is already a matter of little else than idle curiosity. What he is admits of no dispute. So long as the name of America shall endure, the name of Poe will persist, in serene certainty, among those of our approved national worthies.

In all our history, I believe, there is no more salient contrast than this between the man in life and his immortal spirit. Just how or when the change came to be we need not trouble ourselves to dispute. It is enough for us, during this little while when we are together, that we let our thoughts dwell not on the Poe who was but on the Poe who is. Even then we shall do best not to lose ourselves in conjectures concerning his positive magnitude, or his ultimate significance, when you measure his utterances with what we conceive to be absolute truth, or with the scheme of the eternities. We should be content if we can begin to assure ourselves of what he is, and of why.

The Poe whom we are met to celebrate is not the man, but his work. Furthermore, it is by no means all the work collected in those volumes where studious people can now trace, with what edification may ensue, the history, the progress, the ebb and the flow of his copious literary production. His extensive criticism need not detain or distract us; it is mostly concerned with ephemeral matters, forgotten ever since the years when it was written. His philosophical excursions, fantastic or pregnant as the case may finally prove to be, we need hardly notice. The same is true concerning his copious exposition of literary principle, superficially grave, certainly ingenious, perhaps earnest, perhaps impishly fantastic. All of these, and more too, would inevitably force themselves on our consideration if we were attempting to revive the Poe who was. At this moment, however, we may neglect them as serenely as we may neglect scrutiny of outward and visible signs, of such questions as those of where he lived and when and for how long, of what he did in his private life, of whom he made love to and what he ate for dinner, of who cut his waistcoats, and of how—if at all—he paid for them.

The very suggestion of such details may well and truly seem beneath the dignity of this moment. They are forced into conscious recognition, not by any tinge of inherent value, but because of the innocently intrusive pedantry now seemingly inseparable from the ideal of scholarship. We have passed, for the while, beyond the tyranny of that scholarly mood which used to exhaust its energy in analysis of every word and syllable throughout the range of literature. From sheer reaction, I sometimes think, we are apt nowadays, when concerned with literature, to pass our time, even less fruitfully than if we were still grammarians, in researches little removed from the impertinence of gossip; and gossip concerning memorable men and women is only a shade less futile than gossip concerning the ephemeral beings who flit across our daily vision. So far as it can keep us awake from superstitious acceptance of superhuman myth, it may perhaps have its own little salutary function. If it distract us from such moods of deeper sympathy as start the vagrant

fancies of myth-makers, it does mischief as misleading as
any ever wrought by formal pedantry, and without the lingering grace of traditional dignity. Your truly sound scholarship
is concerned rather with such questions as we are properly
concerned with here and now. Its highest hope, in literary
matters, is to assert and to maintain persistent facts in their
permanent values. In the case of Poe, for example, its chief
questions are first of what from among his copious and varied work has incontestably survived the conditions of his
human environment, and secondly of why this survival has
occurred. What contribution did Poe make to lasting literature? Does this justly belong to the literature not only of
America but of the world? In brief, why is he so memorable
as we all acknowledge by our presence here to-day?

   Stated thus, these questions are not very hard to answer.
The Poe of literature is the writer of a good many tales, or
short stories, and of a few intensely individual, though not
deeply confidential, poems. Stories and poems alike stand
apart not only from all others in the literature of America,
but—I believe we may agree—from any others anywhere.
Some profoundly, some rather more superficially, they all
possess, in their due degree, an impalpable quality which the
most subtle of us might well be at pains to define, but which
the most insensitive man imaginable can always, surely,
recurrently feel. The most remarkable phase of the impression they thus make is probably the complete and absolute
certainty of its recurrence. Turn, whenever you will and in
whatever mood, to any of Poe's work which has proved more
than ephemeral. Tale or poem, it may chance either to appeal to you or to repel you. In one mood you may think it
inspired; in another, you may find it little better than prank-
ishly artificial. You may praise it until dissent gape breath-
less at your superlatives; or you may relentlessly point out
what you are pleased to believe its limitations, its artificial-
ities, its patent defects. Even then, a very simple question
must bring you to pause. Let anybody ask you what this piece
of literature is like, or what is like it—let anybody ask with
what we should match it. Whether you love it or are tempted
to disdain it, you must be forced to the admission that it is

almost unique. Whatever its ultimate significance, the better work of Poe remains altogether itself, and therefore
altogether his. This gleams the more vividly when you come
to recognise how his individuality asserts itself to you, whatever your own passing mood, under all imaginable conditions.
The utterance of Poe is as incontestably, as triumphantly
itself as is the note of a song bird—as poets abroad have
found the music of the skylark, or of the nightingale, or as
our own country-folk find the call of the whippoorwill echoing
through the twilight of American woods.

His individuality, the while, is of a kind for which our language hardly affords a name more exact than the name poetic.
The accident that we are generally accustomed to confuse the
spirit of poetry with some common features of poetic structure can mislead us only for a moment. Poetry is not essentially a matter of rhyme or metre, of measure and quantity
in sound or syllable. The essence of it is not material but
spiritual. There are few more comprehensive descriptions
of it than the most familiar in the varied range of English
literature:

> The lunatic, the lover, and the poet
> Are of imagination all compact: —
> One sees more devils than vast Hell can hold, —
> That is, the madman; the lover, all as frantic,
> Sees Helen's beauty in a brow of Egypt;
> The poet's eye, in a fine frenzy rolling,
> Doth glance from heaven to earth, from earth to heaven;
> And, as imagination bodies forth
> The forms of things unknown, the poet's pen
> Turns them to shapes, and gives to airy nothing
> A local habitation and a name.

In the literature of America, and indeed throughout that of
the English language, you will be at pains to point utterances
more illustrative of these lines—I had almost said more
definitive of them—than you shall find in the tales and the
poems of Poe at their surviving best. Momentarily illusory
though his concrete touches may sometimes make his tales—
and he possessed, to a rare degree, the power of arousing

"that willing suspension of disbelief for the moment which constitutes poetic faith"—the substance of his enduring fantasies may always be reduced to the forms of things unknown, bodied forth by sheer power of imagination. To these airy nothings the cunning of his pen, turning them to shapes, gives local habitations and names so distinct and so vivid that now and again you must be loath to believe them, in final analysis, substantially unreal. Yet unreal they always prove at last, phantasmally and hauntingly immaterial. They are like figured tapestries spun and woven, warp and woof, from such stuff as dreams are made of. Only the dreams are not quite our own. The dreamer who has dreamed them is the poet who has woven them into this fabric, making them now forever ours as well as his. Without his own innermost life they could never have come into being at all. Without his consummate craftsmanship, itself almost a miracle, they must have hovered invisibly beyond the range of all other consciousness than his who dreamed them. Dreamer and craftsman alike, and supreme, it is he, and none but he, who can make us feel, in certain most memorable phases, the fascinating, fantastic, elusive, incessant mystery of that which must forever environ human consciousness, unseen, unknown, impalpable, implacable, undeniable.

The mood we are thus attempting to define is bafflingly elusive; it has no precise substance, no organic or articulate form. It is essentially a concept not of reason, or even of pervasive human emotion, but only of poetry—a subtly phantasmal state of spirit, evocable only by the poet who has been endowed with power to call it from the vasty deep where, except for him, it must have lurked in secret forever. If it were not unique, it could not be itself; for it would not be quite his, and whatever is not quite his is not his at all. So much we may confidently assert.

If we should permit ourselves, the while, either to rest with the assertion, or to stray in fancy through conclusion after conclusion toward which it may have seemed to lead us, we should remain or wander mischievously far from the truth. That Poe's imagination was solitary, like so much of the circumstance of his life, we need not deny or dispute.

Clearly, nevertheless, he lived his solitary life not in some fantastic nowhere, but amid the undeniably recorded realities of these United States of America during the first half of the Nineteenth Century. It is equally clear that throughout the years when his solitary poetic imagination was giving to its airy nothings their local habitations and their names, countless other poetic imaginations, at home and abroad, were striving to do likewise, each in its own way and fashion. Solitary, apart, almost defiant though the aspect of Poe may have seemed, isolated though we may still find the records of his life or the creatures of his imagination, he was never anachronistic. Even the visual image of his restless presence, which we tried to call up a little while ago, will prove on scrutiny not only individual, but outwardly cast in the form and the habit of its own time—to the very decade and year of the almanac. With his dreams, and with the magic fabrics into which he wrought them, the case is much the same. Neither dreams nor fabrics, any more than his bodily presence, could have been quite themselves—and still less could the dreams and the fabrics have combined forever in their wondrous poetic harmonies—during any other epoch than that wherein Poe lived and moved and had his being.

What I mean must soon be evident if we stop to seek a general name for the kind of poetical mood which Poe could always evoke in so specific a form and degree. The word is instantly at hand, inexact and canting if you will, but undeniable. It is the word which his contemporaries might carelessly, yet not untruly, have applied to his personal appearance, alluring to the eye if only for the quiet defiance of his temperamental solitude. It is the word by which we might most fitly have characterised such impulsive curiosity as should have impelled us, if we had seen him, to inquire who this mysterious-looking stranger might be. It is the word—misused, teasing, filmily evasive—by which we are still apt indefinitely to define the general aesthetic temper of his time, all over the European and American world. We use it concerning every manner of emotion and of conduct and the countless phases of literature or of the other fine arts throughout their whole protean ranges of expression. You will have guessed already, long before I shall have come to utter it, the word thus hovering in all our minds—the word romantic.

If we should hereupon attempt formally to define what this familiar word means, there would be no hope left us. Turn, as widely as you will, to dictionaries, to encyclopaedias, to volumes, and to libraries of volumes. Each may throw its ray of light on the matter; none will completely illuminate it or irradiate. You might as well seek words which should comprehend, in descriptive finality, the full, delicate, sensuous truth of the savour of a fruit or of the scent of a flower. Yet, for all this, there are aspects of romanticism on which we may helpfully dwell; and of these the first is an acknowledged matter of history. Throughout all parts of the world then dominated by European tradition, the temper of the first half of the Nineteenth Century was predominantly romantic. This was nowhere more evident than in the spontaneous outburst of poetry which, in less than twenty years, enriched the roll of English poets with the names of Wordsworth, Coleridge, Shelley, Keats, Byron, and Scott. Now the way in which this period of poetry was lately described in an American announcement of teaching may help us to perceive, with a little more approach to precision, one feature of what romanticism everywhere means. Some worthy professor, doubtless chary of indefinite terms, chose to describe the romantic poets as those of the period when the individual spirit revived in English literature. Poetic or not, this sound instructor of youth was historically right. The very essence of romanticism lies in passionate assertion of literary or artistic individuality. Wherefore, as we can now begin to feel sure, that romantic isolation of Poe's has double significance; it not only marks him, apart from others, as individual, but at the same time it defines him as an individual of his own romantic period.

We shall not go astray, then, if we ponder for a little while on this whole romantic generation. Before long, we may contentfully agree that the individualism of the romantic poets resulted everywhere from their passionate declaration of independence from outworn poetic authority. The precise form of poetic authority from which they fervently broke

free was the pseudo-classic tradition of the Eighteenth
Century—in matters literary a period of formal rhetorical
decency, and of a cool common-sense which had little mercy
for the vagaries of uncontrolled aesthetic emotion.

Already we may well feel insecure. We are straying, beyond peradventure, into dangerously elusive generalisation,
interminably debatable. Yet, if our present line of thought is
to lead us anywhere, we must not hesitate to generalise more
boldly still. That same Eighteenth Century, from which romanticism broke free, was not a sporadic and intrusive epi-
sode in the history of European culture; it was the culmina-
tion of a period at least five hundred years long. This period
began when the reviving critical scholarship of the Renaissance brought back to the dominant upper consciousness of
Europe a vivid understanding of the facts of classical antiquity;
and when, so doing, it began to suppress the vigorous and
splendid body of intervening tradition and temper to which we
have consequently given the name of mediaeval. In matters
literary, at least, the spirit which began with the Renaissance persisted until the Revolution of the dying Eighteenth
Century prepared the way for that Nineteenth Century, of
romantic freedom, wherein Poe lived and did his living work.

Already we can begin to see that there was some analogy
between the Middle Ages, which preceded the Renaissance,
and the epoch of romanticism which ensued after the Eighteenth Century. Both periods, at least, were free—each in
its own way—from the intellectual control of such formal
classicism or pseudo-classicism as intervened. A little
closer scrutiny of the Middle Ages may therefore help us to
appreciate what Nineteenth Century romanticism meant.
Throughout that whole mediaeval period, we may soon agree,
the intellect of Europe was authoritatively forbidden to exert
itself beyond narrowly fixed and rigid limits. European emotion, meanwhile, was permitted vagrant and luxuriant freedom of range and of expression. It might wander wherever
it would.

In contrast with this period, we can now begin to see, the
Renaissance may be conceived as an intellectual declaration
of independence; and through a full five hundred years, the

intellect of Europe was increasingly free. Its very freedom
made it, in turn, tyrannical. At least in the matters of temper and of fashion, it repressed, controlled, or ignored the
ranges of emotion which had flourished during its subjection.
In literature its tyranny extended far and wide. Though for a
while thought was permitted to range more and more unfettered, emotion was at best sentimentalised. So, when the
centuries of tyranny were past, poetry, if it were ever to
regain full freedom of emotional existence, if it were ever
to enjoy again the fine frenzy of creation, needed more than
independence. To revive the spirit which should vitally re-
animate its enfranchisement it needed to drink again from
the fountains for which it had thirsted for hundreds of years;
it must revert to something like the unfettered emotional
freedom of the Middle Ages.

To put the case a little more distinctly, the romanticism
of the Nineteenth Century could be its true self only when to
the intellectual maturity developed by five hundred years of
classical culture it could add full and eager sympathy with
the tremendous emotions of the Middle Ages, inevitably ancestral to all modernity. So the instinct was profoundly vital
which directed the enthusiasm of poets to mediaeval themes
and traditions, even though these were imperfectly understood. The inspiration derived from them came not so much
from any detail of their actual historical circumstances as
from their instant, obvious remoteness from the common-
sense facts of daily experience—matters judiciously to be
handled only by the colourless activity of intellect. It was
remoteness from actuality, above all else, which made romantic your romantic ruins and romantic villains, your
romantic heroines, your romantic passions, and your romantic aspirations. Yet even your most romantic poet must
give the airy nothings of his imagination a local habitation
and a name. Unreal and fantastic though they might be, they
must possess at least some semblance of reality; and this
semblance, whether bodily or spiritual, normally assumed
a mediaeval guise.

Throughout Europe such semblance could always be guided,
controlled, and regulated by the pervasive presence every-

where of relics, material or traditional, of the mediaeval
times thus at length welcomed back to the light. So far as
the full romantic literature of Europe deals with mediaeval
matters, accordingly, or so far as intentionally or instinctively it reverts to mediaeval temper, it has a kind of solidity
hardly to be found in the poetic utterance of its contemporary
America. For, at the beginning of the Nineteenth Century,
America was not only consciously further than Europe from
all the common roots of our ancestral humanity; it possessed
hardly a line of what is now accepted as our national literature. As patriots and as men of their time, the poets of
America were called on to add their part to romantic expression. To give their expression semblance of reality they
had no mediaeval relics to guide them, nor enduring local
traditions, thick and strong about them. They were compelled to rely on sheer force of creative imagination. Pre-
tentious as that phrase may sound, it is animated by a spirit
of humility. Its purpose is in no wise to claim superiority
for the romantic literary achievement of our country. It is
rather, by stating the magnitude of our national task, to explain our comparative lack of robust solidity, and to indicate
why the peculiar note of our country must inevitably have
been a note of our singular, though not necessarily of powerful, creative purity.

Now just such creative purity is evidently characteristic
of Poe. It may sometimes have seemed that among our eminent men of letters he is the least obviously American. A
little while ago, indeed, when I again turned through all the
pages of his collected works, I was freshly surprised to find
how little explicit trace they bore of the precise environment
where they were written. Throughout all their length, it
seemed, there was not a single complete page on which a
stranger might rest proof that it had come to the light in this
country. The first example which occurs to me—it happens
to be also the most generally familiar—will show you what I
have in mind: the mysterious chamber where the Raven
forces uncanny entrance is not American. The image of it
originated, perhaps, in a room still pointed out. Yet, so far
as the atmosphere of it is concerned, that room might have

been anywhere; or rather, as it lives far and wide, it is
surely nowhere. Yet, all the while, it has a strange semblance of reality. What is true here proves true throughout.
The Paris of Poe's detective stories is no real Paris; the
House of Usher never stood, or fell, on any earthly continent;
Poe's Maelstrom whirls as fantastic as the balloon or the
moon of Hans Pfaal. One might go on unceasingly, recalling
at random impression after impression, vivid as the most
vivid of dreams, and always as impalpable. There is nowhere
else romantic fantasy so securely remote from all constrain-
ing taint of literal reality; there is none anywhere more un-
conditioned in its creative freedom.

Thus, paradoxical though the thought may at first seem,
Poe tacitly, but clearly and triumphantly, asserts his nationality. No other romanticism of the Nineteenth Century was
ever so serenely free from limitation of material condition
and tradition; none, therefore, was so indisputably what the
native romanticism of America must inevitably have been.
Call his work significant, if you like, or call it unmeaning;
decide that it is true or false, as you will, in ethical or
artistic purpose. Nothing can alter its wondrous independence of all but deliberately accepted artistic limitations.
In this supreme artistic purity lies not only the chief secret
of its wide appeal, but at the same time the subtle trait which
marks it as the product of its own time, and of its own time
nowhere else than here in America, our common country.

American though Poe's utterance be, the while, it stays
elusive. When one tries to group it with any other utterance
of his time, one feels again and afresh the impression of its
temperamental solitude. This solitude is far from prophetic
or austere; it is as remote as possible from that of a voice
crying in the wilderness. Nor indeed was America, in Poe's
time, any longer a wilderness wherein a poet should seem
a stranger. Even though when the Nineteenth Century began
there was hardly such a thing as literature in America, the
years of Poe's life brought us rather copiousness than dearth
of national expression. As a New Englander, for example,
I may perhaps be pardoned for reminding you that in the year
1830 Boston could not have shown you a single recognized

volume to demonstrate that it was ever to be a centre of
purely literary importance. Twenty years later, when Poe
died, the region of Boston had already produced, in pure literature, the fully developed characters, though not yet the
complete and rounded work, of Emerson, and Longfellow, and
Lowell, and Holmes, and Whittier, and Hawthorne.

For the moment, I call this group to mind only that we may
more clearly perceive the peculiar individuality of Poe. In
many aspects, each of the New England group was individual,
enough and to spare; nobody who ever knew them could long
confuse one with another. Yet individual though they were,
none of them ever seems quite solitary or isolated. You
rarely think of any among them as standing apart from the
rest, nor yet from the historical, the social, the religious
or the philosophic conditions which brought them all to the
point of poetic utterance. Now Poe was in every sense their
contemporary; yet the moment you gladly yield yourself to
the contagion of his poetic sympathy, you find yourself alone
with him—aesthetically solitary. You might fancy yourself
for the while fantastically disembodied—a waking wanderer
in some region of unalloyed dreams. American though he be,
beyond any question, and a man of his time as well, he
proves, beyond all other Americans throughout the growingly
illustrious roll of our national letters, immune from impris-
onment within any classifying formula which should surely
include any other than his own haunting and fascinating self.

This isolation might at first seem a token of weakness.
Enchanting as the fascination of Poe must forever be—even
to those who strive to resist it and give us dozens of wise
pages to prove him undeserving of such attention—the most
ardent of his admirers can hardly maintain his work to be
dominant or commanding. Except for the pleasure it gives
you, it leaves you little moved; it does not meddle with your
philosophy, or modify your rules of conduct. Its power lies
altogether in the strange excellence of its peculiar beauty;
and even though the most ethical poet of his contemporary
New England has immortally assured us that beauty is its
own excuse for being, we can hardly forget that Emerson's
aphorism sprang from contemplation of a wild flower, in the

exquisite perfection of ephemeral fragility. A slight thing
some might thus come to fancy the isolated work of Poe—the
poet of Nineteenth Century America whose spirit hovered
most persistently remote from actuality.

If such mood should threaten to possess us, even for a
little while, the concourse here gathered together should
surely set us free. That spirit which hovered aloof sixty and
seventy years ago is hovering still. It shall hover, we can
now confidently assert, through centuries unending. The solitude of weakness, or of fragility, is no such solitude as this;
weak and fragile solitude vanishes with its earthly self, leav-
ing no void behind. Solitude which persists as Poe's is per-
sisting proves itself by the very tenacity of its persistence
to be the solitude of unflagging and independent strength.
Such strength as this is sure token of poetic greatness. We
may grow more confident than ever. We may unhesitatingly
assert Poe not only American, but great.

So we come to one further question, nearer to us, as
fellow-countrymen, than those on which we have touched before. It is the question of just where the enduring work of
this great American poet should be placed in the temperamental history of our country—of just what phase it may be
held to express of the national spirit of America.

That national spirit—the spirit which animates and inspires
the life of our native land—has had a solemn and a tragic history. From the very beginning of our national growth, historic
circumstance at once prevented any spiritual centralisation
of our national life, and encouraged in diverse regions,
equally essential to the completeness of our national existence, separate spiritual centres, each true to itself and for
that very reason defiant of others. So far as the separate
phases of our national spirit have ever been able to meet one
another open-hearted, they have marvelled to know the true
depth of their communion. Open-hearted meeting, however,
has rarely been possible; and throughout the Nineteenth Century—the century in which Poe lived and wrought—it was
hardly possible at all. Americans were brethren, as they
were brethren before, as they are brethren now, as they
shall stay brethren, God willing, through centuries to come.

For the while, however, their brotherhood was sadly turbulent. They believed that they spoke a common language. The
accents of it sounded familiar to the ears of all. Yet the
meanings which those accents were bidden to carry seemed
writhed into distortion on their way to the very ears which
were straining to catch them. It was an epoch, we must sadly
grant, of a Babel of the spirit.

So, throughout Poe's time, there was hardly one among
the many whom the time held greater than he to whose voice
the united spirit of our country could ever unhesitatingly and
harmoniously respond. What I have in mind may well have
occurred to you, of Virginia, when a little while ago I named
the six chief literary worthies of New England in the Nineteenth Century. They were contemporaries of Poe. They were
honest men and faithful poets. They never hesitated to utter,
with all their hearts, what they devotedly believed to be the
truth. Every one of them, too, was immemorially American.
Not one of them cherished any ancestral tradition but was
native to this country, since the far-off days of King Charles
the First. In every one of them, accordingly, any American—
North or South, East or West—must surely find utterances
heroically true to the idealism ancestrally and peculiarly our
own. Yet it would be mischievous folly to pretend that such
utterances, speaking for us all, can ever tell the whole story
of the New England poets. They were not only Americans, as
we all are; they were Americans of Nineteenth Century New
England. As such they could not have been the honest men
they were if they had failed to concern themselves passionately with the irrepressible disputes and conflicts of their
tragic times. They could not so concern themselves without
utterance after utterance fatally sure to provoke passionate
response, or passionate revulsion in fellow-countrymen of
traditions other than their own.

Even this sad truth hardly includes the limitation of their
localism. Turn to their quieter passages, descriptive or
gently anecdotic. Strong, simple, sincere, admirable though
these be, they are excellent, we must freely grant, chiefly
because they could have been made nowhere else than just
where they were. In New England, for example, there was

never a native human being who could fail to recognise that
"Snow Bound" was a genuine utterance straight from the
stout heart of his own people; nor yet one, I believe, who,
smile though he might at his own sentimentality, could resist the appeal of the "Village Blacksmith." We may well
doubt, however, whether any Southern reader, in those old
times, could have helped feeling that these verses—as surely
as those of Burns, let us say, or of Wordsworth—came from
other regions than those familiar to his daily life.

The literature of New England, in brief, American though
we may all gladly assert it in its nobler phases, is, first of
all, not American or national, but local. What is thus true
of New England is generally true, I believe, of literary expression throughout America. Turn, if you will, to the two
memorable writers of New York during the first quarter of
the Nineteenth Century—Washington Irving and James Feni-
more Cooper. They were good men, and honest men of letters, and admirable story-tellers. Neither of them, however,
wasted any love on his neighbours a little to the eastward;
both hated the unwinsome surface of decadent Puritanism;
and neither understood the mystic fervour of the Puritan
spirit. So, even to this day, a sensitive reader in New England will now and again discover, in Irving or in Cooper,
passages or turns of phrase which shall still set his blood
faintly tingling with resentment. Whatever the positive merit,
whatever the sturdy honesty of most American expression in
the Nineteenth Century, it lacked conciliatory breadth of feeling. Its intensity of localism marks it, whatever the peace-
fulness of its outward guise, as the utterance of a fatally
discordant time.

Now it is from this same discordant time that the works of
Poe have come down to us; and no work could have been much
less inspired by the local traditions and temper of New England. To his vagrant and solitary spirit, indeed, those traditions must have been abhorrent. New England people, too,
would probably have liked him as little as he liked them. You
might well expect that even now, when the younger generations of New England turn to his tales or his poems, sparks
of resentment might begin to rekindle. In one sense, perhaps,

they may seem to; for Poe's individuality is too intense for
universal appeal. You will find readers in New England just
as you will find readers elsewhere, who stay deaf to the
haunting music of his verse and blind to the wreathing films
of his unearthly fantasy. Such lack of sympathy, however,
you will never find to be a matter of ancestral tradition or of
local prejudice or of any sectional limitation; it will prove
wholly and unconditionally to be a matter only of individual
temperament. Among the enduring writers of Nineteenth
Century America, Poe stands unique.

Inevitably of his country and of his time, he eludes all limitation of more narrow scope or circumstance. Of all, I believe,
he is the only one to whom, in his own day, all America might
confidently have turned, as all America may confidently turn
still, and forever, with certainty of finding no line, no word,
no quiver of thought or of feeling which should arouse or
revive the consciousness or the memory of our tragic national discords, now happily for all alike heroic matters of
the past. The more we dwell on the enduring work of this
great American poet, the more clearly this virtue of it must
shine before us all. In the temperamental history of our
country, it is he, and he alone, as yet, who is not local but
surely, enduringly national.

As I thus grow to reverence in him a wondrous harbinger
of American spiritual reunion, I find hovering in my fancy
some lines of his which, once heard, can never be quite forgotten. To him, I believe, they must have seemed only a
thing of beauty. He would have been impatient of the suggestion that any one should ever read into them the prose of
deeper significance. It was song, and only song, which possessed him when he wrote the words:

> If I could dwell
> Where Israfel
>   Hath dwelt, and he where I,
> He might not sing so wildly well
>   A mortal melody,
> While a bolder note than this might swell
>   From my lyre within the sky.

Is it too much to fancy, nevertheless, that to-day we can hear that bolder note swelling about us as we meet here in communion? None could be purer, none more sweet; and, beyond the shadow of a doubt, none could more serenely help to resolve the discords of his fellow-countrymen into their final harmony.

Democracy

From the very beginning of our national existence, —from the days when independent America first consciously cherished our national ideal of Liberty, and throughout the years when our national ideal of Union was growing to its slow and vital maturity, —our third national ideal, that of Democracy, has been vigorous. But since the Civil War, it has become so much more insistent than it used to be that it sometimes seems to have taken on a form almost new. Almost everywhere throughout recent American utterances about public affairs, or social, you will find Liberty assumed, and Union, too; Democracy, on the other hand, you will be apt to find asserted in terms like those in which the subjects of a sovereign feel bound, on public occasions, to make open professions of personal loyalty. Of course if you like, you may call this a matter of passing fashion; but on sober thought, you can hardly help recognizing it to be something deeper. Our popular professions of loyalty to Democracy often sound impressively like the confession of a creed; and, in truth, the American ideal of Democracy has developed various creed-like qualities. Creeds, for one thing, though not intended to be tyrannical, are apt to prove so when confronted with unsympathetic freedom of speech or even of thought. At best, they are not kindly disposed to searchings for truths which they do not happen to specify. Something like this now seems the case with Democracy as a national ideal of our country. There are moments when the unquestionable truth which inspires it, like the truth which must be at the heart of any creed, seems a little obscured by our unquestioning devotion

to reverend phrase. At such moments America sometimes
seems to be passing into the misty region of superstition.

This superstitious deference to the mere name of Democracy, this almost timorous acceptance of domination by a
venerated word, is perhaps most evident in certain commonplaces now current concerning private affairs. On general
principles, for example, you would suppose that when a
question of policy presents itself to people interested in our
universities,—whether the question concern academic interests, or those perhaps more absorbing ones involved in the
athletic contests now so congenial to American taste,—the
single thing to consider would be how either learning or sport
could most prosper. Yet over and over again you will find
other considerations uppermost. To take a trivial example,
perhaps the more characteristic for its very triviality, it is
not long since an inconspicuous man was chosen to high undergraduate office in one of our older colleges, for no other
evident reason than that he honorably earned money, during
spare hours, by waiting on table at a college restaurant. The
choice was applauded as "democratic." This popular adjective is constantly used as a crushing argument, too. Quite
lately the chairman of a college athletic committee, criti-
cised for having shown "favoritism" towards football, base-
ball, and rowing, to the neglect of other equally respectable
sports, answered in an open letter that his course was dic-
tated by the "democratic" principle that people in general
take most interest in the sports which he favored. The use of
the word "democratic" indeed has gone further still. You will
find it frequently applied in America to any line of human
conduct which happens to present itself as agreeable. When
royal personages have travelled here, for instance, and have
behaved, as they behave everywhere, with pleasant simplic-
ity, our newspapers and the public have frequently been so
complimentary as to describe them as democratic.

Any mention of Democracy which should not imply unquestioning devotion to it is apt, meanwhile, to excite blind in-
dignation. People so prone to idealism as Americans cannot
help imagining that their ideals are absolutely true; and
absolute truth is universal. Not to aspire toward it would be

sinful in anybody, no matter whom or where. Wherefore we
most honestly prate of Democracy in all the glory of its absolute universality; and if any of us chance to raise a question of this universality, we run the risk of trouble. The very
question now before us—a simple attempt to find out what the
word really means among our countrymen—is apt to seem
disloyal; and consequently to excite hot-headed patriots to
utterances concerning tar and feathers.

And yet, universal as we may profess and believe our
American ideals to be, we have already seen that those of
Liberty and of Union cannot be quite understood until we appreciate those phases of them which are distinctly national.
Something similar and even more impressive proves true
when we begin to inquire how, for all its extravagant phrase,
the ideal of Democracy has actually presented itself to the
native American mind. So far as one can define the term
"democracy," it means here, as everywhere else, the rule
of the people,—as distinguished from autocracy, the rule of
an individual sovereign, or from aristocracy, the rule of a
governing class. To this extent, no doubt, Europe and America would be in complete agreement. The connotation of the
word in America, however,—the range of emotion which it
kindles here,—is peculiar to ourselves. To Europe, the rule
of the people means something gloriously Utopian. To America, this rule means something immemorially familiar.
Among us, indeed, the national ideal of Democracy has a
kind of emotional sanction unparalleled elsewhere.

This emotional sanction springs from the special conditions
under which our national history began. From causes into
which we need not now enter,—for it were fruitless here to
dispute how far our forefathers were devoted to this or that
abstract political principle,—the original governments of the
American colonies, from the time of their foundation in the
early seventeenth century, assumed on the whole a democratic form. Though the constitutions of the different colonies
differed from one another, the greater part of the public
officers were everywhere chosen by some form of majority
vote. What is more, although the conditions of suffrage differed with almost every colonial constitution, there was

hardly any colony, or even any town or county where, as a matter of fact, the suffrage was not more widely extended than was generally the case, during the seventeenth and the eighteenth centuries, with similar constituencies in Europe. In Europe, one may generally say, the suffrage was everywhere a privilege. In America, to begin with, it was probably the same; but the course of our history soon began to make the suffrage a privilege so general that people came to regard it as a right. By the time of the American Revolution, accordingly,—by the time when our nation and its ideals reached the stage of conscious vitality,—something like a democratic system had become traditional throughout the colonies. For a full five generations, at least in the elder colonies, the fathers and their children had been in the habit of electing most of the officers who should control the affairs of government. During the years when native America had slowly developed this state of customary law, democratic utterance and indeed the use of the word "democracy" had been infrequent and even unpopular; but more or less democratic practice had been the uninterrupted rule of our political development.

A curious fact results. When revolutionary America, full of the enthusiasm of the later eighteenth century, echoed back the French philosophical declarations of the rights of man, it used concerning Democracy, just as it used concerning Liberty, terms which still sounded radical and destructive. At the same time, the democratic generalizations of revolutionary America really proclaimed no unprecedented policy, hostile to the form of government under which the revolutionists had hitherto been living. Rather, in the case of Democracy as truly as in that of Liberty, the living strength of revolutionary America lay in its determination to maintain unchanged a system of customary law and of established government which had already proved immemorially favorable to American prosperity and American righteousness. There seems to be a popular impression nowadays that the constitutions of the American colonies were tyrannically autocratic. This was so far from the case that, by 1775, a marked departure from some essentially democratic form of government, anywhere throughout the thirteen colonies, would have been as destructively revolutionary as accession to a democratic form of government proved to the old régime of France, or as aspiration toward democracy seems to-day in Russia. Now nothing is more clear to any one who grows familiar with American temper than that, for all our vagaries of utterance, we do not like abrupt breaches of historical continuity. Radical, then, as the terms of our democratic assertion must always sound, radical as our revolutionary forefathers may have believed themselves in the heat of conflict, the fervor with which those idealistic yet orderly ancestors of ours insisted that we must maintain a democratic system of government was really, like so much else in their conduct, an evidence of their political conservatism.

How deep this conservative impulse among native Americans has been,—how deep, indeed, it remains,—must be evident to any one who fully understands the structure of American society, and who is frank enough to admit its nature. Throughout our history, to be sure, there has been less legal distinction between one sort of men and another than has existed almost anywhere else. The generalization, so popularly repeated since it was phrased for us in the Declaration of Independence, to the effect that all men are created equal, undoubtedly records genuine American sentiment. But, on the other hand, there has never yet been a moment in American history when one or another social class has not enjoyed a degree of personal consideration not popularly accorded to others. In the early days of New England, for example, public opinion acknowledged the hegemony of the clergy. A glance at any among the older catalogues of Harvard or of Yale will tell the story. Until a few years ago the names of all graduates of either college who became ministers were printed in italics, to distinguish them from their brethren of the laity. For more than a century after the foundation of Harvard, meanwhile, the names of Harvard graduates were entered in the lists of their classes, not in alphabetical order, but in the order of their established social precedence; and for the first sixty years of Yale, the same practice prevailed there. In both cases, accordingly,

if a student who ultimately became a minister chanced to be
of inferior social origin according to the complicated rules
of colonial precedence, his italicized name stood near the
end of the list of his class. Look for that of his son, however,
a generation later. Whether this son were minister or lay-
man, you will find, his name will have risen well toward the
head of the class list, in recognition of the fact that his
father had occupied a pulpit. The old hierarchy of New England was poor in the goods of this world, to be sure, but it
had, even on earth, what no money could buy,—an edifying
degree of social consideration. What is more, it exerted an
extraordinary degree of almost arbitrary social power. It
was not hereditary; any able man was welcome to join it; and
its privileges and its dignity were sanctioned by little more
than consenting custom. But these privileges were so fixed,
this dignity was so assured, that there is something nearer
truth than fancy in the familiar passage where Dr. Holmes
celebrates the Brahmin caste of New England.

Those same old catalogues of New England record other
forms of recognized social precedence as well. Men who
held high public office in the colonies had the happiness of
seeing their names printed in capital letters, and of seeing
the names of their children head the lists of classes in which
social dignity had not yet succumbed to alphabetic precedence. Yet the system of government which surrounded these
dignitaries was by no means undemocratic in principle; on
the contrary, it was a system in which an almost unprecedented degree of popular suffrage had long existed, and was
on the whole strengthening. The simple fact is that among
the most deeply rooted traditions of New England was the
frank recognition of certain social classes as superior to
others. So long as the higher rank was freely accessible to
able men of whatever birth, and so long as it in no wise em-
powered those who attained to it to transmit their privileges
to unworthy descendants, it never proved unfavorable to
democratic institutions.

At least in New England the days of recognized social distinction came to an end before the Revolution. The last Yale
class of which the list preserves the pristine social order

took its degrees in the year 1768; Harvard modernized its
lists only four years later. But legislation cannot kill tradition. And something like the tradition which had animated the
elder college catalogues has lingered in America to this day.
In the course of years, to be sure, the preëminence of the
clergy has somewhat declined; at this moment they enjoy no
higher consideration than is accorded to members of the
other learned professions. But that very term—"the learned
professions"—must arouse, in any mind familiar with America, associations which will go far toward proving that
something like the pristine hegemony of the Yankee clergy
long persisted throughout the regions which their spirit once
dominated. The minister of any Yankee village in the later
days of his social domination had two pretty clearly recognized fellows. These were the lawyer,—the squire, as Yankee dialect used to call him,—and the doctor. Both were
college men; both had enjoyed the highest opportunities for
education which the America of their time offered. In the
process of enjoying these opportunities they had made friends
with other men of their intellectual class from various parts
of the country. After graduation, these college men dis-
persed themselves widely; but they never forgot their college
training and their college friendships, which made them, like
the elder clergy, a sort of brotherhood. They had no special
or official power; their dignity was protected by no legal
privilege; but it was recognized and respected by public
opinion. It was a social fact as undeniable as the dignity of
any landed gentry of Europe, secured though that gentry
might seem in its position not only by the consent of popular
esteem, but also by positive mandates of law. Though the
days of village triumvirates are doubtless past, almost as
finally as the days when Yankee pulpits were tyrannical, the
tradition which gave dignity to the learned professions seems
vital still. In its modern form it is rather more highly generalized. But no one who really knows American temper
today can doubt its reverence for a college education. There
is something pathetic in the wide and genuine respect with
which Americans who have never been members of a college
regard the degree of Bachelor of Arts.

The truth is that, however fervently Americans may have
believed that all men are created equal, they have never
gone so far as to insist that all men must permanently remain so. Undoubtedly, from the Revolution to this day,
floods of popular utterance have pretended that American
principle does not sanction the existence of any social order.
In these torrents of eloquence there has been so much truth
as is involved in the fact that Americans have always been
jealously careful that social order should not develop into
fixed privilege. But here the truth of them ends. There was
never a more American aphorism than one which chances not
to be of American origin,—the assertion, popularly attributed to Napoleon, that careers should be open to talent.
Whatever a man's origin, any American would agree, he
ought to have every possible chance for a career which
should bring his powers and his usefulness to their fullest
fruition. This word "career" would hardly be disowned by the
most ardent democrat between the Atlantic and the Pacific.
A good many fiery democrats, meanwhile, might not quite
realize all that it implies. The very conception of a career
involves some end or goal for that career to attain; and any
end or goal which should make an earthly career stimulating
in prospect, can exist only where social order is reasonably
recognized. American democratic sentiment has not been
misled by its conventional utterances. Its unconventional utterances are more pregnant. The human race, somebody has
said, is just like any other; it is no fun unless some one
comes out ahead. We have never seriously attacked that
social order which makes careers possible. We have only
maintained that, so far as may be on earth, social order
shall not needlessly obstruct the career of any talent.

From this sentiment two or three results have followed.
To begin with, as we have seen, American conviction has
constantly regarded any sort of privilege with jealous suspicion; for privilege—even though, as often proves the case,
it may stimulate aspirants to better work—can hardly help
seeming like an obstacle in the course of any able man who
does not happen to possess it. An extreme example of this
conviction deeply impressed me, a few years ago.

There was in my part of the country a local politician who
hated Civil Service Reform. To be sure, even his enemies
admitted that he was honest: he did not fill his pockets with
public moneys. For years, however, he had devoted himself
to the task of placing and of maintaining in public office a
great number of persons whose only qualification seemed to
be unswerving devotion to the political party of which his
considerable talent for organization had made him the local
leader. Accordingly all reformers agreed in denouncing him
as unscrupulous, and, as I was apt to read reform newspapers, I made no doubt that he was a very bad man. A friend
of his, with whom I chanced to talk about him, threw a different light on his character.

He was a boss, no doubt; but he was as far from self-
seeking as the best reformer who ever tried to purify the
civil service; any one who knew him in private life could not
fail to recognize his honest devotion to a cherished political
ideal. His ideal, of course, was radically different from that
held by the newspapers which indignantly denounced him. In
their view, the only proper way to govern an American community was to consider as candidate for any office, high or
low, only men who were well equipped for the duties thereof.
To the boss whom they execrated, on the other hand, a contrary principle, held with equal ardor, seemed the only one
which patriotic citizens could conscientiously cherish. This
was that the most precious and inalienable right involved in
American citizenship is the right, undoubtedly possessed by
us all, to be elected or appointed to any office whatever. In
describing this conviction, his friend used a striking, though
perhaps barbarous, Latin term. The deepest conviction of
the boss, he said, —a conviction in the support of which that
earnest patriot was prepared to make any sacrifice, —was
that every American citizen possesses the jus officii, that
is, the right to hold office if he can attain it. And this right
the boss believed so sacred as to hold the principles of civil-
service reformers not only distasteful, but abominable. To
admit for an instant their pretence that citizenship was not
full qualification for any office whatever would be to deny the
universality of our precious American jus officii.

To my unpractical mind, nurtured by academic commonplace, this conception of political principle was rather startling. Would the boss hold as a matter of principle, I ventured
to ask by way of reductio ad absurdum, that a laborer who
had never had a bank-account might properly be put in charge
of the finances of a large city? Beyond question, his friend
answered; if any citizen could get himself regularly in
charge of anything, the boss would earnestly maintain that
he had a right, as indefeasible as any monarch's right of
succession, to keep in charge of it as long as he could. Indeed, this right was the most sacred of all conferred by the
fact of citizenship. No one desired that offices should be
mismanaged, of course; but frequent mismanagement of
office would be preferable to a bureaucratic system which
should deny the jus officii to the humblest of citizens. The
devices of civil-service reformers, —examinations, promotion by merit, and the like, —this eccentric idealist accordingly detested, as nothing more nor less than privilege in
disguise. His views, though sympathetically presented to me
by his friend, did not command my approval. It was impossible to deny, however, that they were enlightening. And I
rather think that, for all their extravagance, they indicate
some honest American impulses too generally ignored by us
of academic habit, who have been apt to accept as gospel the
lucubrations of that eminent foreign journalist, the late Mr.
Godkin.

Again, the public opinion of America has not only been
jealous of all privilege. Perhaps more characteristically
still, it has maintained its jealousy, so obvious throughout
the Constitution, of any preponderant accumulation of power,
no matter where. It is fond of asserting that our government
is a government of laws and not of men; and, assuming this
principle as fundamental, it may often be distracted from
inconvenient scrutiny of any public question by the solemn
assertion—sincere or tricky—that the tendency of the matters
involved is to place undue power in executive hands, or leg-
islative, or judicial, or corporate, as the case may be. Here
again the dreaded word often has more instant effect than any
state of fact. Americans hold formulas very sacred; and our

honest jealousy both of privilege and of power makes us
abruptly sensitive whenever we are told that anybody is
grabbing either. We are very suspicious of any pretence to
superiority on the part of those who endeavor to lead us. And
yet we eagerly admire our true leaders. For all our distrust
of privilege and power, we are not at heart ungenerous. No
people is more humbly willing to recognize and to cherish its
national heroes.

As time passes some of these heroes prove worthy and endure. Others vanish into the obscurity from which chance
plucked them for a little while. Like any other country,
America errs, has erred, and will err again and again, in
estimating contemporaries. Throughout our history, however,
we have never wavered in our willingness to acknowledge
merit. When you stop to think, you will find this fact significant; for all our prating of equality, it means, Americans
have never denied that you and I, ordinary human beings,
are living in a world where for one reason or another some
of our fellows must always be our betters. They are not instantly obvious. They are not always to be found among such
people as in other countries might claim hereditary privilege
or power. But they exist; and it is generally possible for
them to demonstrate their excellence, if we will judge them
by the tests of daily life. Whoever can thus demonstrate excellence will nowhere find more hearty and unstinted recognition than in this America, where all men, though created
equal, are content to admit that careers should always be
open to those who deserve them.

This reverence of America for demonstrated excellence is
so genuine, so deep, so widespread, that when a national
worthy is once established in our popular esteem few Americans stop to think where he sprang from. We have always
had our various social classes,—rich and poor, educated and
uneducated, more or less characterized by rectitude of personal conduct. Among these classes there has been a good
deal of mutual suspicion, sometimes culminating in passionate mutual misunderstanding. Yet, for all these differences
between class and class, Americans of the true tradition
have always been at one in paying honor to fellow-citizens

who have proved themselves worthy. It makes no difference
to Americans of any class whether their heroes sprang from
among themselves or from surroundings which they generally
incline to distrust.

At the same time, any one who knows the America of the
nineteenth century must recognize that throughout the country
we have been apt to delight most in careers which have begun
obscurely. One can easily see why. Such a career is sure to
be varied and picturesque. Besides, our American jealousy
of privilege involves a sympathy with hardship, which sometimes leads to paradoxical results. The very circumstances
which are conventionally assumed to be advantageous—learning, friends, money—often work the other way. Indeed this
preference for the less fortunate in origin appears in private
life as well. A poor young man, starting in any profession,
is far more apt to find practice coming his way than is his
richer fellow next door. Even in matters so far from public
life as college athletics, I have known instances in which the
man who was admitted to be the ablest candidate for the
office of captain of a college team, has been defeated by a
candidate whose decisive claim was that he was a man of less
fashion than his abler competitor. And whoever was an
American boy thirty or forty years ago must surely remember a popular series of juvenile books with titles which imply
exactly the kind of sentiment now in mind. "The Printer
Boy," "The Bobbin Boy," and so on, they were named. You
might well have guessed them to have been sympathetic
studies of infancy in misfortune. Nothing of the kind. One
and all were somewhat legendary, but ardently patriotic
biographies of eminent Americans who had begun their careers in decent obscurity.

That conventional phrase brings us to one deeply human
reason for this popular sentiment. In life, as in painting,
chiaroscuro, a deep contrast of light and shade, attracts the
eye. It excites the attention, particularly of the untutored;
and particularly the untutored have a tendency to dwell on
the shade rather than the light. I remember, for example,
a pious address concerning a Revolutionary general in which
something like half an hour was devoted to the circumstance

that in youth he had been apprenticed to a village blacksmith. You would have supposed that the entire company present was content to linger indefinitely in admiration of this industrious image. Indeed, they may perhaps have supposed themselves so, for most of them would have assured you that no American could claim more honor than is due to an honest day's work. Yet if you had soberly questioned these patriotic people, you would have found them in the end willing to admit less admiration for a man who had remained at the forge all his life, than for this one who, having begun his career as a blacksmith, ended it as a victorious soldier. The true secret of American delight in careers of humble origin lies not so much in the humility of their origin as in the picturesque contrast between their origin and their achievement.

As has often been the case before, we have been generalizing extremely. No concrete instance could better illustrate our generalizations than the career of that American who during the last forty years has grown most secure in his rank among our national heroes,—a rank second only to that of Washington. I mean, of course, Abraham Lincoln. As surely as Washington may be called the Father of our Country, Lincoln may be called the Saviour of our Union. His greatness, as well as the inestimable value of his services to the nation, become more and more evident with time. Already, indeed, his memory is enshrouding itself in something like sanctified tradition,—so sacred that you are often met with indignant protestation if you dwell long on certain facts, plain facts of his career. And yet, stripped of all legend, that career is not only the most interesting, but the most reassuring in all our recent history.

Of the various social classes in America during the nineteenth century, none seems much less promising than the poor whites of the South and of the Southern frontier. Yet as you read the story of Lincoln's early years you are forced to admit that some such dubious environment was that from which he sprang, and amid which he began his career. At that time the dominant class throughout the country, and nowhere more conspicuously than in the regions surrounding his early experience, were the lawyers. Everywhere throughout

America, accordingly, the bar attracted ambitious and able youths, particularly if they were disposed to concern themselves with public affairs. Like all lastingly great men, Lincoln was normal; so he wanted to be a lawyer. He was born in a log cabin. He had little if any chance of formal education. Surrounded by illiterate people, he was virtually compelled to educate himself. As is so often the case in America, his difficulties at once proved stimulating and saved him from the dangers of distracted attention. From the beginning he showed himself to be one of those rare men who have the faculty of somehow or other accomplishing whatever they earnestly undertake. Long before he appeared in public life, accordingly, or at least long before his name was widely known, he had risen to a condition far above the humility of his origin. Yet he would not have been the Lincoln of history, he would not have been even quite the Lincoln of tradition, if he had not retained, to the very end of his heroic life, many uncouth traces of the obscure condition from which he so admirably emerged.

To a great degree, the while, these traces of his origin were superficial. So far as any one was ever disposed to infer from them that he could not deal with social conditions and personal characters strange to his early years, they were completely misleading. Like many other men whom the course of world history has proved enduringly great, he possessed an imaginative power so strong and so sympathetic, that he never found himself confronted by any class of human beings whom he could not sympathetically understand. The quality I have in mind is nowhere more conspicuous than in his magnanimous sympathy with political opponents, even amid all the controversies of the Civil War. But in another sense the rude exterior of Lincoln, which venerating posterity has sometimes tried to disguise, was deeply significant. It never suffered those who knew him, even in the full splendor of his almost imperial career, to forget that he had emerged from very different surroundings.

Born a peasant, he grew to be an almost absolute sovereign. Think what that means, and you can hardly fail to understand how inevitably a life so comprehensive must have

passed in its rising course through every plane of American
society. As a matter of fact this was almost literally true.
At one time or another Lincoln had known on equal terms
every imaginable kind of American, high and low. His rise
from beginning to end was regular, steady, and normal. To
use the tritest of figures, he climbed the ladder of fame with
firm foot, step by step. A less sympathetic man than he
might have been apt, as he rose, to lose vivid memory of
whence he came, or at least to find the circumstances of the
moment distracting. The supreme greatness of Lincoln was
that, as he persevered through circle after circle of his
terrestrial Purgatory, he never forgot the road he had travelled, or whom he had met and passed on the way. With
every phase of American life he had been on equal, friendly,
familiar terms. His career is the most typical in all our
history of what Americans mean when, without defining the
words even to themselves, they use that much abused phrase
"a man of the people."

In certain moods that phrase sounds demagogic. But the
moment we realize how truly Lincoln's career represents
what we mean by the words, we can begin to feel that a man
of the people as Americans conceive him is about as different
from a demagogue as anything of flesh and blood can be.
Demagogues only prate of ideals. Lincoln, a true American
man of the people, cherished ideals, aspiring towards them.
He was a practical politician, and a skilful, —with a robust-
ness of method perhaps beyond the unhesitating reach of men
who nurture their political ideals in the hot-houses of academic culture. Yet he was devoted as unswervingly as Webster himself to our national ideal of Union, which more than
any one else of his time he preserved and consecrated. He
was unswervingly devoted as well to that newer phase of our
national ideal of Liberty, crescent in the North throughout
his life, which more and more emphasized the liberty of the
individual. Believing in these ideals with all his heart, he
early perceived that the institution of slavery was dangerously threatening to both. Slavery disunited our national
interests; and it denied to millions of human beings the freedom which the Declaration of Independence proclaimed as an

inalienable right of all men. Yet his utterances concerning slavery are very different from those of virulent Abolitionists. However honest and enthusiastic, those apostles of liberty ran to excesses of speech which often make you wonder whether they were more stirred by love for slaves or by hatred of slave-holders. With Lincoln the case was different. Of all the evils of slavery the greatest in his mind was the fact that its growth, its extension, and indeed, as he came at last to see, its very existence, imperilled our national Union.

This Union, with all its increasingly ideal sanction, was what he had most deeply at heart. No Abolitionist deplored the social evil of slavery more earnestly than he; yet I believe that he is somewhere recorded to have said that if the Union could have been saved without freeing a single slave, he would have been content with the saving of the Union. He never forgot, in short, that slave-holders had rights as precious, in their way, as the rights of the slaves whom Northern Abolitionists seemed to think the only factor in the question. Popular Northern tradition—the cant of crude oratory and unintelligent school-teaching—has misrepresented his most memorable act as President. His Emancipation Proclamation, which marked the end of negro slavery, was in no wise the doctrinal assertion of the rights of men which Yankee children are taught to suppose it; in purpose and in specific terms alike, it was an official declaration, published by the executive magistrate of a sovereign power at war with dangerous opponents, that unless those opponents laid down their arms, the chief source of their wealth should be confiscated, as a measure of warfare. Lincoln was no such radical as would ruthlessly sweep away vested rights, just because he happened to think them deplorable. If he had really done so,—always supposing that such a deed could have been brought within the range of his official power,—he would perhaps have been a great man. The complexion of his greatness, however, would not have been so fine as that which we can discern in the magnanimous greatness which he really embodied. It would have lacked the final grace of imaginative sympathy with those whom his fate compelled him to oppose even to the death.

During his career as President, circumstances more than once required him to assume and to exert a degree of personal power hardly paralleled by any other sovereign of the nineteenth century. And yet, all the while, he remained as far from arbitrary as if everything he did had been duly sanctioned by unanimous consent. He looked upon himself not as an irresponsible dictator, nor yet as the representative of a single section of the country or of a single political party; he felt, rather, that the sad necessities of his time had imposed on him the grave duty of embodying the nobler spirit and of carrying out the deeper purposes of our whole people. That phrase "the people" he often used. And two of the instances in which he used it have lingered living in popular memory. Of these characteristic utterances perhaps the more familiar may seem trivial. It persists, indeed, chiefly because of its high place among those shrewd saws which will always remind us how Lincoln could sweeten the bitterness of life with unexpected infusions of humor. On some occasion when popular opinion looked dangerous, —when the team of the Union was plunging and rearing, —Lincoln is said to have cheered some alarmed companions by remarking that "You can fool some of the people all the time, and you can fool all the people some of the time; but you can't fool all the people all the time." In which humorous words there lies hardly hidden one of the most devout extant confessions of our national democratic creed.

His other utterance about the people which Americans will never forget is widely different. There is no note of humor in it. There could have been none without some discord which should have impaired its harmony. At least in popular memory, the crucial moment of the Civil War still seems to have been that when the only serious invasion of the North by Southern arms was finally repulsed on the soil of Pennsylvania. A few months after that decisive Union victory, they held a solemn service on the battlefield of Gettysburg, where a permanent burial-place had been set aside for the Northern soldiers who had fallen there. President Lincoln came to the ceremony, for the purpose of delivering the

chief speech of the day. It is generally believed that, amid
his pressing duties he had made small preparation for this
occasion. The little manuscript which contained his words is
said to have been hastily and carelessly written, almost if
not quite on his way to the spot where he uttered them. Yet
among all the occasional speeches in our history that Gettysburg address stands unique, not only for its gravely
intense beauty and power, but also for the classic brevity
which makes every syllable of it emotionally significant. It
is so short that we may read every word of it here and now:

"Fourscore and seven years ago our fathers brought forth
on this continent a new nation, conceived in liberty, and
dedicated to the proposition that all men are created equal.
Now we are engaged in a great civil war, testing whether
that nation, or any nation so conceived and so dedicated, can
long endure. We are met on a great battlefield of that war.
We have come to dedicate a portion of that field, as a final
resting-place for those who here gave their lives that that
nation might live. It is altogether fitting and proper that we
should do so. But, in a larger sense, we cannot dedicate—
we cannot consecrate—we cannot hallow this ground. The
brave men, living and dead, who struggled here have consecrated it, far above our poor power to add or detract. The
world will little note, nor long remember what we say here,
but it can never forget what they did here. It is for us the
living, rather, to be dedicated here to the unfinished work
which they who fought here so nobly advanced. It is rather
for us to be here dedicated to the great task remaining before
us—that from these honored dead we take increased devotion
to that cause for which they gave the last full measure of
devotion—that we here highly resolve that these dead shall
not have died in vain—that this nation, under God, shall have
a new birth of freedom—and that government of the people,
by the people, for the people, shall not perish from the
earth."

Exactly what Lincoln meant by "the people" one might be
at pains to say. At unthinking moments the words undoubtedly
suggest only folks of the lesser sort or the humbler,—of the
kind, in short, whom we have in mind when we talk of the

masses as distinct from the classes. Lincoln may thus seem
to imply that men in this world, whosoever and wheresoever
they be, ought to strive toward the end of flat equality. And
yet, on reflection, we can hardly believe that he intended to
make any such blindly generous denial of all human experience. We must remember that when he spoke of "the people"
he was not merely a public official or an occasional orator;
for the moment he was in a position of almost absolute sovereignty. He was the chief magistrate of a nation at war for
its very life. And just as surely as the previous life of that
nation had been possible only because all classes therein had
accepted the necessity of public order, so the actual persistence of that nation through the awful stress of civil war was
possible only if every citizen should stay content humbly to
hold his merited place in a public order which must be sustained unless the Union were to become chaotically extinct.

What is more, if we allow the radical utterances so frequent in America to betray us into the fancy that Americans
have ever insisted on an impossible degree of equality among
mankind, we have failed to understand the ancestral spirit of
our country. The very phrase of the Declaration of Independence which Lincoln interweaves in his Gettysburg Address,
asserts that men are created equal, not that men must remain so. And we have already reminded ourselves, enough
and to spare, that the more characteristic spirit of America
has never abandoned itself to excessive insistence on equality
in daily practice. Every man, it has stoutly held, should
have the best possible chance for such a career as his talents
make him fit for. Beyond this, American feeling has never
generally maintained anything more radical than that all men,
insomuch as they are created equal, should be protected, so
far as may be, in their equal right to register their consent
to the firmly established form of government under which
alone our society and our nationality can prosper.

These conceptions may really be discovered in the word
"people," as Lincoln used it. Whether he was conscious of
the fact or not, his wonderfully comprehensive life had en-
abled him sympathetically to know the whole range of American society. He himself was a man of no one class, high or

low; he was truly a man of the people. If he had remained in
the humble station from which he originated, he would have
been, not a man of the people, but only one of a worthy, but
limited section thereof. If he had remained a practising lawyer, or a local politician, in the Middle West, he would have
been, not a man of the people, but a man of a distinct kind
in one section of our country. If throughout his public career
he had been what he was in his final years, a virtual sovereign, he would have been, not in any true sense a man of the
people, but only a magnificent embodiment of efficient personal government. For our people of America are not the
rich, nor yet the poor; they are not the learned, nor yet the
ignorant; they are not the wise, nor yet the foolish; not the
good, nor yet the erring. From the beginning to this day the
true people of America has been composed of all alike, —
rich and poor, learned and ignorant, and all the rest together, each in his place, none unworthily secure, however high
his place, none undeservedly oppressed, however low. And
what makes Lincoln our most magnificently comprehensive
man of the people, in whose name he spoke so earnestly, is
that among all the varied and changing classes of which that
people has been and shall be composed, there was none
which he could not meet on equal terms, as one of themselves.

   Something like this must everywhere mark the difference
between a true man of the people and a demagogue. But by
no means everywhere need a man of the people be all that
Lincoln was. For he was peculiarly, inevitably American.
He was not only a completely representative man of the entire people whose national existence his career preserved;
he was a man of our American people as distinguished from
any other in the whole course of history. And this he could
not have been unless in his more earnest moods he had been
stirred to the very depths of his grave and tender being by
a kind of idealism which could not help regarding the passing
facts of this troublous earthly existence as poignant symbols
of some infinite, eternal truth beyond and above any transitory experience of humanity. In all his utterances there is
none which Americans must feel in spirit more fully and

significantly native than the very short address which he
delivered in March, 1865, when for the second time he was
inaugurated as President.

As a war measure, we may remember, and by no means
as a tyrannical imposition upon others of his personal con-
victions concerning abstract right, he had proclaimed, two
years before, that all slaves in all States which remained
under arms against the Union should thenceforth be free. The
result of that proclamation had already been the complete ex-
tinction of slavery throughout the regions subject to the law
of the United States. And when for a second time Lincoln took
upon himself the responsibilities of the chief magistracy, it
was to this fact that his mind recurred. The terms in which
he spoke of it are deeply characteristic not only of him but
of all his America, which is ours as well. And what makes
those words so deeply characteristic, —what made Lincoln so
comprehensively American, as he uttered them, — is the
almost mystic idealism which pervades them. The more
familiar you grow with them, the more surely you group
them in memory with those Hebrew prophecies which the
consent of twenty centuries has held to be divinely inspired.

"Fellow-countrymen," he said, ". . . on the occasion
corresponding to this four years ago, all thoughts were anx-
iously directed to an impending civil war. All dreaded it—all
sought to avert it. While the inaugural address was being
delivered from this place, devoted altogether to saving the
Union without war, insurgent agents were in the city seeking
to destroy it without war—seeking to dissolve the Union, and
divide effects, by negotiation. Both parties deprecated war;
but one of them would make war rather than let the nation
survive; and the other would accept war rather than let it
perish. And the war came.

"One-eighth of the whole population were colored slaves,
not distributed generally over the Union, but localized in the
Southern part of it. These slaves constituted a peculiar and
powerful interest. All knew that this interest was, somehow,
the cause of the war. To strengthen, perpetuate and extend
this interest was the object for which the insurgents would
rend the Union, even by war; while the government claimed

no right to do more than to restrict the territorial enlarge-
ment of it.

"Neither party expected for the war the magnitude or the
duration which it has already attained. Neither anticipated
that the cause of the conflict might cease with, or even before, the conflict itself should cease. Each looked for an
easier triumph and a result less fundamental and astounding.
Both read the same Bible, and pray to the same God; and
each invokes His aid against the other. It may seem strange
that any men should dare to ask a just God's assistance in
wringing their bread from the sweat of other men's faces;
but let us judge not, that we be not judged. The prayers of
both could not be answered—that of neither has been answered fully.

"The Almighty has His own purposes. 'Woe unto the world
because of offences! for it must needs be that offences come;
but woe to that man by whom the offence cometh.' If we shall
suppose that American slavery is one of those offences
which, in the providence of God, must needs come, but
which, having continued through His appointed time, He now
wills to remove, and that He gives to both North and South
this terrible war, as the woe due to those by whom the offence came, shall we discern therein any departure from
those divine attributes which the believers in a living God
always ascribe to Him? Fondly do we hope—fervently do we
pray—that this mighty scourge of war may speedily pass
away. Yet, if God wills that it continue until all the wealth
piled by the bondsman's two hundred and fifty years of unre-
quited toil shall be sunk, and until every drop of blood drawn
with the lash shall be paid by another drawn by the sword, as
was said three thousand years ago, so still it must be said,
'The judgments of the Lord are true and righteous altogether.'

"With malice toward none; with charity for all; with firmness in the right, as God gives us to see the right, let us
strive on to finish the work we are in; to bind up the nation's
wounds; to care for him who shall have borne the battle, and
for his widow, and his orphan—to do all which may achieve
and cherish a just and lasting peace among ourselves, and
with all nations."

Six weeks later the war was at an end, and Lincoln was
dead, murdered by the hand of a mad or half-mad actor, who
fancied himself the Brutus of local liberty. Truly, "the Almighty has His own purposes." Lincoln was spared the task
of reconstructing the Union which he had saved. He died
heroic in the moment of his heroic triumph with all his virtues dominant, with all his trivialities and failings momentarily forgotten. And that momentary forgetfulness of all in
him which was not admirable is deepening into the oblivion
where all of him that is not best shall finally sink from sight.
What was best in him lives and shall live, so long as our
America shall persist to enshrine it. For beyond any other
figure in our history that great and constant man of the people reveals himself as the true embodiment of our own
American democracy.

From the very beginning, as no one can deny, the surface
of this American democracy has often seemed worse than
careless. When a people so emotional as Americans find
themselves perforce addicted to material pursuits, they are
sure to show themselves vagrant and impulsive, in a thousand perversities of thought, of speech, and of conduct.
Americans have constantly done things which shall provoke,
according to your mood, either cynicism or despair. They
will do so to the end of their time. Yet, all the while, this
story of their lesser lives has never been the whole. More
even than many of ourselves can yet quite realize, the American people have striven to keep their aspirations pure, and
their heroes worthy. The heart of a democracy devoted to
orderly idealism can never be vulgar. There is no vulgarity
in our national heroes, nor yet in the sentiment which has
chosen them. For this sentiment is one of humble and honest
reverence for the superiority of a few human beings who
have risen above the mass of mankind. As such superiors,
we cherish the memories of Washington, of Lincoln, and of
Grant. The true spirit of America is magnanimous, too. In
their own critical days Lincoln and Grant seemed only sectional heroes; to-day they belong to our reunited nation. And
there are not lacking signs that, in times not so very far
away, our reunited nation shall cherish equally such other

heroic memories as those of Jackson and of Lee. At heart,
in its nobler moments, American democracy is at one. It
has never yet refused respect and reverence to those who
have proved themselves worthy.

All this sounds vague again. I can hardly illustrate it better than by recounting a little experience of my own, not very
long ago. While travelling in Europe, I was deeply impressed
by the manner in which an American newspaper, regularly
sent me, discussed public affairs. If a foreigner asked what
kind of people Americans really are I found myself apt, instead of attempting to set forth psychologic abstractions, to
call his attention to its pages, and to tell him that he could
there discover much of what is best in the temper of our
country. In a mood like his, I wrote to one of the editors that
his work seemed to me truly and deeply native.

The personal letter which he wrote me back contains a
passage so characteristic that, quite without his leave, I
shall venture to set it down here; for I know of nothing anywhere which better expresses our national temper. Here are
his words: "Faith in democracy,—if I may be allowed to define that terribly abused word,—is a part of my religious
faith. That is, I believe in the undeveloped capacity of every
man to comprehend the divine laws under which he lives, the
divine order of which he is or should be a part. To understand those laws and to give to them a joyful and loyal obedience is self-government and is the secret of liberty both for
the individual and for society. To promote this self-government, I think I may truly say, is the aim of my life. Because
with all her faults there is more of this ideal in the national
consciousness of America than in that of any other people,
I rejoice in and believe in 'what is most truly and most
deeply native.'"

That little passage, so simple, yet so admirably expressive of our real American spirit, was carelessly thrown off
in a casual letter. Had it been expressed more deliberately,
it might hardly have seemed quite so truly and deeply native
as it is.

In view of this, there is one phrase in my friend's letter
which may set us to pondering. In his first sentence he speaks

of democracy as a "terribly abused word." So it is among us
at this moment, in more senses than one. We prate about
democracy in more and more wildly general terms, forgetting what in more solemn moments it has truly signified to
the American forefathers who have left their heritage in our
care. We have long allowed the word to tyrannize over us
even in our private lives, until it sometimes seems as if
half our fellow-countrymen would be disposed to assert that
we could not be American unless we conducted our family
affairs with due respect to a majority vote,—ordering no
dinner until some process of domestic suffrage had ascertained what three out of five children might prefer to eat that
day. This unresisted tyranny of the word "democracy" is
perhaps our most instantly palpable abuse of it.

Terrible, all the same, is hardly the word for an abuse so
laughable as this. Another phase of this abuse may more
justly be described by the solemn adjective. Our pratings
concerning democracy nowadays are apt to sound as if they
totally neglected that divine order on which my friend so admirably insisted. One can see why our tongues and even our
wits thus run away with us. Orderly though American idealism may have been at heart, the most deeply characteristic
phase of our national temper is not that it has been thus
orderly, but that it is so intensely ideal. This national idealism, we have seen, has sprung in no inconsiderable degree
from the intense self-searching of our ancestral Calvinists,
who spent their whole higher lives in striving to discern that
solemn fact, the unalterable will of God. Now the will of God
may perhaps be recognized; but once recognized it may
never be scrutinized or questioned without sin. Once perceived it blazes with all the inscrutable splendor of eternally
absolute truth. And it blazed thus before ancestral America,
as the archetype of all ideals. Wherefore it has dazzled us
to this day. Lesser ideals, like this loftiest of all, are in
their nature ideal; they are not material facts; and so, confusing the lesser with the greater, we have been apt to
conceive all ideals as essentially beyond dispute—as absolutely and eternally true. We have confused the ideals of
earth with the immortal ideal of divinity; we have unwittingly

made for ourselves idols. Thus, truly, there is something terrible in the manner in which we permit the mere word "democracy" to tyrannize over us, bowing down to it as to a graven image, abusing ourselves, and terribly abusing, the while, the name of the national ideal which we now most ardently cherish.

Again, there is another reason why our modern pratings of democracy should give rise to what among ourselves must seem an increasingly terrible abuse of the word. Any one who contemplates the tendency of European history can hardly deny that the whole world which we have called civilized is beginning, for better or worse, to relax its grasp on its old systems of government. Content until revolutionary days with its historic structure, European civilization has been disposed for more than a hundred years to prefer as the constitution of the future a system of democracy based on the dogmatic assumption of the rights of man. However noble its formulas and its aspirations, this European democracy still remains to a great degree doctrinarian and untested. At this moment, for example, there is no more important fact in French politics than the separation of the Church and the State; and in the very last article on this subject which I chanced to read—an article by a man deeply sincere, but fervently devoted to the principles of the French Revolution—my eye has lighted on such passages as these: "The laity of France is making ready to write the book of which the declaration of the rights of man is only a chapter." . . . "The circumstances of the moment make our legislators think that this crisis is only a rupture with all churches; in truth it is the normal and necessary result of democracy which means the rule of the laity, that is of the people." . . . "And finally there are at this moment in France only two kinds of people, —those who have received from the past centuries a treasure which they jealously preserve without being willing that it should be scrutinized either by themselves or by others; and those who, whatever treasure the centuries have left them, seek, march, surge toward the future."

The commonplaces of our American democracy harmonize with these wider generalizations of modern Europe. And

surely the dreams of European democracy, doctrinarian and
untested though they be, are full of generous aspirations.
However noble these aspirations, nevertheless, there lurk
within them deep and almost obvious dangers. One of these
dangers is implied in those fervid sentences from the French
at which we have just glanced. Democracy, this writer feels,
as distinguished from hierarchy, means the rule of the laity
as distinguished from the rule of the church. It means, in
other words, not that each class shall share in the government; but that one class shall dominate over another. The
only difference between democracy and hierarchy proves to
be that in democracy the dominating class shall be a larger
and more comprehensive, a less carefully trained and cultivated, a less cohesive and on the whole a lower. Now the fact
of class domination, whatever the class which dominates,
must tend toward tyranny. And when you come to tyranny,
the tyranny of democracy is probably the most intolerable
which the human mind can imagine. However generous its
intentions, they cannot exceed the initial benevolence of a
thousand monarchs and oligarchies, who have flourished and
fallen through the changing course of history. Nor is there
any reason to expect that a dominant laity or proletariat shall
be a whit less arbitrary than a dominant individual. The most
dangerous and most destructive kind of tyranny you can conceive of, indeed, is that which should be based on the whims
of a mob. Toward something like this the impulses of European democracy now seem tending.

There is another danger in the utterances of this generalized democracy,—less material no doubt, but perhaps for
that very reason more terrible. The dangers of the spirit exceed beyond compare the dangers of the flesh. There is no
assertion of European democracy now more incessant—more
eloquent or more blatant, as you chance to find it—than that
which maintains the absolute dogma of human equality. Liberty, equality, and fraternity are the watchwords of the
French republic, and of European democracy throughout the
elder continent. Nowadays equality is the watchword of the
three on which European democracy is most disposed to
dwell. And to the European mind equality seems to mean

something different from what it meant to the authors of the Declaration of Independence. It does not mean that all men are created equal; it means that everybody must remain equal from the cradle to the grave. This conception is doubtless generous; the moment you scrutinize it, however, you cannot fail to perceive that it denies the right of any man to strive for superiority, for excellence, for that which may distinguish him from the mass of his fellows. In the seeming generosity of this impulse, accordingly, there lurks damnable spiritual danger—a danger never better phrased than in those words of the Anglican Litany, "From envy, hatred, and malice, and all uncharitableness, Good Lord, deliver us."

These dangers, so deeply inherent in the democracy of modern Europe, are dangerous in America too. They lurk venomous in the utterances of all demagogues, and demagogues you shall find throughout our history, so long as our democracy shall exist. There are moments, happily enough, when we of America can deride them as comic; but in the heat and danger of any critical political contest, our humor tends to fade; and those of us who begin to feel grave find these demagogues and their utterances discouraging things and despairing. Now and again they seem like the evil prophets of some socialistic anarchy to come. And yet, all the while, whoever knows the course of our history may there find comfort. From the beginning to this day the tempests of our demagogic folly have so far proved only passing. The names of the demagogues have loomed large; but again and again they have vanished into nothingness. Each in turn is swiftly forgotten. There is not yet one of them among our heroes. You shall search history in vain for a less demagogic worthy than Lincoln, the most comprehensively typical man of our American people.

Yet Lincoln, you may say, was only a man; and he has been dead and gone these forty years. For all the pricelessness of his memory, we are now exposed, almost as if he had not been, to the dangers of democratic tyranny,—of a class tyranny, the more ruthless for the very reason that the class which threatens to tyrannize over us shows itself constantly lower and lower. In these fears there may be truth.

One thing surely is true; there is nothing more essentially
sacred in the power of a sovereign people than there is in
the power of a sovereign individual. Any sovereignty, if it is
to endure, must be just, wise, generous, moderate, self-
restrained. If Democracy, which is everywhere assuming
the control of the modern world, is to endure, it must govern wisely, moderately, with generous self-restraint.
Whether any consciously sovereign people can thus conduct
itself is the deepest question which now confronts the modern
world.

And here it behooves us of America to see ourselves as we
are bound to be seen in the history of the centuries to come.
At this moment we are the only living people to whom democracy has been confided, not as a philosophical abstraction,
but as an ancestral practice. Democracy, as we conceive it,
is so deeply rooted in our tradition that to those who have
been nurtured in the full spirit of our native America, any
departure from a democratic system of government would be
the most fundamental of revolutions. This is what to-day
makes our country so solemn a fact. It is not because of our
wonderful material powers and resources that we are now
significant; it is because with us, and with us alone, democracy can show what it can achieve, when free from the savage dangers of destructive revolution.

To our history, past and to come, the world must accordingly turn with the greatest concern, in the times which are
at hand. For on the course which our history takes, more
than upon that of any other, must depend the course which
must be inevitably taken by the history of the coming world.
Whither this democratic era is truly tending, neither you nor
I can ever live finally to know; but of one thing we may feel
confident. When the years to come are past, and when those
who contemplate the century now beginning can see it in final
completeness, the course of the single traditional democracy
now existing—of our own America—shall prove most tremendously whether at this moment of crescent democratic force
our world is passing into the dusk of a new barbarism, or
into the dawn of a new dispensation.

The Relation
of Literature to Life

In this effort to give some account of the French as I found them, I have followed, so nearly as might be, the course of my experiences in France. Beginning with the universities, my official connection with which opened my opportunities, I have touched on what I next came to observe, the structure of society; I have then told of that more intimate social fact, the family; and finally I have tried to make clear my impression of the French temperament, as these various phases of life in France revealed it to me. Our considerations henceforth will be of somewhat different character. We shall occupy ourselves with the manner in which this national temper displays itself in connection with some of the chief interests of modern French life, —literature, religion, and politics. And first with literature.

One thing must instantly be evident. French life and character, as we have here approached them, have not appeared quite as foreigners, and particularly English-speaking foreigners, are accustomed to expect. At least in America, the French are supposed to be frivolous and unprincipled. And in our present considerations we have found them so remarkable for seriousness and for regularity that I may well seem to have been writing deliberately <u>virginibus puerisque</u>.

If I had been, I should not have written much otherwise. And here arises perhaps the most perplexing question which must beset anyone who, having been familiar with foreign prejudice concerning France, finds himself among French

people in their daily lives. The France evident to casual
travellers and generally set forth in such French literature
as comes to foreign notice is very different from the France
you come to know for yourself. The external aspect of them
is identical, no doubt; just as the language is. In both, too,
as everywhere else on earth, there is a regularly organized,
orderly society, side by side with various vagary from social
order. The true difference lies in the fact that those who
know France from report are apt to suppose vagary to be the
rule of French life, while those who know France from personal experience will probably agree that the most profound
characteristic of the French is rather their conscientious
devotion to their regular duties. The question accordingly
becomes that of how such divergent impressions can result
from a common cause.

To begin with, we may well put aside some obvious reasons
for the opinion usually held by foreigners. One general authority for it may be found in the gossip of tourists. It is
honest, gleeful or indignant as the case may be, and reduc-
ible to a simple fact true of travel anywhere. No matter
where a stranger may stray, he will see instantly the most
irregular, the least respectable, the most broadly commonplace phase of the society which surrounds the hotel where
he has taken up his momentary abode. Throughout the nineteenth century Paris has been perhaps the most attractive
capital in Europe. It has attracted to itself, at least, more
visitors than any other. More than any other, accordingly,
it has developed into what seem permanently established
forms those various catch-penny devices for the allurement
of strangers which make any great city, in certain aspects,
more like a mere watering-place than one always quite understands. In fact, however, the Paris of travel—the hotels
and the theatres, the streets, the museums and the restaurants, together with endless other places of public entertain-
ment—is the least Parisian, and the least French Paris
imaginable. It is only one more of the great places of amusement, open—for human good or ill—all over the world.

Not long ago a friend happened to tell me a bit of experience which just here may be illuminating. He was himself

a respectable citizen of New York. Something had called him
to Brazil, where, without personal introduction, he had
passed two or three weeks at Rio de Janeiro. He had returned
home with the honest conviction that there was not a decent
human being in the whole Brazilian republic. Every prospect
had been pleasing, but men and women had displayed an ultimate vileness of character in which the corruption of Europe
and the crudity of America seemed indistinguishably blended.
So Brazil was not sweet in the nostrils of this reputable
American, who honestly believed that he knew Brazil from
personal observation. The limits of his experience were
startlingly revealed to him a year or two later. On a steamer
going to Europe he had the pleasure of meeting a congenial
fellow-traveller, of about his own age. This gentleman presently turned out to be a Brazilian, who had passed a month
or so in America on his way to Paris. He had come to the
United States as a stranger, with no means of access to society; he had spent a few days at the chief hotels of our principal Eastern cities; and his honest conclusion, derived from
personal observation, had been that nothing imaginable could
exceed the social corruption of Boston and New York. Personal respectability he conceived unknown in either, just as
my American friend had conceived it unknown in Brazil. On
the voyage they grew to be great friends; and as each was
blest with a sense of humor, they corrected each other's
impressions instead of quarrelling about them. They parted
happier men and wiser, having come to understand that what
each had seen in the other's country was only what casual
travellers must always find everywhere. Vice is less various, far less individual, than virtue. Of all commonplaces,
it is the most irredeemably monotonous.

Once for all, then, we may put aside the disrepute of
France so far as it comes to us from travellers' tales. It is
no more French than it is Brazilian or American. We can
hardly deal in so summary a way with another source of our
impression of this deplorable social fact. Whoever has
looked into the windows of French shops, where books and
prints are displayed, whoever has glanced at such French
comic papers, and the like, as stray into restaurants and

barbers' shops, and into club reading-rooms elsewhere than
in France, can hardly fail to have found endless warrant for
our conventional faith in French naughtiness. He may have
been attracted; he may have been shocked; the one sure
thing is that he will not have been enlightened. For full enlightenment, indeed, he will need an experience open only to
those who come to know French people as they actually live.
Then he will slowly grow aware that in decent French opinion
this kind of publication is no more reputable than it seems to
him, or to anybody else. It does not express life in any comprehensive sense; it is so far from expressing life, as life
presents itself to Frenchmen of the better sort, that it does
not even appeal to them. They ignore it, just as respectable
Americans ignore the obnoxious advertisements of patent
medicines so frequent in the cheaper sort of newspapers or
on flaming bill-boards. The simple truth is that all over the
world you will find disreputable objects of commerce, kept
technically within the law. Those most obvious among ourselves are devices for encouraging teetotalers to drink adul-
terated alcohol; those most obvious in France are designed
rather to encourage effrontery; but both alike, and all other
such matters, are really to be classed together. Any American would be surprised and pained to find a worthy French
family fuddling itself with one of those proprietary nostrums
which help debase country folks and tired shop-girls in so
many parts of the United States. The sentiments of Frenchmen, when brought face to face with certain Parisian publications in the reading-rooms of American clubs, are said to
be even more bewildering. They sometimes permit themselves to wonder, I am told, whether their surroundings can
really be consonant with self-respect.

So far, accordingly, as our notions concerning the French
may be traced either to travellers' stories or to objects of
shady commerce, we may dispose of them once for all. They
are simply stupid. Very clearly, however, this fails to cover
the whole matter. What remains for us to explain is considerable. It consists of novels written by men who have attained the highest degree of personal recognition as serious
masters of literature—a seat among the forty immortals of

the Académie Française. It consists of plays which everybody in Paris, French as well as foreign, flocks to see, and
eagerly discusses. It consists of that great body of literature
—in many respects the most admirable of all modern times—
which any student of modern French must eagerly and seriously study. Whoever has tried to teach French in American
institutions of learning where co-education prevails, must
have found himself aghast. Countless writers who cannot be
neglected will bring him before long to dangerous ground. In
general, there can be no denial that the novelists and the
dramatists of modern France set forth a state of society
deeply different from that described in English or American
works by writers of equal dignity. Any foreigner would naturally infer that the society on which their work is based must
be far more corrupt than ours. Of course, it may be. In
matters so intimate as this no one can ever feel sure of anything more than personal conviction. Beyond question, however, no one who is cordially received by the modern French
would derive from his intercourse with them any such impression as we have all derived from what they write about
themselves; and anyone familiar with society in modern England or America would probably find it about what literature
had led him to expect. Our precise purpose now is to account, as well as we can, for this deep difference.

In trying to account for it we must soon remind ourselves
of a fact asserted whenever this question arises. Throughout
the modern English-speaking world, at least so far as living
memory extends, there has been a general assumption that
standard literature is addressed to everybody who can read,
—men and women, old and young, boys and girls. The very
restiveness occasionally displayed by English or American
writers in the presence of this convention only serves to
define it. Most of us accept the limitations of it just as we
accept those of the language in which we are forced to express our meaning as best we may. How completely different
this assumption is from that of modern France, I may best
indicate perhaps by a specific instance. After one of my lectures at the Sorbonne, a French lady, accompanied by her
daughter, a girl of eighteen or so, did me the honor to

present herself to me with a request for a little expert advice. The daughter, it appeared, had learned to read English fluently and desired to extend her reading beyond the classic novels of Cooper and of Sir Walter Scott. Could I name some contemporary works which she might find interesting? My impromptu answer took the form of a few hasty memoranda setting forth the names of some standard writers, and of three or four popular magazines. The good lady was perplexed. I could hardly have understood her, she thought; she had not asked me what authors were eminent, she had asked what books were suitable for a young girl; as to the magazines, she was right, she believed, in supposing them to be addressed to the general public—in which case they were, of course, not the kind of thing she had in mind. I tried to explain that any young girl might range securely throughout the work of the novelists in question, and that our most respected magazines would not cloud the innocence of a nursery. My efforts seemed fruitless. She attributed my opinions, I think, to my obviously imperfect command of French. The fact that a popular literature could anywhere be addressed to a public so comprehensive as to include respectable youth seemed to her inconceivable. And how her daughter's education proceeded in the matter of English, I have never been privileged to know.

The public to whom French literature is addressed, in short, is always assumed to be mature. To grown-up people anywhere you may obviously say things unmentionable to children. Maxima reverentia debetur pueris; nobody questions that, either in France or among ourselves. The difference is that we are disposed to display our reverence for youth by excessive attention to our library shelves, and that the French display theirs by the more summary process of keeping the library door shut.

Such differences of national impulse as this are never without cause. The cause in this case may be traced pretty readily to the different conceptions of education, and particularly of domestic education, entertained by the French and by ourselves. The fundamental question of education everywhere is how to prepare children for maturity. In English-

speaking society, which, as we have seen, is far less systematic than that of France, this is held to mean that we must
train them to make their way. In the much more systematic
society of France, on the other hand, it seems rather to
mean that we should fit them to take their places in the
world. Slight as the difference between these assumptions
may seem, it tends to widely different conclusions of principle. Everybody knows everywhere that all things are not
what they seem. Everybody knows that preaching and practice can nowhere quite agree. Everybody knows that so long
as civilization persists we must keep on both preaching and
practising—bringing precept and practice into some semblance of harmony, each for himself, as best we may. We
try to meet these conditions by giving our children the greatest degree of experience which is within the range of safety;
the French prefer to surround theirs with the greatest degree
of protection which is within the range of prudence. Each of
us is prone to excess. Our children are sometimes left too
much to themselves; theirs sometimes appear distorted by
undue control. You will feel the difference when you compare
a French Lycée with an English public school. You will feel
it just as much, and hardly more, when you compare a Yankee play-room with the children's corner of any French
foyer. We try to make our children face fact, insisting less
than we used to on abstract principle. The French still insist
on principle, dissembling, so far as they can, discordant or
unwelcome fact. We desire to develop the individual; with
them the prime impulse is to maintain the social system.

In any such contrast as this it is hard to avoid the appearance of urging one side as better than the other. I have been
trying not to do so. The reward of our methods is found, perhaps most surely, in the frank personal candor of our young
people. The reward of theirs is found most surely in the deep
intensity of their family affections. In each process there
must be a stage disturbing and even alarming to people who
believe in the other. But when we come to the end and ask
ourselves which of the methods makes the better men and
women, there is no answer. Each, honestly pursued, leads
to the same result. What almost surely ends ill is an attempt

to train the children of either society in the manner generally upheld by the other.

F ar as we may have seemed to stray from literature, we
have only been reminding ourselves of one reason for the
widely different assumptions concerning its function among
ourselves and in F rance. Our whole conception of education
implies our belief that literature should be addressed to
everybody who can and will read it. Their whole conception
of education implies their contrary belief that literature
should be addressed only to those who have outgrown domestic supervision. Our custom compels more reticence than
theirs. To each of us his own custom is bound to seem a law
of nature. So they think our novels hypocritical, and theirs
seem to us corrupt; and both of us are wrong.

When we foreigners fully agree that F rench literature is
addressed only to mature people, we may, perhaps, begin
to understand it better. One delightfully evident feature of it
is clearly due to this fact. I mean the beautiful precision and
finish of F rench style. Whatever a F rench writer's topic, he
must never forget that his readers will be of such age and
disposition as to be competent and scrupulous critics of his
literary manners. When, like any English writer, you are
addressing so widely general a public that you cannot feel
sure of their intelligence, you may permit yourself, even
without quite realizing that you do so, considerable carelessness in expression. When, like all F rench writers, you are
addressing only a mature and highly cultivated public, you
must be more careful, even though you do not deliberately
try to be, of duly accepted conventions. In consequence you
will generally be more agreeable. Observance of convention
is always pleasant; surprising people are not comfortable
companions; good style is a phase of good manners. Our
certainty that F rench books will be well written affects us
like the certainty with which we expect and find civilized conventions in the homes of some of our friends, and not glad-
dening our essentially cordial relations in those of others.
American books and English are not always careless; but you
never know what to expect of them. Some, and parts of many,
are delightfully written; some, inoffensively; most of them

seem written anyhow. A kind of restless insecurity results each time we take up a new one. Our own life, our own style, are wanting in civilized grace and amenity. These qualities in the style of the French are very welcome to our foreign taste.

At the same time there can be no doubt that these conventions of French style often impress us as artificial. At least in matters of form, the literature of France seems far less at liberty than ours to stray where it will. And the impression which it thus makes on us is strengthened by some obvious features of its substance. A novel or a play, for example, almost always presents definite pictures of social life. Take a scene from any standard comedy. A man enters to make a call on a lady. He wears his gloves and he carries his hat—circumstances evidently affording him opportunity for a little easy stage business with his hands. Obviously, we think, these details are literary conventions, like the pleasantly formal phrases with which he is received. Or a company is assembled, each in his own chair, and each takes part in the general conversation, with no symptom of such division into groups of two as is pretty sure to take place among ourselves. Again, we think, this is a piece of literary convention, pleasantly like that which requires these creatures of conventional imagination to talk in happier style than we are used to at home, and in English novels. There seems, too, on reflection, a sound artistic reason for the conventional regularities of French literature and the French stage. Nothing could more strongly emphasize, by contrast, the rather irregular lines of conduct to which punctiliously decorous persons prove to be addicted.

As you grow to know France better, your notion of these conventions of manners will be quietly modified. Conventions they remain, of course,—matters of civilized system, as distinguished from momentary impulse. But they prove to be conventions of quite another character than you had supposed. They had seemed, like the conventions of style through which they were made known to you, amenities of literature, and hardly anything more. They turn out to be the accepted amenities of French behavior. The manners presented on the stage

and in novels are photographically true to the social habits
of the present day. You were right, no doubt, in supposing
that gloves and a hat furnish an actor with easy business for
his hands; but that is not the reason why he comes on the
stage with them. A man enters a room with them throughout
France; not to do so would be to make himself unceremoni-
ously at home, almost to the point of scandal. You were right
in supposing that conversation addressed to everybody within
hearing is inevitable on the stage and convenient in fiction;
but that is not the reason why you will find it everywhere in
French literature. To talk to your neighbor in a French
drawing-room, instead of addressing the whole company,
would be almost as uncouth as if at home you should plant
your chin on his shoulder and whisper in his ear. These
French conventions, at first blush so evidently literary, turn
out to be conventions not of literature but of life.

Beyond question they are among the conditions which make
French life agreeable. You will find them in all ranks of
French society. What is more, you will find them in all degrees of French friendship, even to the domestic privacy of
the foyer. You must stray further in France than ever I did
if you would seek such unsocial carelessness of behavior as
you shall often find at home without the seeking. Wherefore,
you may safely conclude that French life in its daily detail is
pleasanter than life among ourselves—far more deeply permeated with the graciousness of civilization. To find yourself,
wherever you are, in a little company,—one of an affable
group,—is a less perplexing experience than to find yourself
in a collection of casual couples trying to think of something
to say to each other. And yet you presently begin to perceive
that this is not the whole story. More agreeable in any given
instance, this precision of conduct tends to grow a shade
monotonous. The formal comedy of daily life in France re-
peats itself as interminably as the pleasant pictures of it on
the French stage repeat one another. Though it never ceases
to please, its charms soon fail to include the charm of nov-
elty. One interior is so like the last, or the next, that when
you have made six or eight calls in Paris, you will be at
pains to remember which was which. The ease and the grace

of French life depend on a degree of convention unfavorable
to variety. Unless you pry far beneath the surface of daily
life in that pleasant France, you grow to feel, it offers rather less scope for obvious individuality than you have been
used to elsewhere.

Here at last we can begin to understand the full significance
of an epigram which, a few years ago, startled a company of
Americans assembled to welcome an eminent French man of
letters. When the speeches of formal greeting were over, the
after-dinner eloquence took a more familiar turn, and one of
our own novelists ventured to ask the Parisian writer why the
heroines of French fiction are so generally given to misbehavior. He could not believe, he politely added, that miscon-
duct was general among the women of France; in reality, he
could not doubt that French women are among the best creatures a good God ever made; why should they not appear so
in French literature? The French writer replied with that
delightful ease of manner and of phrase which makes post-
prandial discourse in France a matter rather of anticipation
than of dread. Our friend, he assured us, could not have
generalized French womanhood more happily if he had enjoyed the privilege of knowing from infancy how completely
it justified the reverence in which all who understand it must
hold it. And, in explaining why this aspect of it was not more
salient in the long historical perspective of French literature,
he could not find a happier phrase than one uttered under
similar circumstances by his lamented friend, Monsieur Guy
de Maupassant. When that most eminent of literary artists
was once asked, in a familiar company, whether he might not
some time gladden us with a heroine more sedate, if not
more alluring, than those with whom we were all familiar,
he had resolutely said, No—for "l'honnête femme n'a pas de
roman."

The idea that good women are not interesting baffled this
company of intelligent Americans. They were familiar only
with their own society, where young girls have their blameless romances as regular preliminaries to happy and faithful
marriages, where good married women—young and old—have
their friendships and their interests, apart from domestic

life, as innocent as the romances of their girlhood. To these
Americans, accordingly, Maupassant appeared to assert that
no woman could be interesting, in any aspect, until she took
to mischief. This I conceive to be far from the true meaning
of his epigram. His comment was concerned not with human
character in general but with a state of society extremely
different from that to which Americans are accustomed. We
all know how deeply foreigners misapprehend our manners;
few of us stop to think that we may equally fall to misunderstanding theirs.

Such social conventions as ours, or such lack of them, if
you choose,—such freedom from fixed system,—make life,
in its every-day aspects, a tolerably varied thing. Even the
most innocent young girl properly has her little secrets, her
pretty perplexities; and this with no disregard of the customs
in which she has been brought up. Social conventions, on the
other hand, so precise and so systematic as those of the
French, go far to keep young girls and good women from such
experiences as should avert the drowsiness of monotony. Our
ideal of womanly conduct demands little more than rectitude
and candor. Theirs demands that a good woman attend unre-
mittently to the obvious business of her useful life. Each of
us would probably agree in respect and admiration for the
ideal most cherished by the other. Each might well believe
that the ideal of the other was implied in his own. But the
emphasis would differ, just as we have seen the emphasis of
America to differ in other respects from that of France. And
no matter how much Americans may prefer their own emphasis, they cannot deny that the emphasis of the French on
obedience to conventional system must tend to prevent, in
every-day life, that sort of individuality among good women
which often makes them, among ourselves, happy subjects
for literary treatment. The moment that we reach this point
of view we can see—whether we resent the epigram or not—
what a French novelist means when he declares that good
women afford no opportunity to a writer of fiction.

The honnête femme of France, in short, is a devoted woman who has more things to do than waking hours suffice for.
These she does cheerfully, faithfully, beautifully. She has

the cares of her household; she is passionately devoted to
her children; so long as her parents live, she is devoted
to them as well; the interests of her brothers and her sisters
are her own; more still her own are the interests, in every
sense, of her husband. She is the central fact in the national
life of her country. But from the point of view of the story-
teller her career is not interesting.

The essence of any interesting literary problem, indeed,
may perhaps be reduced to this: it involves a conflict, more
or less impelled by personal passion, between individual impulse and social surroundings. The question, in its simplest
and most comprehensive terms, is one of adjustment between
an organism and its environment. The more rigid the environment, the more sternly it represses and controls individual
tendencies to variation. What would be normal in a society
which cherishes above all the ideal of individuality becomes
exceptional in a society which cherishes, with almost religious fervor, the ideal of system. When any question of
individual variation from an accepted type declares itself in
France, accordingly, it involves a far more abrupt diver-
gence from general presumption than is necessarily, or even
usually, the case among ourselves.

For various reasons, too, these exceptions to the rule of
social life, interesting anywhere, make exceptional appeal
to interest among the French. One condition of a systematic
habit of life is that whoever is addicted to it must grow, by
very force of habit, to feel it at once a phase of the law of
nature and, like other such conditions of existence, exasper-
atingly repressive. We human beings, compelled to live on
the surface of the earth, would now and then like to soar in
the air, partly because we know that if we could do so at will,
we should be workers of miracles. And with people to whom,
for generations, social restraint has been the unbroken rule
of life, vagaries from such restraint, though not miracles,
have a touch of miraculous fascination. When New England
was given to godly austerities, small boys thought it a fine
thing to say damn; nowadays, amid more relaxed surroundings, this expletive has lost its charm and is getting out of
fashion.

Again, and far more characteristically, when such fixed
lines of conduct as prevail in France become the regular rule
of existence, they are bound to present themselves, to people
who accept them, as generalizations. Any system tends to
reduce itself to a series of propositions; and when propositions are once stated and received as true, it is not only in
mathematics that we are disposed to regard them as universal. Now, the propositions which govern the social life of the
French, even in their most whole-souled domesticity, have
gone beyond any mere formulas of language. They have embodied themselves in the forms, the manners, the details of
all terrestrial habit. Take any French family, for example,
whom you may have had the privilege to know. Every one of
its members will have some stated occupation for every hour
from morning till night. The old lady in Pailleron's comedy,
who regularly makes her appearance in the drawing-room at
four in the afternoon, might be taken, in this respect, as an
incarnation of France. And, even among people who live in
the simplest way, there is very little personal, as distinguished from domestic, privacy. A Frenchman's house is
his castle, even more than an Englishman's; it is his own,
inaccessible except to those whom he favors with the pass-
word of the day. But within it he is so little alone that, if he
wants to be by himself, his only resource is some holy of
holies, where he can lock himself in. Among his own family
he has his open and regular part to play, as surely and as
socially as the least of them. He plays it cheerfully, willing-
ly, happily, as they play theirs. Human nature and human
life generalize themselves unopposed. Love of system makes
system the stronger, and the growing strength of system
strengthens the love for it with all the security of habit.

Amid such strength of beloved environment, the persistent
tendency of human nature to variation presents something
more than a specific problem; it gives rise to many general
considerations, which people unused to such conditions would
hardly suspect. One reason why this is not instantly evident
lies in the fact that, whether in literature or in life, any
individual variation from an accepted type—any assertion of
personal independence from the control of accepted custom—

is bound to seem peculiar to the individual involved. Otherwise human beings would be no more stimulating facts than
algebraic symbols or tin soldiers. The precision of the
French mind, too, demands that when the problem of any
such variation is presented in literary form it shall be stated
concretely. You must read far in standard French novels or
plays before you shall discover there a character who shall
not seem to be somebody in particular as distinguished from
somebody in general. And yet, all the while, this individuality, this vivid personality, of the characters in French
literature or on the French stage is itself a matter of convention. It is a phase of the same mental habit, the same immemorial tradition of expression, which makes the style of
France so admirably, so brilliantly precise. In point of fact,
you will find, these characters—vividly individual though they
be—are accepted by the public for whom they are imagina-
tively created not quite as individuals, but far more instantly
as types, as abstractions, as terms to be used in social reasoning rather than as objects of sympathetic contemplation.

What I have in mind must be familiar to anybody who has
heard French people discuss current literature among themselves. You make a call in Paris, for example, and find six
or eight people accidentally gathered together in a pleasant
drawing-room. They prove to be talking about a play just
brought out at one of the better theatres. You have happened
to see it—with alert interest, and at the same time with a
distinct emotion of such sort as used to impel the English of
French caricature to summarize their impressions of the
Parisian stage in the single word shocking. Rather to your
dismay, some of the ladies present appear to have shared
your interest without a tinge of your emotional reaction.
They say acute things, which would never have occurred to
you, about details of the acting. You begin to perceive the
standard of art to which a French actor is held by the critical
intelligence of his public. In reflecting on this aspect of the
situation, you forget for an instant your Yankee displeasure
at the lines of conduct which these admirable histrionic artists had called to your attention. You lose the thread of the
conversation. When you try to catch it again, you find that it

has led to another phase of the drama in question. These excellent women—there are no young girls in the company—are no longer discussing the art of the actors; they are eagerly expressing their opinions concerning what the characters in the play were about. And here comes your enlightenment. To you the situation in question had seemed vividly individual; Armand was Armand, Germaine was Germaine. To them, for all the precision of the terms which set forth the loves of Armand and Germaine, the situation had evidently seemed generalized. You had been thinking of it in arithmetical terms; to them the terms had rather been algebraic. It is ten to one that where you would have said Armand in discussing the situation, they will say a man; that where you would have said Germaine they will say a woman, or a wife, or an honest woman. Before you have quite realized this difference, the conversation will very likely have pursued its way still further. It will have generalized itself, you hardly perceive when and how; and these volatile people will be gravely, animatedly, yet dispassionately discussing an abstract problem of psychology, of conduct, of morals. That now and again they revert to a man or a woman, to Armand or Germaine, does not alter the case. What has really interested them, what they will discuss until some more apposite topic distracts them, might just as well have been suggested by a sermon, or by an open lecture at the Sorbonne, as by a dramatic performance which had seemed to you, in certain respects, abominable.

In almost every instance, meanwhile, at least nowadays, such general discussions as arise from novels or plays will be found to turn on the fundamental point which we have been trying to keep in mind. There is a fixed system—social, religious, moral, whatever you will. The accepted conventions of this would relentlessly repress the impulses of some individual; and very probably they would go far, at the same time, to repress or to contradict some impulses common to the human race. To make this situation clear, an author has stated it in concrete terms of Armand and Germaine. Armand and Germaine, however, bear to the point at issue no more comprehensive relation than that borne to a proposition

in geometry by the figure used to illustrate the reasoning
involved. They are necessary to the process; but once so
used, they remain important only for the precision of line
with which they may have been drawn. The real question is
whether, in a case where the rigidity of system and the impulse of human variation are at odds, the system or the
individual should yield.

Obviously and everywhere assertions of individuality are
apt to take licentious form. You may illustrate this truth, if
you prefer, by blameless reference to the poetic license indulged in by men of letters impatient of academic restraint.
How far from dreary such purely literary discussion may
become in France anyone knows who has read of the devotees
of classic tradition endeavoring, when "Hernani" was new, to
to suppress the unorthodox metaphor,

> "Vous êtes <u>mon lion</u>, superbe et généreux."

Without appreciating episodes like this you can never understand the French point of view, when systems and individuals,
organisms and environment, come in conflict. But all the
distraction of your attention in the world to poetic license can
never avoid the truth that the questions of license involved in
such conflicts are apt rather to involve license of personal
conduct, such as our English habit is disposed not to talk
about in general society.

Just here we are confronted again with the deep contrast
between the intellectual candor of the French and the personal candor of English-speaking peoples. In certain respects,
one sometimes conjectures, the French are less scrupulous
concerning statements of concrete fact than our own convic-
tions would generally approve. When, on the other hand, the
matter in question is either a general proposition, or the
implications which it involves, they become unflinching. With
us the case is precisely the opposite. In discussing concrete
fact we mercilessly demand truth from ourselves and from
everybody else; but when it comes to scrutinizing general
propositions, we permit ourselves a degree of mental indo-
lence regrettable in the eyes of our alertly intellectual
neighbors; and when the further question arises of what our

general propositions may logically imply, we are not only
disinclined to think it out, but even resentful if we are
pressed to do so. In a specific case, the right sort of a
Frenchman might be rather more disposed than we to assert
the spotlessness of a lady who had the misfortune to be discovered in an equivocal situation; on the other hand, he would
be far more ready than we to admit the unhappy truth that
wherever men and women are gathered together equivocal
situations frequently occur. So the French, to the end of
time, will think us hypocritical; just as we, with equal error,
shall think them mendacious.

It is in no small degree this intellectual candor of the
French which permits them, throughout their literature, to
deal with topics on the whole forbidden among ourselves.
Among other things, it leads them to assume as a matter of
course what is everywhere true, namely, that the most instantly suitable subjects for literature are not the commonplaces of every-day life. Otherwise a shopkeeper's ledger
might serve the purpose of a novel. Literature, in general,
must concern itself with interesting exceptions to the commonplace. Of these the most interesting, on the whole, arise
from the vagrant tendencies of affection between men and
women. If such incidents were not exceptional, they would
not be interesting; you can imagine a state of society where
monogamy might have all the fascination of romance, but
that is not the society of European civilization. To deny these
general truths would be, from the French point of view, perverse; worse still, it would be silly.

Meanwhile, there can be little doubt that another reason
why the substance of French literature misrepresents
French life may be found in another phase of French attachment to tradition. The intellectual candor of the French,
their insistent admission of generalized fact, is no new trait
of theirs; it has persisted ever since they have been a nation. And though in its present form, which happens to be
intensely serious on the surface, it may seem different from
what it used to be, the nature of it stays much the same. The
old folk tales of France, and the like, are full of ribald fun—
"gaieté gauloise," they sometimes call it now. France has

always had its systems, and has always admitted the persistent recurrence of exceptions. Of old it used to laugh at
them; just now it is disposed rather to philosophize about
them. Whether you laugh or whether you reason is a question
of mood. What they reason about now is what they used to
laugh about, and what very likely they will laugh about again
in days to come. In any event, it is not only something which
their intellectual candor must admit to be of perennial human
interest; it is something which the immemorial convention of
their race has assumed to be the normal subject of literature. The frailty of woman is as old as Eve, and the place of
it in French literature has analogies to the place of Harlequin
in Christmas pantomime.

All of these considerations should help us toward the end
of which we are now in search—the understanding of why the
life of modern France, when you come to know it, seems so
different from the same life as set forth in the most highly
developed literature of modern Europe. We have seen that
convention has much to do with this paradox. We have seen,
as well, that it springs in no small degree from the insistent
intellectual candor of the French. We have seen that this
candor, or any semblance of it, involves the admission that
the subject of literature in general should rather be interesting exceptions to a rule than the rule itself. And thus we find
ourselves led toward a conclusion, or at least a suggestion,
astonishingly remote from our original assumption. There is
reason, in short, for believing that the pervasive licentiousness of literature in France so far from proves licentiousness
to be the rule of French life that it may rather be held to
imply the reverse.

Another consideration, on which we have not yet touched,
should strengthen this conclusion. As the whole world knows,
the French are not a sluggish people. They are probably the
most alertly intelligent in the modern world, and this both
from native impulse and from the training consequent upon
the circumstances of their intensely competitive life. The
intensity of their competition, so evident in the details of
their university system, demands incessant, unremittent,
intellectual work. So does their attachment to their social

system. A good Frenchman must not only do his utmost to
maintain and to advance his own position in the world; he
must occupy himself as well with the interests of his family.
He must provide for the careers of his sons; he must provide
for the dowries of his daughters; he must see to it that his
household, large or small, is conducted prudently; he must
end each year in a little more security than he enjoyed when
he began it. He can never remit his attention to detail. Well
and good. This means that when the day's work is over he
would not be human if he were not pretty well tired out. He
needs amusement, diversion, distraction, recreation. To
recruit his powers of attention, he needs something different
from what has engaged them yesterday and today, and must
engage them again tomorrow. He would not be French, either, if he did not demand this stimulating distraction in a
rigorously precise form. He is more fond of generalization
than we are, I dare say; but he likes to base his generalization on concrete terms, and on concrete terms of a kind
which shall readily hold his tired attention. And what is true
of him is just as true—perhaps more true still—of his honest
and devoted wife. She would not be French, again, any more
than he would, if she lacked the strong habit of an intellectual
candor which at once admits the existence of things we Englishmen or Americans are apt to ignore, and maintains the
perhaps deplorable but surely undeniable truth that such
things have an enduring power of exciting interest, of holding
the attention, of making us forget for the instant such monotonies as have engaged us all day and as must engage us
again, day after day, until the melancholy day arrives when
they send out notice of the funeral. As a mere matter of recreation, the French demand in their literature something
different from what they find in life—just as Yankee factory-
girls like to read about duchesses. They turn instinctively to
the ranges of fact least familiar in their daily experience,
and least likely to strain their attention. Obviously such a
range of fact is apt to be licentious.

A vivid instance of what I have in mind was lately told me
by a French friend who has lived for some years in America. During a visit to Paris, he strayed into a small popular

theatre, frequented by petty shopkeepers and the like. At his
side he found a stout, motherly person, whose daily duties
were evidently absorbing; for he could not help overhearing
her voluble discourse about housekeeping, the shop, and the
children; where you could buy your groceries cheapest, what
promised to sell well or ill, in terms of pocket-money, and
whether it was necessary to buy Louis a thicker pair of shoes,
in view of his tendency to colds in the head. The curtain rose.
The one-act play proved to be of a freedom which, after my
friend's prolonged habit of America, impressed him as 'ap-
palling. The good matron by his side felt no such scruples.
Beyond question, it was very funny, and you could not help
attending to it. She laughed with a merriment which did your
heart good. And when the curtain fell, to rise again in due
time for a farce as unrestrained as the first, she filled the
interval with the same sort of devoted domestic chatter as
had served her for prologue. A good soul, tired with assid-
uous attention to duty, she found innocent pleasure—and
nothing else—in giving herself up to what honestly amused
her. You could no more feel her to be depraved than you
could feel a pretty girl to be, delighting in the waltz.

The phenomenon is not peculiar to the French. A famously
austere American senator, remarkable for conscientious
work in Congress, was lately asserted by a librarian to have
been in the habit of reading himself out of torpor in books
which would have made his constituents and his family shud-
der. This does not mean that he ever relaxed his conduct,
for an instant, either in public or in private; it rather proves
the contrary. So, I believe, the persistent irregularities of
conduct incessant in French literature may most sensibly be
regarded as the intellectual counterparts of lives benumbing
in their general regularity.

One phase of this regularity must often surprise a foreigner who finds himself in a company of Frenchmen famil-
iarly talking to each other. I can best illustrate what I mean
by an anecdote told me by an American in Paris. He liked to
read French novels, and believed himself by no means
squeamish. Certain incidents in the works of one popular
French author, however, had been too much for him. The

man, he had been given to understand, was personally respectable. It seemed incredible. He put him on his unwritten
index expurgatorius. Wherefore, he was startled one evening
to find himself sitting next to this deplorable person at a
dinner-party. The aspect of the novelist was irreproachable.
His personality and manners were attractive. The talk was
general and animated. It began with the soup, and kept on
till late in the evening. All the company, but my friend, it
happened, were French. He took little part in the conversation, partly for want of command of their fluent language.
To all appearances, they talked with perfect freedom, saying
whatever came into their heads. The novelist talked most of
all. My friend avers that he never passed a more delightful
evening. And it was only after he got home that he quite appreciated an astonishing fact. Through all the hours when
these Frenchmen had been talking together, not a word had
been uttered which might not have been uttered in the presence of a young girl. So far as my friend's memory could
serve him he had never enjoyed quite this experience among
any company of English-speaking men. He reminded me, with
a sigh, of a line from an imitation of Elizabethan comedy in
which I had indulged myself some years ago: "When knew you
a company of men left to themselves but that straight they
fell to talking bawdy?"

     And yet not only the novelist who had been the leader of
this animated talk about politics, and fine art, and philosophy,
and travel, had written things which no self-respecting American would sign; others in the company had sinned likewise,
if not so deeply. The conclusion at which my friend arrived
I am inclined to think true. The French are given to writing
things which they would not say; English-speaking men are
given to saying things which they would not write. Comments
on a truth like this may be various. Six of one, you might
conclude, and half a dozen of the other; it is only that people
of decent life approach things differently, according as they
are familiar with the customs of French society or of ours.
A good American woman in whose presence I ventured to
make this remark declared it to signify, in absurdly minced
words, that all the men in question ought to be ashamed of

themselves. I should be the last to deny this proposition as
a matter of principle. I refrained from pointing out to her
that if I had assented to it as a statement of fact I should
have exposed myself—at least in the just opinion of such intellectual candor as prevails among the French—to the
charge of English-speaking hypocrisy.

Still another consideration may throw light on the conventional subjects of literature in France. As we reminded ourselves when we were discussing the structure of French
society, the artists of France—using the term artists in its
most comprehensive sense—are a class apart. With us the
word artist suggests a man who devotes his life to the art of
painting. In French, I believe, it has hardly any such limitation; it implies, to begin with, only that a man's life is
devoted rather to contemplation and expression than to the
kind of labor which the political economies of my youth used
to call productive. An artist's effort is not to increase the
wealth of society, but to enlarge its intelligence, and above
all to intensify its aesthetic pleasure. Painter, sculptor,
architect, musician, actor, man of letters—it is all one.
There are grades, no doubt, in the hierarchy of art, just as
there are in the learned professions or in the army. At one
time one service may be the more in fashion; at another
time the same may be the less favored. These shades of difference do not obscure the great difference of all. The world
of fine art in France is a world by itself with a pretty distinct existence of its own.

Artists may be of noble origin; oftener they come of
bourgeois stock; sometimes they spring from the common
people. Once artists, they belong first of all to their own
class—I had almost said their own caste. In their art they
are consummately serious, untiringly industrious. In superficial aspect, their lives are as orderly, as regular, as
punctilious as the lives of anybody else. Beneath the surface,
however, the question of regularity is in many aspects a
matter of more indifference than is the case with people of
similar character among ourselves. I permitted myself to
compare this state of things with what we generally recognize
in America to be the case with the dramatic profession. So

long as an actor plays well and conducts himself agreeably,
we ask fewer questions about him than about other people.
And if our taste lead us away from a society where questions
might perhaps be awkward, we are not quite disposed to cul-
tivate his acquaintance in private. This is no reflection on
his numerous excellences of heart. It is only a candid admission that his standards of daily conduct will probably differ—
for better or for worse—from those which we have happened
to find most congenial.

The case of a father and a son almost equally eminent in
the French literature of the nineteenth century will illustrate
what I mean. Among the perennial books are the novels of
Alexandre Dumas. If you ever think them trivial when you
are well, turn when you are ill to "Monte Cristo" or "The
Three Musketeers," and you will never want other diversion.
As is generally known, the life of Dumas, while full of ami-
ability, was not conspicuously austere—a fact which has no
more bearing on the charm of his narrative than the personal
morals of an opera singer have on the quality of the notes
produced by her vocal organs. You would not have chosen
him as private tutor for your sons, no doubt; there it ends.
The whole world may forever enjoy his animated romances.
You may feel, however, a shade of embarrassment if they
ask you too definitely about his son, the younger Alexandre
Dumas. His origin, regular in the course of nature, was not
preceded by all the legal formalities conventionally assumed
among ourselves to be preliminary to such incidents; and the
circumstances of his youth were such as to find normal expression—at an age when most of our boys are still at college—in "La Dame aux Camélias."

Whatever the ultimate moral of this classic work, no one
can deny its astonishing power, nor yet that this power
springs from two qualities deeply characteristic of its author. It enlists your sympathy for the moment; without stop-
ping to inquire whether you approve of these people, or agree
with them, you understand them and share their griefs.
More conspicuously still, it is apparently serious; it discusses matters with intense gravity. In this aspect it could
hardly be outdone by any sermon.

Both of these traits persisted throughout the admirable
artistic career of the younger Dumas. What is more, as he
grew in maturity he became the serious expounder of a moral
code as simple and as sound as you should find in any orthodox Sunday-school. He preached it, no doubt, in terms of his
own, instinct with the animation inseparable from lasting
literary work in France. He preached it, too, with something of the fervor which animates the spirits of converts or
of moral discoverers. The commonplaces of our nurseries
blazed for him with the splendor of new, self-revealing
truth. His career as an artist was honorable, conscientious
and distinguished. It was remarkable for popularity, for en-
durance, and for recognition. Among the members of the
Académie Française in his time hardly any was more widely
known, or more secure in public esteem. As a man of letters, he commanded not only admiration but respect; and I
have been given to understand that he commanded them
equally from those who had the privilege of knowing him in
private life.

Yet, from the "Dame aux Camélias" to "Denise" and
"Francillon," he set forth his principles in terms of social
surroundings and conduct conspicuous for irregularity. He
rose from a world of frank disrepute, through that ambiguous
society to which he gave the name of Demi-monde, to the established social system of the middle and the upper classes
of France. Throughout he showed you everywhere the mischief which must ensue from misbehavior, and showed it by
means of pitiless detection and analysis thereof. Partly, no
doubt, this was a matter of his art, due to the conditions
which we have already taken into account. Partly, on the
other hand, it seems a question of his own personal experience. Born in the artist class, he lived in it, worked in it,
and attained in it a dignity respected not only in Paris and in
France, but all over the world. Yet the facts of his personal
career might almost be inferred from the subjects of his art,
as we recalled them a moment ago. Much of his life was
passed amid surroundings where vagaries of conduct are
more usual than most of us habitually find them. This would
have been true of any actor among ourselves; it has nothing

whatever to do with his personal character or principles. It is true, in general, of all artists in France—from the Academy to the cafés of the Champs Elysées. Anybody, artist or not, must generally assume as normal the phase of life he knows best. Thus we have found another, and a different, reason for the range of topic which pervades French literature.

And yet, after all, it is possible that we have long been straying too far afield. We have been trying to account for the wide differences between French life as one finds it and French life as it is set forth in the literature on which foreign notions of France are based. We have discovered for this difference various reasons—traditional, psychologic, social. Very likely we might better have illustrated it by an analogous difference, equally obvious to any foreigner who should first travel in America and then come to know Americans as they are. If I may trust my own experience, after more than one journey abroad, the most salient literary fact in America, when you view things with a fresh eye, is the prevalence of newspapers. You see them everywhere, in everybody's hands; and of late the custom of filling space with huge headlines has so flourished that you cannot help remarking what they offer as the principal subjects of interest. When I last returned to Boston, after a year's absence, this happened to concern the identity of an unhappy girl whose body had been discovered in two or three separate packages floating about the harbor. Day by day the accounts of this incident were copiously illustrated in the newspapers which confronted you in every public place. It may be taken as typical. Murders, burglaries, elopements, accidents, rascalities stare you in the face, in monstrous type, morning, noon, and night. Railway trains are full of people with their noses buried in these savory sheets. Any stranger might well infer this America of ours to be a land where his most respectable neighbor would probably be a pickpocket. Wealth here appears to be regarded as the result of robbery applied to purposes of deliberate corruption. Political eminence seems to be, at best, demagogic arrogance devoting itself to oppression of the deluded poor. The principal

occupation of those who purvey food is presented in the light
of an endeavor to strike a working balance between rapacity
and poisoning. And so on. I do not intentionally exaggerate
the probable impression produced on any foreigner by the
muck-raking and the yellow journals now so popular throughout the United States of America.

In the matter of taste, nothing can be said for this phase
of depravity. Psychologically, on the other hand, it is both
interesting and instructive. It is only a vulgar example of the
same human impulse which, in anything but vulgar form,
may be detected in the topics most frequent throughout the
standard literature of France. The inference to be drawn
from it is not that you are in the presence of a society so
corrupt as to be obviously on the verge of dissolution. It is
rather that tired human beings, fatigued by lives of conscientious regularity, find diversion in contemplating something
different from the monotonies of their daily routine. Literature affords them this chance. In France, the literature has
great intrinsic merit; in America, it has only the ephemeral
vivacity of popular journalism. In both cases its relation to
every-day life is about the same. It sets forth irregularities,
for the purpose of counterbalancing the benumbing torpor of
recurrent regularity. If you imagine otherwise, you will fall
into the fatal error of supposing the exception to be the rule.

At least, I hope, the manner in which I have tried to set
forth this analogy will serve to define my purpose. This has
not been in any sense apologetic. I have not meant either to
commend or to condemn the subjects most frequent in French
literature, any more than I have meant to praise or to blame
the course at present taken by the daily newspapers of America. I have attempted only to point out the likeness between
a paradox which we all understand and one which has generally misled us. American life is not such as American newspapers would lead a stranger to infer. Neither does French
life seem such as strangers infer who know it only from
French novels. In each case the facts set forth are substantially true; in each case they are comparatively unusual; in
each the vast strength of social regularity is, for the moment, ignored. In each, as one grows to know the nation

better, this strength proves so vital, so incessant, that in generalizing the life which it animates one is apt to think of little else.

For human life everywhere is a conflict between good forces and evil—constructive and destructive. It is the same with physical organisms, with moral, with social. Without the evil it could not exist; without the good it could not persist anywhere.

Sources

COTTON MATHER, THE PURITAN PRIEST

The copy-text is Cotton Mather, the Puritan Priest (New York, 1891), pp. 300-307.

SOME NEGLECTED CHARACTERISTICS OF THE NEW ENGLAND PURITANS

Read before the American Historical Association in December, 1891, and subsequently printed in the Annual Report of the American Historical Association for 1891 and in the Harvard Monthly (April 1892); the copy-text is Stelligeri, and Other Essays Concerning America (New York, 1893), pp. 47-62.

THE ELEMENTS AND THE QUALITIES OF STYLE

Delivered as part of the Lowell Institute lectures, Boston, November and December, 1890; the copy-text is English Composition (New York, 1891), pp. 1-40.

ELEGANCE

Delivered as part of the Lowell Institute lectures, Boston, November and December, 1890; the copy-text is English Composition (New York, 1891), pp. 272-307.

WILLIAM SHAKSPERE

The copy-text is William Shakspere, a Study in Elizabethan Literature (New York, 1894), pp. 395-425.

A LITERARY HISTORY OF AMERICA: INTRODUCTION

The copy-text is A Literary History of America (New York, 1900), pp. 1-10.

NATHANIEL HAWTHORNE

The copy-text is A Literary History of America (New York, 1900), pp. 425-435.

WALT WHITMAN

The copy-text is A Literary History of America (New York, 1900), pp. 465-479.

A LITERARY HISTORY OF AMERICA: CONCLUSION

The copy-text is A Literary History of America (New York, 1900), pp. 521-530.

EDGAR ALLAN POE

Delivered at the Poe Centenary at the University of Virginia, January, 1909; the copy-text is The Mystery of Education, and Other Academic Performances (New York, 1909), pp. 197-254.

DEMOCRACY

Delivered as part of the Hyde Lectures at the Sorbonne, Paris, 1904-1905, and then as part of the Lowell Institute lectures, fall, 1905; the copy-text is Liberty, Union, and

Democracy, the National Ideals of America (New York,
1906), pp. 249-327.

THE RELATION OF LITERATURE TO LIFE

Delivered as part of the Lowell Institute lectures, November and December, 1906; the copy-text is The France of Today (New York, 1907), pp. 191-238.

Selected Bibliography

PRIMARY SOURCES

I. Books by Wendell

The Duchess Emilia: A Romance. Boston: Osgood, 1885.
Rankell's Remains: An American Novel. Boston: Ticknor,
    1887.
Cotton Mather, the Puritan Priest. Makers of America
    Series. New York: Dodd, Mead, 1891.
English Composition. New York: Scribner's, 1891.
Stelligeri, and Other Essays Concerning America. New York:
    Scribner's, 1893.
William Shakspere, a Study in Elizabethan Literature. New
    York: Scribner's, 1894.
A Literary History of America. The Library of Literary His-
    tory. New York: Scribner's, 1900.
Ralegh in Guiana, Rosamond and a Christmas Masque. New
    York: Scribner's, 1902.
A History of Literature in America. In collaboration with
    Chester Noyes Greenough. New York: Scribner's, 1904.
The Temper of the Seventeenth Century in English Literature.
    New York: Scribner's, 1904.
Selections from the Writings of Joseph Addison. Edited, with
    introduction and notes, in collaboration with Chester Noyes
    Greenough. Athenaeum Press Series. New York: Ginn, 1905.
Liberty, Union, and Democracy, the National Ideals of Amer-
    ica. New York: Scribner's, 1906.

The France of Today. New York: Scribner's, 1907.
The Privileged Classes. New York: Scribner's, 1908.
The Mystery of Education, and Other Academic Performances.
    New York: Scribner's, 1909.
La France d'aujourd'hui. Translated by Georges Grappe.
    Paris: Floury, 1910.
The Traditions of European Literature from Homer to Dante.
    New York: Scribner's, 1920.
Einhard. The History of the Translation of the Blessed Mar-
    tyrs of Christ, Mercellinus and Peter. Translated by Bar-
    rett Wendell. Cambridge: Harvard University Press,
    1926.

II. Articles by Wendell

Editorial Contributions to Harvard Lampoon, I-VII (1876-
    1879).
"On Dinners and Dining." Harvard Lampoon, I (June 1876),
    102-104.
"Notes on the Pedigree of Some of Our Contemporaries."
    Harvard Lampoon, III (May 1877), 689.
"Letters to a Freshman." Harvard Advocate, 2 February
    1881, pp. 10-12.
"From a Looker-on in Chicago." Boston Daily Advertiser,
    10-11 July 1884, pp. 1, 2.
"Social Life at Harvard." Lippincott's Magazine, XXXIX
    (January 1887), 152-163.
"The Last of the Ghosts." Scribner's Magazine, III (Febru-
    ary 1888), 227-239.
"Mr. Lowell as a Teacher." Scribner's Magazine, X (No-
    vember 1891), 645-649.
"Some Neglected Characteristics of the New England Puri-
    tans." Annual Report of the American Historical Associa-
    tion for 1891. Washington: American Historical Associa-
    tion, 1892.
"The Dean of Bourges." Scribner's Magazine, XI (January
    1892), 117-120.
"Were the Salem Witches Guiltless?" Historical Collections

of the Essex Institute, 29 (February 1892), 129-147.
"How He Went to the Devil." Two Tales, 30 April 1892,
   pp. 4-8.
"John Greenleaf Whittier." Proceedings of the American
   Academy of Arts and Sciences, XXVII (May 1893), 431-441.
"Impressions at Chicago." Harvard Monthly, IX (October
   1893), 7-8.
"English Work in the Secondary Schools." School Review, I
   (1893), 638.
"English at Harvard." The Dial, 16 (March 1894), 131-133.
"Francis Parkman." Proceedings of the American Academy
   of Arts and Sciences, XXIX (May 1894), 435-447.
"Harvard University." English in American Universities.
   Edited with an introduction by William Morton Payne.
   Boston: Heath, 1895.
Introduction to Shakespeare's As You Like It. Longman's
   English Classics. New York: Longman, Green, 1896.
"Cotton Mather." American Prose. Edited by George Rice
   Carpenter. New York: Macmillan, 1898.
"Composition in the Elementary Schools." New York Teach-
   ers' Monographs, I (November 1898), 68-76.
"Samuel Eliot." Proceedings of the American Academy of
   Arts and Sciences, XXXIV (May 1899), 646-651.
"The Relations of Radcliffe College with Harvard." Harvard
   Monthly, XIV (October 1899), 3-11.
Introduction to John Hays Gardiner's The Forms of Prose
   English. New York: Scribner's, 1900.
Review of A Life of Francis Parkman by Charles H. Farn-
   ham. American Historical Review, VI (January 1901),
   376-377.
"Memoir of William Whitwell Greenough." Proceedings of
   the Massachusetts Historical Society, 34 (February 1901),
   1-17.
Review of The Clergy in American Life and Letters by Daniel
   D. Addison. American Historical Review, VI (April 1901),
   576-579.
Review of The Transit of Civilization from England to Amer-
   ica in the Seventeenth Century by Edward Eggleston.
   American Historical Review, VI (July 1901), 802-805.

"A Review of American Literary Phases." Studies in Amer-
    ican Literature. Edited by Frederic Spiers. Philadelphia:
    Booklovers' Library Press, 1901.
Review of The Literary Diary of Ezra Stiles, D.D., LL.D.,
    President of Yale College. American Historical Review,
    VII (July 1902), 769-772.
"The American Intellect." The Cambridge Modern History,
    VII. Edited by A. W. Ward, et al. New York: Cambridge
    University Press, 1903.
"Our National Superstition." North American Review,
    CLXXIX (September 1904), 388-401.
"Le Président Roosevelt." Revue Politique et Parlementaire,
    10 February 1905, pp. 7-15.
"Impressions of Contemporary France: The Universities."
    Scribner's Magazine, XLI (March 1907), 314-326.
"Impressions of Contemporary France: The Structure of
    Society." Scribner's Magazine, XLI (April 1907), 450-464.
"Impressions of Contemporary France: The French Temper-
    ament." Scribner's Magazine, XLI (June 1907), 741-753.
"Impressions of Contemporary France: The Republic and
    Democracy." Scribner's Magazine, XLII (July 1907),
    53-65.
"The Influence of the Athenaeum on Literature in America."
    The Influence and History of the Boston Athenaeum from
    1807 to 1907. Boston: Boston Athenaeum, 1907.
"The Privileged Classes." Journal of Education, 27 Febru-
    ary 1908, pp. 11-24.
"A Fantasy Concerning an Epitaph of Shakspere." Anniver-
    sary Papers of Colleagues and Pupils of George Lyman
    Kittredge. Boston: Ginn, 1908.
"The United States and France." International Conciliation,
    9 (August 1908), 3-9.
"Charles Eliot Norton." Atlantic Monthly, CIII (January
    1909), 82-88.
"Abbott Lawrence Lowell, Twenty-Fourth President of Har-
    vard College." Harvard Graduates' Magazine, XVII
    March 1909), 397-403.
"De Praeside Magnifico." Harvard Graduates' Magazine,
    XVIII (September 1909), 26.

"Henry Cabot Lodge, Statesman." Boston Herald, 1 May
    1910, p. 2.

Introduction to John A. Lomax's Cowboy Songs and Other
    Frontier Ballads. New York: Sturgis and Walton, 1910.

"Cotton Mather." American Prose: Selections with Critical
    Introductions. Edited by George Rice Carpenter. New
    York: Macmillan, 1911.

"Edmund March Wheelwright." Harvard Graduates' Maga-
    zine, XXI (December 1912), 240-242.

"A New England Puritan." The Quarterly Review, 218 (Jan-
    uary 1913), 32-48.

Speech at the Alumni Luncheon. Columbia University Quar-
    terly, 15 (September 1913), 355-356.

"The Mystery of Education." Representative Phi Beta Kappa
    Orations. Edited by Clark Sutherland Northrup. Boston:
    Houghton Mifflin, 1915.

"William Roscoe Thayer." Harvard Graduates' Magazine,
    XXIV (September 1915), 19-22.

"Henry James: An Appreciation." Boston Evening Tran-
    script, 16 March 1916, p. 20.

"The Ideals of Empire." Harvard Graduates' Magazine, XXV
    (June 1917), 458-474.

"Japan and Righteousness." Scribner's Magazine, LXIV
    (July 1918), 71-79.

"Thomas Raynesford Lounsbury (1838-1915)." Proceedings
    of the American Academy of Arts and Sciences, LIII (Sep-
    tember 1918), 831-840.

"The Conflict of Idolatries." Harvard Graduates' Magazine,
    XXVII (September 1918), 1-16.

"Law and Legislation." Scribner's Magazine, LXV (February
    1919), 177-181.

"A Gentlewoman of Boston, 1742-1805." Proceedings of the
    American Antiquarian Society, 29 (October 1919), 242-
    293.

"Sunrise." Scribner's Magazine, LXVI (October 1919),
    467-472.

"James Russell Lowell." Commemoration of the Centenary
    of the Birth of James Russell Lowell. New York: Scrib-
    ner's, 1919.

SECONDARY SOURCES

I. Reviews of Wendell's Books

"A Literary History of America." The Saturday Review,
    19 January 1901, p. 81.
"An American Contribution to Cambridge Scholarship" (re-
    view of The Temper of the Seventeenth Century in English
    Literature). The Saturday Review, 27 May 1905, pp. 904-
    905.
"Barrett Wendell's 'English Composition.'" The Critic,
    14 November 1891, p. 259.
"Barrett Wendell Low in His Mind" (review of The Privileged
    Classes). New York Times Saturday Review of Books,
    31 October 1908, p. 635.
Barry, William. "American Literature" (review of A Liter-
    ary History of America). The Bookman, XIX (January
    1901), 128.
Boynton, Henry W. "The American Character" (review of
    Liberty, Union, and Democracy). The North American Re-
    view, DCIV (December 1906), 1182-1186.
————. "Poetry and the Stage" (review of Ralegh in Guiana).
    Atlantic Monthly, XCII (July 1903), 121-122.
Bronson, Walter C. Review of A Literary History of America.
    The American Historical Review, VI (July 1901), 807-811.
Browne, W. H. "Wendell's Literary History of America."
    The Nation, 7 March 1901, p. 200.
"English Composition." Atlantic Monthly, LXIX (January
    1892), 129-133.
"English Literature in the Seventeenth Century." The Spec-
    tator, 1 October 1906, pp. 468-469.
"The France of Today." The Spectator, 23 November 1907,
    pp. 822-823.
Gates, Lewis E. "Professor Wendell's 'Literary History of
    America.'" The Critic, 14 April 1901, pp. 341-344.
Greenslet, Ferris. "Wendell's Seventeenth-Century Liter-

ature." The Nation, 29 December 1904, pp. 526-527.

Hale, Edward E., Jr. "A New Book on Shakespeare." The Dial, XXVII (January 1895), 13-15.

Horwill, Herbert W. Review of The Temper of the Seventeenth Century in English Literature. The Forum, XXXVI (January-March 1905), 406-410.

Howells, William Dean. "Professor Barrett Wendell's Notions of American Literature." North American Review, CLXXII (April 1901), 623-640.

Jusserand, J.A.J. "Barrett Wendell's France" (review of The France of Today). New York Times Saturday Review of Books, 23 November 1907, p. 742.

Kraus, Horatio S. "As We See Ourselves, New Books by Professor Wendell, Dr. Van Dyke, and President Eliot" (review of Liberty, Union, and Democracy). Putnam's Monthly, II (April 1907), 107-112.

"Literary America" (review of A Literary History of America). The Independent, 10 January 1901, pp. 99-101.

"Literary History and Criticism" (review of A Literary History of America). World of To-Day, VII (January 1905), 108-109.

Loyd, Mary. Review of The Privileged Classes. The Annals of the American Academy of Political and Social Sciences, XXIII (March 1909), 478-479.

McDonald, P.B. Review of The Traditions of European Literature. The Springfield Republican (Springfield, Mass.), 29 May 1921, p. 9.

MacDonald, William. "Wendell's Privileged Classes." The Nation, 21 January 1909, pp. 69-70.

————. Review of Liberty, Union, and Democracy. The Nation, 22 November 1906, p. 444.

Macy, John. "Professor Wendell's 'The Privileged Classes.'" The Bookman, XXVIII (December 1908), 357-359.

Mann, D.L. Review of The Traditions of European Literature. Boston Evening Transcript, 16 February 1921, p. 4.

Matthews, Brander. "Our Literary Heritage from Europe." New York Times Book Review and Magazine, 26 December 1920, p. 3.

Moore, Charles Leonard. "Three Books on Shakespeare."

The Dial, XXXVII (December 1904), 413-416.

Murdock, Kenneth B. "Cotton Mather, the Puritan Priest, by Barrett Wendell, '77." Harvard Graduates' Magazine, 34 (June 1926), 662-663.

Porter, Charlotte. "A 'Literary History of America.'" Poet-lore, 13 (July 1901), 439-448.

————. "A New Book on Shakespeare." Poet-lore, 7 (January 1895), 37-40.

Powell, G. H. "The Mind of America" (review of A Literary History of America). Contemporary Review, LXXXII (July 1902), 111-125.

"Professor Wendell's Essays" (review of Stelligeri). The Critic, 26 May 1894, p. 353.

"Professor Wendell's Lectures" (review of Liberty, Union, and Democracy). The Independent, 24 January 1907, pp. 213-214.

"Professor Wendell's Optimism" (review of Liberty, Union, and Democracy). Putnam's Monthly, I (February 1907), 639.

"Reconstructive Criticism" (review of William Shakspere), Atlantic Monthly, LXXV (April 1895), 559-560.

Review of Cotton Mather. The Dial, XII (March 1892), 393.

Review of English Composition. The Dial, XII (January 1892), 332.

Review of English Composition. The Nation, 8 October 1891, pp. 281-282.

Review of The France of Today. The Athenaeum, 30 November 1907, pp. 686-687.

Review of The France of Today. Literary Digest, December 1907, p. 876.

Review of The France of Today. The Nation, 28 November 1907, pp. 498-499.

Review of The France of Today. The Outlook, 2 November 1907, p. 479.

Review of Liberty, Union, and Democracy. Literary Digest, 2 February 1907, p. 178.

Review of A Literary History of America. The Athenaeum, 23 February 1901, pp. 233-234.

Review of The Mystery of Education. Literary Digest, 29

November 1909, p. 970.

Review of The Mystery of Education. The Outlook, 18 December 1909, pp. 875-877.

Review of The Privileged Classes. The Outlook, 23 January 1909, pp. 150-151.

Review of Stelligeri. Atlantic Monthly, LXXIII (February 1894), 266-267.

Review of Stelligeri. The Nation, 23 November 1893, p. 391.

Review of The Temper of the Seventeenth Century in English Literature. The Critic, 2 July 1905, pp. 92-93.

Review of The Temper of the Seventeenth Century in English Literature. The Independent, 4 May 1905, p. 1016.

Review of The Traditions of European Literature. The New Statesman, 13 August 1921, p. 526.

Review of The Traditions of European Literature. Times Literary Supplement, 24 June 1921, p. 406.

Review of William Shakspere. The Nation, 10 January 1895, p. 36.

Riley, Thomas J. Review of The Privileged Classes. American Journal of Sociology, XIV (January 1909), 539-540.

Rowe, L. S. Review of Liberty, Union, and Democracy. The Annals of the American Academy of Political and Social Science, XXX (November 1907), 624.

Saintsbury, George. "From Homer to Dante" (review of The Traditions of European Literature). Bookman (London), LXI (October 1921), 19-20.

Swift, Lindsay. "Cotton Mather." The Nation, 1 December 1892, pp. 414-415.

"Three Centuries of American Literature" (review of A Literary History of America). The Dial, XXIX (December 1900), 485-487.

Traubel, Horace. "Liberty Union and Democracy." The Conservator, 17 (November 1906), 140-141.

"Wendell's 'Cotton Mather.'" The Critic, 2 January 1892, pp. 1-2.

Withington, Robert. Review of The Traditions of European Literature. Harvard Graduates' Magazine, XXIX (March 1921), 494-495.

II. Commentary on Wendell's Life and Work

Atkinson, Brooks, ed. College in a Yard, Minutes by Thirty-
    Nine Harvard Men. Cambridge: Harvard University Press,
    1957.
Baker, George Pierce. "Barrett Wendell (1855-1921)."
    Harvard Graduates' Magazine, XXIX (June 1921), 571-
    576.
Baldensperger, Fernand. "Barrett Wendell: American 'Dis-
    coverer' of France." The Living Age, 30 April 1921, pp.
    280-284.
"Barrett Wendell." The Outlook, 23 February 1921, pp. 287-
    288.
"Barrett Wendell and His Letters, by M.A. DeWolfe Howe,
    '87." Harvard Graduates' Magazine, XXXIII (December
    1924), 348-350.
Beer, Thomas. The Mauve Decade. New York: Knopf, 1926.
Bolce, Harold. "Polyglots in the Temples of Babel." Cosmo-
    politan, XLVII (June 1909), 52-65.
Boyd, Ernest. "Readers and Writers." The Independent,
    8 November 1924, p. 373.
Briggs, LeBaron R. "Enviable Record Here." Harvard
    Crimson, 30 March 1917, p. 5.
Brooks, Van Wyck. The Confident Years, 1885-1915. New
    York: Dutton, 1952.
————. New England: Indian Summer, 1865-1916. New York:
    Dutton, 1940.
Burlingame, Roger. "A Harvard Tradition." Saturday Review
    of Literature, 18 October 1924, p. 199.
Castle, William R., Jr. "Barrett Wendell, Some Memories
    of a Former Student." Scribner's Magazine, LXX (July
    1921), 60-66.
————, and Paul Kaufman, eds. Essays in Memory of Bar-
    rett Wendell by His Assistants. Cambridge: Harvard
    University Press, 1926.
Dimnet, M. Ernest. "Results of a Literary Invasion." Har-
    per's Weekly, 29 July 1905, p. 1092.

Eaton, Walter P. "Barrett Wendell." The American Mercury, V (August 1925), 448-455.

Eliot, T. S. "American Critics." Times Literary Supplement, 10 January 1929, p. 24.

————. "American Literature." The Athenaeum, 25 April 1919, pp. 236-237.

Fitzpatrick, Frank A. "Reflections of an Iconoclast." Educational Review, XXIX (February 1905), 151-162.

Giraud, Victor. "La France d'aujourd'hui vue par un Américain." La Troisième France. Paris: Hachette, 1917.

Grant, Robert. "Tribute to Barrett Wendell." Proceedings of the Massachusetts Historical Society, 54 (February 1921), 198-199.

Greenough, Chester Noyes. "Tribute to Barrett Wendell." Proceedings of the Massachusetts Historical Society, 54 (February 1921), 199-202.

Hall, Frederick G., et al. "Barrett Wendell." Harvard Celebrities. Cambridge: Harvard Lampoon, 1901.

Heimart, Alan. Introduction to Cotton Mather, The Puritan Priest. New York: Harcourt, Brace, and World, 1963.

Herrick, Robert. "Barrett Wendell." The New Republic, 10 December 1924, pp. 6-7.

Howarth, Herbert. Notes on Some Figures Behind T. S. Eliot. Boston: Houghton Mifflin, 1964.

Howe, Mark A. DeWolfe, ed. "A Packet of Wendell-James Letters." Scribner's Magazine, LXXXIV (December 1928), 675-687.

————. Barrett Wendell and His Letters. Boston: Atlantic Monthly Press, 1924.

————. "From a Graduate's Window: A Personality." Harvard Graduates' Magazine, XXIX (June 1921), 583-586.

Jones, Howard Mumford. The Theory of American Literature. Ithaca: Cornell University Press, 1965.

Kinne, Wisner Payne. George Pierce Baker and the American Theatre. Cambridge: Harvard University Press, 1954.

Legouis, Émile. "Barrett Wendell et la France." Harvard et la France. Paris: Revue d'histoire moderne, 1936.

Lewis, R. W. B. Edith Wharton, a Biography. New York:

Harper and Row, 1975.

Littell, P. "Barrett Wendell." The New Republic. 6 February 1915, pp. 15-17.

Lodge, Henry Cabot. "Tribute to Barrett Wendell." Proceedings of the Massachusetts Historical Society, 54 (February 1921), 202-203.

Lowell, Abbott Lawrence. "Memoir of Barrett Wendell." Proceedings of the Massachusetts Historical Society, 55 (December 1921), 174-185.

May, Henry F. The End of American Innocence, a Study of the First Years of Our Time, 1912-1917. Chicago: Quadrangle, 1959.

"Memoir" (of Barrett Wendell). The New England Historical and Genealogical Register, LXXXVI (1922), 1-liii.

Mencken, H.L. Prejudices, Fifth Series. New York: Knopf, 1926.

Morison, Samuel Eliot, ed. The Development of Harvard University Since the Inauguration of President Eliot, 1869-1929. Cambridge: Harvard University Press, 1930.
————. Three Centuries of Harvard, 1636-1936. Cambridge: Harvard University Press, 1930.

Nevius, Blake. Robert Herrick, the Development of a Novelist. Berkeley: University of California Press, 1962.

Noxon, Frank W. "College Professors Who Are Men of Letters." The Critic, XLII (February 1903), 124-135.

Osborne, Edith Wendell. Recollections of My Father, August 23, 1855-February 8, 1921. Privately published, 1921.

Phelps, William Lyon. Autobiography, with Letters. New York: Oxford University Press, 1939.

Platt, Isaac Hull. "Wendell on Whitman: Criticism or Libel." The Conservator, 13 (October 1902), 118-119.

Review of Barrett Wendell and His Letters. The Bookman, LX (December 1924), 511.

Review of Barrett Wendell and His Letters. The Outlook, 31 December 1924, pp. 731-732.

Rhodes, James Ford. "Tribute to Barrett Wendell." Proceedings of the Massachusetts Historical Society, 54 (February 1921), 195-198.

Santayana, George. The Letters of George Santayana. Edited

by Daniel Cory. New York: Scribner's, 1955.

————. Persons and Places. Vol. II: The Middle Span. New York: Scribner's, 1945.

Self, Robert T., ed. "The Correspondence of Amy Lowell and Barrett Wendell, 1915-1919." New England Quarterly, 47 (March 1974), 65-86.

Sherman, Stuart P. Critical Woodcuts. New York: Scribner's, 1926.

Smith, George. "A Harvard View of Whitman." Part 1, The Conservator, 13 (August 1902), 85-87; part 2, The Conservator, 13 (September 1902), 102-104.

Stimpson, Mary Stoyell. "The Harvard Lampoon: Its Founders and Famous Contributors." New England Magazine, XXXV (January 1907), 579-590.

Thwing, Charles Franklin. Friends of Men. New York: Macmillan, 1933.

Traubel, Horace. "Barrett Wendell Versus." The Conservator, 15 (November 1904), 141.

Waldo, Fullerton. "A Distinctive Teacher." New York Evening Post Literary Review, 25 October 1924, p. 4.

ROBERT T. SELF, Associate Professor of
English at Northern Illinois University, earned
his doctorate at the University of North Carolina.
He teaches film, fiction, and American
literature, and is the author of Barrett Wendell
in Twayne's United States Authors Series.

A₃